David Brock, Ari Rabin-Havt,
and Media Matters for America

The Fox Effect

David Brock, the founder and Chairman of Media
Matters, is the author of five books, including *The
Republican Noise Machine: Right-Wing Media and How It
Corrupts Democracy* and his bestselling memoir *Blinded
by the Right: The Conscience of an Ex-Conservative*.

Ari Rabin-Havt is Media Matters's executive vice president.

www.mediamatters.org

The Fox Effect

How Roger Ailes Turned a Network

into a Propaganda Machine

**David Brock, Ari Rabin-Havt,
and Media Matters for America**

ANCHOR BOOKS

A Division of Random House, Inc.

New York

AN ANCHOR BOOKS ORIGINAL, FEBRUARY 2012

Copyright © 2012 by David Brock, Ari Rabin-Havt, and Media Matters for America

Library of Congress Cataloging-in-Publication Data
Brock, David.
The Fox effect : how Roger Ailes turned a network into a propaganda machine /
David Brock, Ari Rabin-Havt, and Media Matters for America.
p. cm.
Includes bibliographical references.
ISBN 978-0-307-27958-3 (trade pbk.)
1. Ailes, Roger. 2. Fox News. 3. Television broadcasting of news—United States.
4. Television broadcasting of news—Objectivity—United States.
5. Television and politics—United States. I. Rabin-Havt, Ari. II. Title.
PN4888.T4B76 2012
791.450973—dc23
2011042839

Book design by Debbie Glasserman

www.anchorbooks.com

Printed in the United States of America
10 9 8 7 6 5 4 3 2 1

Contents

The Fox Effect

Introduction:
Not Necessarily the News

It is their M.O. to undermine the administration and to undermine Democrats.
They're a propaganda outfit but they call themselves news.

—a former Fox employee

On August 2, 2009, on board the "Six-Star Luxury Liner" *Crystal Serenity,* somewhere in the middle of the Mediterranean Sea, Fox News's Washington, D.C., managing editor, Bill Sammon, rose to address supporters of Hillsdale College, a conservative institution located just over one hundred miles west of Detroit. His audience had paid between $11,800 and $37,600 per couple to listen to an all-star lineup of conservative journalists and scholars as they traveled from Venice to Athens, via Istanbul. Sammon was the featured speaker. He began with some joking remarks, speculating that conservative political consultant Mary Matalin, who was on board the ship simply on vacation, might have "mischievously arranged" to have her husband, liberal James Carville, along to "save his ideological soul." Then Sammon made a startling admission:

You know, speaking of mischief, last year, candidate Barack Obama stood on a sidewalk in Toledo, Ohio, and first let it slip to Joe the Plumber that he wanted to, quote, "spread the wealth around." At that time, I have to admit that I went on TV, on Fox News, and publicly engaged in what I guess was some rather mischievous speculation about whether Barack Obama really advocated socialism, a premise that privately I found rather far-fetched.[1]

At the time Sammon made these "mischievous speculations," he was Fox News's Washington deputy managing editor, and it

was his job to oversee the reporting of the news on one of our country's major cable networks. Yet here, in front of a friendly audience, on a luxury cruise an ocean away from the United States, he was candidly, nonchalantly admitting to consciously misrepresenting the ideology of a presidential candidate to Fox's audience days before an election.

E-mails we obtained from that time, written by Sammon and a Fox producer, show that this calculated smear against Obama was not an on-air slip but part of a coordinated campaign of deception. Not only had Sammon personally appeared on the network to make these charges against Barack Obama, but he had also sent an e-mail to journalists who worked for him, encouraging them to cover the Democratic candidate's "racial obsessions" and supposed connections to Marxism.

From: Sammon, Bill
Sent: Monday, October 27, 2008 1:02 PM
To: 069 -Politics; 169 -SPECIAL REPORT;
    030 -Root (FoxNews.Com)
Subject: fyi: Obama's references to socialism, liberalism, Marxism and Marxists in his autobiography, "Dreams from My Father." Plus a couple of his many self-described "racial obsessions" . . .

- "To avoid being mistaken for a sellout, I chose my friends carefully. The more politically active black students. The foreign students. The Chicanos. **The Marxist professors** and structural feminists." (Obama writing about his time at Occidental College in "Dreams.")
- After his sophomore year, Obama transferred to Columbia University. He lived on Manhattan's Upper East Side, ven-

turing to the East Village for **"the socialist conferences I sometimes attended** at Cooper Union," he recalled, adding: "Much of what I absorbed from the sixties was filtered through my mother, who to the end of her life would proudly proclaim herself an **unreconstructed liberal."**

- After graduating from Columbia in 1983, Obama spent a year working for a consulting firm and then went to work for "a Ralph Nader offshoot" in Harlem. "In search of some inspiration, I went to hear Kwame Toure, formerly Stokely Carmichael of SNCC and Black Panther fame, speak at Columbia. At the entrance to the auditorium, two women, one black, one Asian, **were selling Marxist literature."**

  During this period, according to Obama, he began a serious romantic relationship.

- **"There was a woman in New York that I loved. She was white,"** Obama wrote in "Dreams." "We saw each other for almost a year. On the weekends, mostly. Sometimes in her apartment, sometimes in mine. You know how you can fall into your own private world? Just two people, hidden and warm. Your own language. Your own customs." But Obama said their relationship was doomed by the racial difference. "I pushed her away," he recalled. **"The emotion between the races could never be pure;** even love was tarnished by the desire to find in the other some element that was missing from ourselves. Whether we sought out our demons or salvation, **the other race would always remain just that: menacing, alien, and apart."**

- In June 1985, Obama was interviewed in New York by Marty Kaufman, a community organizer from Chicago. Obama recalled: **"There was something about him that made me wary. A little too sure of himself, maybe. And white."**[2]

Less than ninety minutes later, Sammon was on Fox engaging in "mischievous speculation" claiming Barack Obama "was drawn to Marxists, and he was drawn to liberals, and he was drawn to socialists by his own admission as a young man."[3]

The next morning, Sammon appeared on the network's morning show, *Fox & Friends,* to reiterate his "far-fetched" theory about Obama's Marxism and racial obsessions. Memos from the show's producers reveal that the entire third segment was built around his e-mail.

From: Cunningham, Jennifer

To: 044—Web Show Producers; 064—Desk Assignment;
    069—Politics; 081- Radio; 085—DC Booking;
    100—Media Relations; 162—Promos; Brown, David;
    Glick, Alexis; Magee, Kevin; Moody, John; Scott,
    Suzanne; Shine, Bill; Tammero, Michael; Wallace, Jay

Sent: Mon Oct 27 18:17:41 2008

Subject: FOX & FRIENDS GUESTS FOR TUESDAY OCTOBER. 28—
EXACTLY 1 WEEK BEFORE ELECTION DAY

FOX & FRIENDS GUESTS FOR TUESDAY OCTOBER. 28—
EXACTLY 1 WEEK BEFORE ELECTION DAY

5:59 (A-BLOCK) COLD OPEN // QUICK TEASE// News
HEADLINES // TALKING POINTS WX BUMP OUT TO
TEASE——————————————

6:15 (B-BLOCK)—2 STORIES AMANDA CARPENTER—
DEMS PLAYBOOK SHOWS DIRTY TACTICS
((DC BUREAU))—————————————

**6:22 (C-BLOCK)—2 STORIES ((ANCHOR)) & BILL
SAMMON—FYI: OBAMA'S REFERENCES TO SOCIALISM,
LIBERALISM, MARXISM AND MARXISTS IN HIS
AUTOBIOGRAPHY, "DREAMS FROM MY FATHER."**

PLUS A COUPLE OF HIS MANY SELF-DESCRIBED
"RACIAL OBSESSIONS" . . . ((FOX DC)) >>
BDAY IN TEASE————————————[4]

As Sammon spoke, the chyron, the graphic appearing on the lower section of the screen, read: "The Real Barack Obama; Aligned W/ Marxists, Socialists"; "Obama's Radical Past; Close Friends W/ Marxist"; "Obama's Chosen Friends; Marxist Profs & Structural Feminists"; and "Obama's Racial Divide; 'Emotion B/W Races Never Be Pure.' "[5]

That same day Sammon published a piece claiming that "Obama laughs off charges of socialism . . . [but] Obama himself acknowledges that he was drawn to socialists and even Marxists as a college student."[6]

It was a peculiar amount of attention to give to a story Sammon

THE REAL BARACK OBAMA
ALIGNED W/ MARXISTS, SOCIALISTS

didn't really believe, particularly since the information involved was neither new nor particularly newsworthy—the contemporary political relevance of Obama's candid account of his early years as described in *Dreams from My Father* (which had been published in 1995) had already been thoroughly covered by the press, including by Sammon himself in a book published earlier that year. Why, a week before Election Day, were years-old, out-of-context quotes suddenly being treated as a major, breaking story on "fair and balanced" Fox News?

When criticized for such on-air behavior, Fox News and its defenders will often assert that the network maintains a firewall between its news and opinion programming similar to that between a newspaper's front page and its opinion section. But as a "news" executive, Bill Sammon clearly crossed this line, as veteran journalist Marc Sandalow, a former bureau chief at the *San Francisco Chronicle*'s Washington office, points out. "[Sammon] is overseeing the news operation," he said in an interview with *Media Matters.* "For news gatherers, credibility is everything. You should never deceive viewers or readers."[7]

After his e-mails were revealed in 2011, Sammon defended his actions to *The Daily Beast*'s Howard Kurtz, who wrote of the affair:

> Sammon says his reference to "mischievous speculation" was "my probably inartful way of saying, 'Can you believe how far this thing has come?'" The socialism question indeed "struck me as a far-fetched idea" in 2008. "I considered it kind of a remarkable notion that we would even be having the conversation." He doesn't regret repeatedly raising it on the air because,

Sammon says, "it was a main point of discussion on all the channels, in all the media"—and by 2009 he was "astonished by how the needle had moved."[8]

But a review of the media coverage at the time shows that Fox and Sammon, far from responding to a media narrative, were the driving force behind the reporting of Barack Obama's supposed attraction to socialism. Two weeks before sending his memo to producers, Sammon appeared on Fox's afternoon news program *The Live Desk* to discuss how Barack Obama's comment to Joe the Plumber, an Ohio man, who became a conservative movement fixture after confronting the future president at a campaign stop—that "when you spread the wealth around, it's good for everybody"[9]—was "tantamount to socialism."[10] A few days later Sammon was on Greta Van Susteren's show discussing the same topic, and later that week on *Fox & Friends,* he again reported on the political ramifications of Obama's supposed links to socialism.

Other journalists are not so willing to accept Sammon's explanation to Kurtz. "I don't think deception is ever acceptable in journalism," John Walcott, McClatchy's Washington bureau chief during the 2008 election, remarked of the Fox executive's conduct. "I think there are times when we don't say everything we've learned for reasons of personal security and national security. But outright deception, saying something that you know to be untrue or have no basis for believing is true, is not journalism, it is propaganda."[11]

Sammon's transgressions at the tail end of the 2008 election only marked the beginning of a larger transition at the network, one that would see Fox News change from a network that provided a conservative outlook on the news to an active and unapologetic mouthpiece for the Republican Party.

Media Matters for America, our organization, produces thousands of pieces of research a year focused on correcting conservative misinformation in the media. Our efforts to squelch such lies and distortions initially were distributed over a wide range of news sources—various conservative websites, radio programs, and television shows. But in early 2009, we noticed a marked increase in politically motivated misinformation coming from Fox News. Our attention was thus drawn increasingly to that channel—not only because they were serial violators of responsible journalism, but because their influence and reach within the media and with the public at large as the most-watched cable news network made it even more important to counteract their distortions of the truth. In early 2009, for instance, approximately 33 percent of our work focused on Fox News and its affiliates; in 2010, that number rose to 44 percent. By the beginning of 2011 we were spending more than 54 percent of our time focused on the network. This was not intentional; it was a matter of responding to this growing trend: the vast majority of the lies, smears, and distortions from conservative media flowed from or through Fox News.

We live in a cynical time, when words like "fair" and "balanced" are used as slogans to sell content that is anything but. When the words of lobbyists and the politicians they support are given equal weight with the consensus of scientific experts, by journalists who think a news story is a competition between opposing narratives rather than a judicious search for truth. Reporters often ask why they should trust Media Matters any more than Fox, given that both are ideological institutions. But this is precisely our point: Media Matters makes no claim of being neutral; we proudly wear our progressive ideology on our sleeve. We make decisions about the issues we focus on and the lies we debunk, just as newspapers choose what stories to cover. But our research and reporting stick to the facts and are painstakingly documented. Fox, on the other hand, claims to be a "fair and balanced" news network while brazenly broadcasting demonstrable lies and distortions, always with a conservative spin.

It is critical that the media, Democrats, opinion makers of all stripes, and the public at large understand what Fox News is. Too many reporters and commentators have continued to treat Fox as a news organization. By doing so, they enable the network to conduct a political campaign under the guise of a media outlet, influencing the outcome of legislative debates and elections.

It is all the more important to keep an eye on Fox because the rhetoric the network wields as a political weapon is filled with violent imagery and demonization. This is never a good practice, particularly at a time of economic instability, when social unrest and passions are high. Fox News personalities, unfortunately, have a habit of portraying their ideological opponents in outrageously negative ways. In the past few years its hosts have, among other things, compared President Obama, members of Congress, and progressive leaders to Nazis and genocidal dictators such as Adolf Hitler, Joseph Stalin, and Mao Zedong, and have referred to the president as a racist. Glenn Beck, one of Fox News's most popular personalities from 2009 to 2011, even simulated the assassination of House Speaker Nancy Pelosi on air by miming giving her a glass of poisoned wine, without any repercussions from network management. It's all harmless amusement until an unbalanced individual is riled up to perform an unspeakable act against a public official who has been reduced by media images into a two-dimensional, cardboard-cutout villain. The history of the United States—both early and recent—includes many examples of the unintended horrors that can result from this type of relentless and careless demonization.

Then there is the deliberate spread of misinformation. Polls consistently find Fox News viewers among the most ignorant on a variety of issues. For example, NBC News's online publication *First Read* reported in April 2009 that "72% of self-identified FOX News viewers believe the health-care plan will give coverage to illegal immigrants, 79% of them say it will lead to a government takeover, 69% think that it will use taxpayer dollars to pay for abortions, and 75% believe that it will allow the government to make decisions about when to stop providing care for the elderly."[12] As *First Read* pointed out, this was "rampant misinformation" that large numbers of Fox News viewers believed.

Following the 2010 election, the University of Maryland released a study finding that Fox News viewers were the most misinformed audience of any major news network. Compared with those who never watch Fox, frequent viewers of the network were:

- Thirty-one percentage points more likely to agree that "most economists have estimated the health care law will worsen the deficit." In fact, the nonpartisan Congressional Budget Office said just the opposite: that health care reform would actually decrease the deficit.

- Thirty-one points more likely to agree that "it is not clear that Obama was born in the United States." In fact, the birther claims had been repeatedly debunked during the 2008 election by numerous nonpartisan and even Republican sources, including former Hawaii governor Linda Lingle.

- Thirty points more likely to agree that "most scientists do not agree that climate change is occurring." In fact, there is broad scientific consensus that not only is climate change occurring but human activity is the cause.

- Fourteen points more likely to agree that "the stimulus legislation did not include any tax cuts." The nonpartisan PolitiFact .com noted that the stimulus bill provided tax cuts to 95 percent of workers.

- Fourteen points more likely to agree that "their own income taxes have gone up." Most Fox viewers could have confirmed this to be false by looking at their own tax return.

- Thirteen points more likely to agree that "the auto bailout only occurred under Obama." In fact, it had begun under George W. Bush.

- Twelve points more likely to agree that "most economists estimate the stimulus caused job losses."[13] *USA Today* reported with a banner headline in August 2010, "Economists Agree: Stimulus Created Nearly 3 Million Jobs."[14]

When confronted with this study, Michael Clemente, Fox's senior vice president for news, reacted in a telling way. Instead of expressing concern about Fox's apparent failure to inform their viewers, or arguing with the substance or methodology of the study, Clemente attacked the messenger, sarcastically impugning the reputation of the University of Maryland. Acting more like a political attack dog than a major media executive, Clemente told *The New York Times,* "The latest Princeton Review ranked the University of Maryland among the top schools for having 'Students Who Study the Least' and being the 'Best Party School,'" adding, "Given these fine academic distinctions, we'll regard the study with the same level of veracity it was 'researched' with."[15]

But this was hardly the first time Fox's viewers had been revealed to be conspicuously misinformed. In 2003, the Program on International Policy Attitudes conducted "a series of national polls between January and September." The results, as reported by *The San Diego Union Tribune,* found:

- "A majority of Americans (52 percent) believed evidence was found linking Iraq to September 11."
- "A large minority (35 percent) believed weapons of mass destruction were found in Iraq."
- "A majority (56 percent) believed most world opinion supported the war."
- "Fox led the list for those with at least one misperception (80 percent). It also led for those holding all three—45 percent, compared with 12 percent to 15 percent for the other networks."[16]

Misinformation has consequences, especially in a democracy. "In general, you end up with citizens who are acting on bad information when they carry out their civic duties," says Kelly McBride, an expert on media ethics at the Poynter Institute, speaking about the media in general. "It affects the governing of a nation. It inspires people to make their voting decisions on fear or lies."[17]

And the network's partisan misinformation has not been limited to the dry facts of reporting on political or legislative issues—some of the consequences of its poorly vetted and politically motivated investigations have unjustly and seriously damaged lives and careers. In the past few years Fox News has been involved in several high-profile attacks on progressive leaders, such as White House Special Advisor for Green Jobs, Enterprise and Innovation Van Jones; Assistant Deputy Secretary of Education Kevin Jennings; and Agriculture Department official Shirley Sherrod; as well as progressive organizations such as ACORN and Planned Parenthood. While it is completely appropriate for a news organization to investigate malfeasance by political appointees and major groups, instead of seeking to get to the bottom of these stories, Fox based its work on distortions, smears, and heavily edited video, often used out of context. These "news" stories had little to no journalistic value and were aired simply to harm progressives. Too often, these efforts were successful.

When discussing the problems of Fox, media watchers often get into conversations about bias. However, bias is not Fox News's core defect; nor is it what separates the network from CNN, MSNBC, or any other major news source. Nor is its main problem that it promotes tabloid journalism. Fox, rather, is something unprecedented in the United States: a news business that is willing to put politics above all else. While Rupert Murdoch, CEO of Fox's parent company, News Corp, is driven mostly by his bottom line, the management of Fox News, led by Roger Ailes, takes an active role in shaping the politics of the country and is willing to use Fox News's enormous platform to do so. Murdoch's discomfort with Fox News, while denied in on-the-record settings, has been widely reported. In his biography of the mogul, Michael Wolff describes a Murdoch who despises some of his most popular on-air talent, such as Bill O'Reilly, and whose politics, tough to pin down, can occasionally flirt with liberalism. "In steady, constantly discomfiting ways," Wolff writes, "Murdoch shares the feelings about Fox News regularly reflected in the general liberal apoplexy."[18]

Fox News began with a simple concept: build a network based on the triumph of conservative talk radio. This model was successful at the tail end of the Clinton administration and was even better suited to cheerlead for George W. Bush. In less than a decade, Fox News president Roger Ailes created for Rupert Murdoch a network with a built-in audience driven by its conservative ideology.

From the start, Fox had a profound effect on its viewers. In 2007, *The Quarterly Journal of Economics* published a study looking at differences between populations that received Fox News and those that did not. The authors found "a significant effect of exposure to Fox News on voting":

> Towns with Fox News have a 0.4 to 0.7 percentage point higher Republican vote share in the 2000 presidential elections, compared to the 1996 elections. A vote shift of this magnitude is likely to have been decisive in the 2000 elections. We also find an effect on vote share in Senate elections, which Fox News did not cover, suggesting that the Fox News impact extends to general political beliefs. Finally, we find evidence that Fox News increased turnout to the polls. Based on this evidence and on micro level audience data, we estimate that exposure to Fox News induced a substantial percentage of the non-Republican viewers to vote for the Republican party, 3 to 8 percent according to the more inclusive audience measure, and 11 to 28 percent according to the more restrictive measure.[19]

While the network already was having a significant impact, Fox began a transition in 2008. With conservatives out of power, no longer would it be merely a cheerleader for the conservative movement and the Republican Party. Now the network would wag the elephant, transforming itself from a news and opinion outlet into the leading communications, fund-raising, and mobilizing arm of the Republican Party. Or, as David Frum, then a fellow at the American Enterprise Institute and former George W. Bush speechwriter, told ABC News's Terry Moran, "Republicans originally thought that Fox worked for us and now we're discovering we work for Fox. And that the balance here has been completely reversed."[20]

The interview in which Frum made this comment followed a post on his blog, *Frum Forum,* in which he declared, after the passage of Barack Obama's health care plan, "Conservatives and Republicans today suffered their most crushing legislative defeat since the 1960s."[21] Frum placed the blame for this defeat squarely at the feet of one faction of his party: "There were leaders who knew better, who would have liked to deal. But they were trapped. Conservative talkers on Fox and talk radio had whipped the Republican voting base into such a frenzy that deal-making was rendered impossible." Frum continued, "How do you negotiate with somebody who wants to murder your grandmother? Or—more exactly—with somebody whom your voters have been persuaded to believe wants to murder their grandmother?"[22]

Part I

Attack and Destroy

Chapter 1
Roger's Rise

Let's face it, there are three things that the media are interested in: pictures, mistakes, and attacks.

—Roger Ailes

In 1968, at the beginning of his second presidential campaign, Richard Nixon stopped by the nationally syndicated variety program *The Mike Douglas Show* to make a guest appearance. So that he wouldn't have to share the green room with a burlesque performer named "Little Egypt," Nixon waited before his spot in the office of the show's twenty-seven-year-old executive producer. There Nixon, who had famously lost the first televised presidential debate to John F. Kennedy eight years earlier, bemoaned campaigning in the TV age. "It's a shame a man has to use gimmicks like this to get elected," he said.[1]

Nixon might have been a former vice president on his way to his second Republican nomination, but in that makeshift green room of *The Mike Douglas Show,* he was not top dog. That young producer, a man named Roger Ailes, turned to the future president and said, "Television is not a gimmick, and if you think it is, you'll lose again."[2]

Impressed, Nixon hired Ailes as his campaign media adviser. In this role, he managed Nixon's television strategy, which included the production of the candidate's "Man in the Arena" appearances, during which Nixon took questions from "citizen" panels in front of vetted studio audiences. Today, Ailes downplays his role in the '68 campaign, claiming, "People think I was involved in politics. I had no politics with Nixon. I was a television producer. Now *The New York Times* likes to make it like I was in charge of Southern strategy or something. I was in charge of back-lighting. Cameras. But I always saw a way to daylight."[3]

However, speaking to *The Washington Post* in 1972, Ailes described a much more involved role within the campaign. "I did (Nixon's) regional shows, television spots and that sort of thing. The whole 'man in the arena' concept was mine. Thirteen hours of live programming," said Ailes. "I produced and directed a one-hour rally from Madison Square Garden on the ABC network and then I produced and directed the four hours live from NBC the night before the election. I did all his live and tape stuff, the commercials per se."[4]

With his limited campaign experience, Roger Ailes had already gained an understanding of several fundamental truths that would drive not only future political campaigns, but also the future success of Fox News. Prior to the Nixon campaign, Ailes's experience on *The Mike Douglas Show* had taught him that, in the age of mass media, production value matters as much as, if not more than, substance or even truth. "I don't go out purposely and try and fool voters," said Ailes. "Sure, I know certain techniques: such as a press release that looks like a newscast. So you use it because you want your man to win."[5]

Working for Nixon in 1968, Ailes had his first opportunity to use these lessons and his ample media talent to subtly (and occasionally not-so-subtly) play on people's prejudices and fears in order to win their support for his candidate. Reporter Joe McGinniss witnessed Roger Ailes's manipulation of race firsthand during that Nixon campaign. In his book *The Selling of the President,* McGinniss recounts an exchange he had with Ailes during the process of casting a "Man in the Arena" appearance in Philadelphia. Ailes's first job was to find a diverse set of constituents for Nixon to interact with, fostering a realistic exchange for viewers on TV, while at the same time creating an environment where Nixon would thrive. In Philadelphia, he managed to recruit "an Italian lawyer from Pittsburgh, a liberal housewife from the Main Line, and a Young Republican from the Wharton School of Business."

But Ailes still had seats to fill. "Now we need a newsman," he told McGinniss. McGinniss suggested "the name of an articulate political reporter from the *Evening Bulletin* in Philadelphia." Ailes was excited and asked McGinniss to call him. However, the recommended reporter was African-American, which gave Ailes pause. "Oh, shit," he told McGinniss, "we can't have two. Even in Philadelphia. Wait a minute—call him, and if he'll do it we can drop the self-help guy." The newsman turned out not to be available for the event.

Joe McGinniss had an additional suggestion for Ailes's panel, a psychiatrist he knew who was "the head of a group that brought Vietnamese children wounded in the war to the United States for treatment and artificial limbs."[6] After booking the man, Ailes learned that Nixon hated psychiatrists and would not even appear in the same room as one. He also said the Nixon campaign wanted "to go easy on Jews for a while"—the psychiatrist in question being Jewish. "I guess Nixon's tired of saying 'balance of power' about the goddamn Middle East." Ailes called up and canceled, but now had an extra spot on the panel.

"You know what I'd like?" Ailes later told McGinniss. "As long as we've got this extra spot open. A good, mean, Wallaceite cab driver. Wouldn't that be great? Some guy to sit there and say, 'Alwright mac, what about these niggers?' "[7]

In a perfectly choreographed moment, according to Rick Perlstein's *Nixonland,* the candidate "could abhor the uncivility of the words, while endorsing a 'moderate' version of the opinion."[8] Out on the streets of Philadelphia, Ailes found his man, a cab driver named Frank Kornsey, who "was not really for Wallace, but he wasn't against him either."[9]

Kornsey ended up asking Nixon what he would do about North Korea's capture of the USS *Pueblo* spy ship, to which Nixon gave a rehearsed answer. Earlier in the program Nixon had been forced to answer an unfriendly question about the Vietnam War. While Frank Kornsey did not fill the role Ailes originally prescribed, his softball question still served a purpose.

Roger Ailes grew up in a working-class household in Warren, Ohio, where his father was the foreman of the Packard Electric plant. He suffered from hemophilia, which played a large role in his childhood. According to Ailes, his parents "always would drive me to school and sometimes I['d] have to sit on a pillow in class because I'd have hematomas in my leg. And I couldn't go out for play period, sometimes, and that was bad."[10]

His parents' fears were justified—one seemingly minor incident almost turned fatal:

The worst thing I ever had, which almost killed me, is I cut my lip and hurt my tongue. I cut through my tongue by jumping off a garage. I didn't hurt my legs, but I cut my tongue. I bit my tongue. They didn't think I was going to make it. They couldn't stop it—it was really bad. I was seven or eight, somewhere in there. And I was in the bed, I heard the doctor say—I wasn't sure what it meant, but I heard him say, "We really can't do anything." I thought, Oh shit. My dad grabbed me out of the bed, in the sheets—he had a guy with him, a lodge buddy. And they grabbed me and put me in a car, took me downstairs, threw me in the back seat . . . And I remember the guys that used to come up, Frank La-something and Dirty Neck Watson, guys that worked for my dad who were giving me direct transfusions from their arms to my arm. This was 1946, '47, '48, something around there. And they were scrubbing these guys down. They were filthy, they were just filthy guys. They all worked for my dad—it was maintenance work—and anybody who had a type O positive, my dad would bring them up and they [would] hook me up to them. And I remember lying in the bed and they put it in me and they put it in Dirty Neck Watson and he dumped some blood down, and they'd go to the next guy. "Well, son, you have a lot of blue-collar blood in you, never forget that," my father said after I got through it, and I never have. A lot of what we do at Fox is blue-collar stuff.[11]

Ailes attended Ohio University in Athens because, in his words, "they told me I could drink."[12] While he was away at school, his parents divorced. This came as a shock to Ailes, who recounted, "I went back, the house was sold, all my stuff was gone. I never found my stamp collection."[13] Ailes stayed at a friend's house;

his mother moved to California, and his father fell into a deep depression.

Only twenty-one years old, Ailes took a job with *The Mike Douglas Show* at a Cleveland television station. Five years later, he was the executive producer and the show had grown from a local hit to being seen by "6,000,000 housewives in 171 cities."[14]

After Nixon was elected with Ailes's help, conservatives set out to build an ideological infrastructure that would help them dominate political debate for decades. Institutions such as the Heritage Foundation popped up in Washington, D.C., funded by millionaires such as Richard Mellon Scaife and Joseph Coors.

For the moment, Roger Ailes stuck around Nixon land, serving as an adviser to the White House and the Republican National Committee. Ailes also launched a consulting company, REA Productions, which worked for numerous Republican campaigns. In February 1971, bragging about his work, he sent a note to White House Chief of Staff H. R. Haldeman, telling him, "I worked my tail off but by and large I think we were pretty successful."[15] To his note he attached congratulatory letters from senators, congressmen, governors, and state party chairmen.

Ailes was not universally liked in the Nixon White House. After an appearance by Ailes on a CBS morning news show in March 1970, Press Secretary Ron Ziegler wrote a memo to Haldeman noting that "too close a public association between Ailes and the President could lead to problems,"[16] due to the media consultant's ties to candidates in Republican primaries.

In May 1970, the Republican National Committee ended Ailes's contract, citing "severe budgetary problems."[17] However, in 1971, Ailes was granted an office in the Executive Office Building right next to the White House for use during "consultation visits to the

White House."[18] In a letter sent in June 1971, H. R. Haldeman congratulated him on his "new political trouble shooter role."[19]

When Ailes was fired from the Nixon White House, Haldeman was given talking points that claimed, "We have not been able to build the relationship between you and the president which we had hoped to see. It is no one's fault."[20] The memo also suggested Ailes could be involved in the creation of a "TV series with a pro-administration plot"[21] or a talk show starring Attorney General John Mitchell's wife.

Throughout his tenure in the Nixon administration, Ailes fought to convince his colleagues of the power of television. In November 1968, while Nixon was president-elect, Ailes wrote a "Confidential Report" that began by stating, "Television will play a major role in the Presidency of Richard M. Nixon." He continued, "When it is necessary to run for re-election, it will be the public's composite impression of the President (formed over four years) that will influence them."[22]

A little more than a year later, in December 1969, Ailes sent another "confidential" memo to Haldeman, pitching his company, telling the chief of staff: "It is contingent upon you appointing a person to be responsible who can organize and supervise [the White House's television operation]. Who knows the answers and where to find the answers and who is always 'thinking' and presenting ideas for you to use."[23]

Just under a year later, Ailes sent yet another memo to Haldeman with an apocalyptic warning: "In my opinion, Richard Nixon is in danger of becoming a one-term President. Further, he is in danger of leaving office, even if he is re-elected, with a stigma of leadership failure much as President Johnson did: not because of what he has done—his accomplishments are many—but because of what the people 'think' he has done, and because of the way he sounds and looks to them."[24]

Ailes further elaborated on his ideas in handwritten notes on an unsigned, undated memo titled "A Plan for Putting the GOP on TV News."[25] The memo, later released by the Nixon Presidential Library, sought to create a news dissemination organization to "avoid the censorship, the priorities and the prejudices of network news selectors and disseminators."

The concept was to create news packages featuring "pro-Administration, video tape, hard news actualities"[26] that could then be transmitted to and subsequently broadcast by local stations, which, at that point, were wholly dependent on the major networks for Washington stories. Ailes scribbled copious notes on the fourteen-page memo, at one point writing: "basically a very good idea." Later in the document, Ailes writes to "Bob"—presumably Haldeman: "If you decide to go ahead we would as a production company like to bid on packaging the entire project."[27]

It was during this period that the mega-donor Joseph Coors recognized the same missing piece of conservative infrastructure and set out to build that very network. An idea before its time, Television News Incorporated, or TVN, was set up to sell packages of national news to local stations to air on their nightly newscasts. The packages would be transmitted across phone lines, a slow and expensive process in 1972.

While much of TVN's story has faded into history, the *Columbia Journalism Review* documented the problems at the fledgling network in a March/April 1975 article titled "Coors Brews the News." From the start, Coors's ideological bent created difficulties for the network.

In the twenty-two months that TVN has been in business, the company has had four news directors (two were fired and an acting news director quit) and one mass firing of news staffers . . . Much of the fighting arose from management's feeling that journalists slanted the news in the direction of knee-jerk liberal beliefs and a feeling on the part of many TVN newsmen that management (the Coors family) wanted a right-wing news network.[28]

TVN became an organ for Joseph Coors's political views. He told the *Rocky Mountain News,* "[We] got into it because of our strong belief that network news is slanted to the liberal left side of the spectrum and does not give an objective view to the American public."[29]

To head the operation, Coors appointed Jack Wilson, who previously was news director of a station in Illinois. Wilson injected TVN with a very clear ideology, writing a series of memos with pronouncements such as:

- "Martin Luther King was an avowed communist revolutionary. It is not necessary for us to cover him or any of his subordinates (Abernathy) just because other networks do so."[30]
- "David Rockefeller. Nothing like this should ever be allowed on our air. Rockefeller took a communist public relations tour."[31]
- "The American Civil Liberties Union is generally recognized as the legal arm of the extreme left if not the Communist Party in the United States."[32]
- "The Environmental Protection Agency again raises the specter of deadly pollution. Our typical journalist is putting the government on a pedestal."[33]

Wilson also apparently had it in for Dan Rather. "I hate Dan Rather," former TVN news director Tom Turley quoted Wilson as saying. "I hate all those network people. They're destroying the country. We have to unify the county. TVN is the moral cement."[34]

These dictates were not just coming from Wilson. Joe Coors once approached a member of the TVN staff and asked, "Why are you covering Daniel Ellsberg? He's a traitor to his country."[35] Ellsberg, the informant who leaked the Pentagon Papers to lawmakers and *The New York Times* in 1971, certainly warranted coverage.

Memos from Wilson were just the tip of the iceberg. According to the *Columbia Journalism Review,* the interview process for employment at TVN sometimes included a screening by a Heritage Foundation official:

> Ex-staffers say at least three applicants for key TVN editorial jobs were jointly interviewed by Jack Wilson and by a member of the Heritage Foundation advisory board, John McCarty. McCarty is also on the board of the American Conservative Union. "It was a political litmus test," said Tom Turley, a former CBS assignment editor who became TVN's third news director in June 1974.[36]

Sometimes these conservative allies could control TVN's broadcasts. Paul Weyrich, the Heritage Foundation's first president, had returned to government, serving as an aide to the Republican senator Carl Curtis of Nebraska. At a news conference for the senator, Weyrich "produced a three-by-five index card listing questions he wanted asked and handed them to a TVN reporter, who then asked the questions."[37]

The first three news directors of TVN were reporters with a background in television news. The fourth would have an ideology that aligned with the Coors family's and no pesky journalistic integrity to get in the way. After doing some public relations consulting work for TVN, Roger Ailes transitioned to become the network's news director. The reason for his appointment was clear, according to a TVN staffer: "The Coors people trust Ailes because of his affiliation with the Republicans, and because he's not a newsman. They don't trust newsmen."[38]

The parallels with Fox News could not be more striking.[39] At TVN, Ailes helped run a network built on defaming liberals as communists, attacking environmentalists, and demonizing mainstream journalists, all the while carrying on the pretense of impartial reporting. The *Columbia Journalism Review* concluded, "News Director Ailes says he wants a non-partisan news service. Perhaps he, like his predecessors, will resist any pressure to the contrary. Or perhaps the pressure will cease. But will it? The record indicates that it has been management policy to strengthen, not weaken, the role of Wilson (and therefore, one assumes Coors) while diminishing the role of independent journalists."[40]

TVN was an idea before its time. Covering the news was expensive, and stations carrying the network's signal had to pay AT&T an additional $2,500[41] a month in transmission costs. This further limited the pool of stations willing to pay for TVN's services. The network fell into debt, and operations were no longer financially feasible. In 1975, TVN was essentially shuttered.

Thirteen years later, during George H. W. Bush's 1988 campaign for president, Ailes was a hardened political operative who knew how to use television perfectly to manipulate voters. He would script every moment of his candidate's performance. In a June 1988 profile, *Time* magazine captured Ailes's relationship with the future president: "George Bush eases into a hotel armchair for an interview with Tom Brokaw. Suddenly a burly, bearded figure bounds across the room and, without a word, yanks an errant hair from the vice-presidential eyebrow. 'That hurt,' winces Bush as a grinning Roger Ailes leaves the room, satisfied that he has put his finishing touch on the scene."[42]

In Bush, Ailes had found a reverse Eliza Doolittle, as he attempted to turn the blue-blooded vice president into an everyman. "Roger smoked out the fact that Bush was surrounded by bland, upper-class, middlebrow, tennis-playing second raters," one former Bush adviser said. "Roger would tell Bush, 'You can't wear a short-sleeve shirt—you'll look like a fucking faggot.' "[43] Ailes denies using the slur.

Time also provided an example of Ailes's ability to manipulate the media. When tipped off[44] that Dan Rather would ambush his candidate during an interview, Ailes advised Bush to tell the newsman: " 'It's not fair to judge my whole career by a rehash on Iran. How would you like it if I judged your career by those seven minutes when you walked off the set in New York?' The tactic illustrates an Ailes axiom: when attacked, hit back so hard your opponent rues the day he got nasty."[45]

It's that aggression that veteran operative Lee Atwater, who brought Ailes onto the Bush campaign, was referring to when he remarked that Roger Ailes "has two speeds. Attack and destroy."[46] This occasionally included people and inanimate objects. Once, angry that a table at Bush campaign headquarters had not been repaired, Ailes walked into the conference room, grabbed the piece of furniture, and flipped it over, in full view of the staff.[47]

What history remembers of the 1988 campaign was its ugly turn into racial politics, exemplified by the infamous Willie Horton ad. Willie Horton was a convicted murderer serving a life sentence in Massachusetts. He was permitted to leave prison as part of a weekend furlough program supported by Governor Michael Dukakis. After failing to return to jail, Horton committed multiple crimes, including armed robbery and rape. George Bush repeatedly raised the case in campaign speeches, and an independent group called the National Security PAC spent $8.5 million running an ad featuring Horton that was widely condemned for its crude racial overtones. While the Bush campaign always maintained it was not responsible for the infamous ad, in the midst of the summer leading up to the election, Ailes's interest in exploiting the issue was no secret. He even told a reporter, "The only question is whether we depict Willie Horton with a knife in his hand or without it."[48]

Following the campaign the Federal Election Commission launched an investigation to determine whether the Bush campaign had coordinated with the independent group, which would have been illegal. Ailes claimed during a deposition that he had only been joking when he made the remark, telling investigators, "I never say anything to the press I'm actually going to do."[49]

While being questioned by FEC attorneys, Ailes once again made his views on race and politics clear:

Q: Did the Bush committee have any policy about not using Mr. Horton's photograph?

A: I have no knowledge of that. I personally rejected the use of Mr. Horton in the advertisement.

Q: How is that?

A: A young researcher brought me a picture of him sometime and I tore it up and threw it in the wastebasket and said we're not going to do that.

Q: And why is that?

A: I knew the issue would backlash because of the liberal media.[50]

The real problem with the Willie Horton ad was, of course, its use of race to frighten voters and divide the country along racial lines. The FEC's attorneys continued their line of questioning:

Q: And what was that about?

A: When Republicans see Willie Horton they see a criminal, and when Democrats see Willie Horton they see a black.[51]

On his next major campaign, Roger Ailes picked up right where he left off. He served as media consultant for Rudy Giuliani's first New York City mayoral campaign, which placed an ad in a prominent Jewish newspaper, the *Algemeiner Journal,* featuring an image of Giuliani's opponent, David Dinkins—who would become New York City's first African-American mayor—alongside Jesse Jackson. The ad also showed Giuliani with President George H. W. Bush, and the headline read: "Let the People of New York Choose Their Own Destiny."[52]

At the time, Howard Kurtz wrote, "Ira Silverman, vice president of the American Jewish Committee, said the Giuliani ad seemed a 'legitimate campaign tactic,' but said that he found it 'troubling' because it 'preys upon the fears of the Jewish community.' "[53]

National Public Radio explained, "Giuliani also tagged Dinkins as a 'Jesse Jackson Democrat.' That was an appeal to the city's large contingent of Jewish voters, who had despised Jackson ever since he used an anti-Semitic epithet to describe New York. In this context, Giuliani's signature issue of crime took on racial overtones, says political consultant Norman Adler."[54]

The campaign also had its own Willie Horton, a kidnapper named Robert "Sonny" Carson. Carson "and several others were convicted in 1974 of kidnapping a man they suspected of stealing money. The kidnapped man was shot in the head, but Carson was acquitted of murder and attempted murder."[55] Out of prison, he "became a community organizer" and worked for a group that had received funds from the Dinkins campaign "to help get out the vote."[56]

Giuliani used Carson to rebuke Dinkins, telling audiences, "Imagine if this fellow Dinkins is sitting in City Hall, and he starts hiring Sonny Carsons on us, and he starts paying out $8,000 to $10,000 without receipts."[57]

The New York Times also reported, "A new Giuliani television advertisement, aimed largely at wavering Democrats, features six apparently ordinary New Yorkers, who describe Mr. Dinkins as 'a follower.' They complain, among other things, about 'the crowd' around Mr. Dinkins, including Robert (Sonny) Carson, a former campaign functionary who later proclaimed himself to be anti-white. Another person in the commercial says, 'I'm tired of living in New York and being scared.' "[58]

When asked about the "parallels" to the Willie Horton ads, Ailes replied, "They're both felons and they're both black, but that's not my fault."[59] Democratic consultant Bill Cunningham was quoted in the same news account, painting a picture of Ailes as a political consultant: " 'This is where he makes his money. If you go into the alleyway with him, he comes after you with a bottle or a brick.' "[60]

After Giuliani's campaign, Ailes returned to TV, producing a syndicated show starring Rush Limbaugh. The show remained on the air for four years but never matched the audience or influence of his radio platform.

In August 1993, while still executive producer of the program,

Ailes moved over to CNBC, which he helped turn into the dominant force in business news.

At NBC, Ailes unsuccessfully tried to create another channel. Launched on Independence Day in 1994, *America's Talking* built its lineup around low-budget talk shows. The softer network featured shows like *Pork,* "a political talk show focusing on government waste,"[61] and *Bugged!,* a "comedic look at what bugs people."[62] Ailes even hosted a celebrity talk show called *Straight Forward.* However, *America's Talking* failed to catch on. The network's most enduring legacy was a show called *Politics with Chris Matthews,* which became *Hardball* on MSNBC. When NBC began the process of creating MSNBC, it failed to include Ailes, freeing him to launch a competing network.

After his stint at CNBC, Ailes decided he would attempt to resurrect the Limbaugh model. This time, though, he wouldn't create a single conservative show. Instead, with the support of Australian media mogul Rupert Murdoch, he would mold an entire network based on his Limbaugh television experiment.

Ailes's recipe for success with the Fox News Channel, for the first decade of its existence, was to take conservative talk radio and move it onto cable television. While this programming annoyed the left and galvanized the right, it didn't operate with a set of organizing goals in mind. Furthermore, the right was in power. Although Fox News was founded while Bill Clinton was still in the White House, it rose to prominence during the George W. Bush administration. During this period, Bush was the singular leader of both the Republican Party and the conservative movement—the president's chief political adviser, Karl Rove, made sure of that. In post-9/11 America, Fox News was to be a cheerleader, not a campaigner, and definitely not a critic.

Ailes's broadcast philosophy followed his political philosophy, which he outlined to Judy Woodruff during the Campaign Managers Forum at Harvard following the 1988 election:

ROGER AILES: Let's face it, there are three things that the media are interested in: pictures, mistakes, and attacks. That's the one sure way of getting coverage. You try to avoid as many mistakes as you can. You try to give them as many pictures as you can. And if you need coverage, you attack, and you will get coverage.

It's my orchestra pit theory of politics. If you have two guys on stage and one guy says, "I have a solution to the Middle East problem," and the other guy falls in the orchestra pit, who do you think is going to be on the evening news? (Laughter)

One thing you don't want to do is get your head up too far on some new vision for America because the next thing that happens is the media runs over to the Republican side and says, "Tell me why you think this is an idiotic idea."

JUDY WOODRUFF: So you're saying the notion of the candidate saying, "I want to run for president because I want to do something for this country," is crazy.

ROGER AILES: Suicide.[63]

Running Fox News has made Ailes an extremely rich man. And Rupert Murdoch has given him an unheard-of level of control at the network. According to Michael Wolff, Murdoch "gives Ailes what he has never given any of his editors—never given the *Times* of London, even though his pledge has the force of law, and likely never will give the *Wall Street Journal*, although he'll swear he will: fundamental editorial independence. . . . Ailes himself can't be overruled about what goes on air."[64]

Fox News is primarily a reflection of Roger Ailes, and the conservative movement has noticed. In 2009, speaking at a Boy Scouts dinner honoring Ailes, Rush Limbaugh commented, "One man has established a culture for 1,700 people who believe in it, who follow it, who execute it. Roger Ailes cannot do everything. Roger Ailes is not on the air. Roger Ailes does not ever show up on camera, and yet everybody who does is a reflection of him."[65]

Politics, from the start, was Ailes's primary passion. "I didn't have to go into politics. I was a successful $60,000-a-year executive with Westinghouse producing their largest show," he told *The Washington Post* in 1972. "I had it made, in effect, where I was. I took a hell of a gamble with my own career."[66]

Now he would return to his first love—the art of public persuasion. As Ailes himself said in a 1971 speech titled "Candidate + Money + Media = Votes," "Being deeply interested in and involved in television and politics, I find it difficult to divorce the two from the rest of our life."[67] Thirty-five years later, Ailes had more money and a larger platform to launch a campaign than ever before, and there was no candidate to screw it all up.

On January 20, 2009, the Republican Party was left leaderless. George W. Bush was aboard Air Force One, heading back to Texas for good. His father, never a favorite of the conservative base, was happily ensconced in retirement and for the better part of two decades had shown no interest in the day-to-day tussle of electoral politics.

The party's 2008 presidential candidate, Senator John McCain, was in no position to remain the standard-bearer following his resounding defeat. The conservative base of the Republican Party had merely settled for John McCain at the top of the ticket. While their support was firmed up by the selection of running mate Sarah Palin, they would never accept McCain as their leader.

Palin, for that matter, had won the love of the conservative base, but by January 2009, she was back in the governor's mansion in Alaska. It was not until the following summer that she would step down in order to take on a higher national profile and cash in on her newfound celebrity. Additionally, Palin was too much of a political neophyte for even her most ardent supporters to argue persuasively that she was ready to be the party's leader.

Michael Steele, who would be elected chairman of the Republican National Committee ten days after Obama's inauguration, soon proved himself cursed with the inability to appear on camera without embarrassing himself. Many insiders doubted he would survive even a year, while others were working behind the scenes to make sure his term would never be successful.

Mitch McConnell and John Boehner, the Republican leaders in Congress, were too busy with the parochial concerns of running a legislative caucus. Congress, in any case, has never been an ideal platform for leading a movement, given that its leaders' primary constituencies are the members of their own caucuses, whose individual interests often diverge from those of the party's base.

Had it been 1993, Rush Limbaugh might have stepped in to fill the void. His platform had grown, and he certainly tapped into the Republican id when he proclaimed, "I hope he fails," just days before President Obama's inauguration.[68] But Limbaugh didn't have the desire or energy to run the kind of sustained campaign required to lead the party. Broadcasting an enormously profitable radio show one hundred yards from the ocean in West Palm Beach, Florida, is one thing; traveling around the country ginning up the base is another.

The only conservative pundit with the energy and desire to

take on such a mission might have been Glenn Beck. But Beck had begun his new show at Fox News the day before Obama was sworn in, and he had yet to build his army of followers.

At the very moment the conservative movement was leaderless, it desperately needed one. Its grassroots—from the libertarians who wanted the government small enough to drown in a bathtub; to the religious right who feared what America would become with a liberal and, in their minds, possibly a Muslim, in the White House; to the neocons who saw their foreign policy aims in Iraq and Afghanistan crumble before their eyes—were left adrift, confident only of two things.

First, the Republican establishment had failed them. Eight years in power, four of which were completely unchecked, had bred corruption. The promise of the 1994 Republican revolution was now a distant memory. The size of the federal government had ballooned under Republican control. Instead of eliminating entitlements such as Medicare, George W. Bush oversaw the largest expansion of the program since its inception. Instead of tearing down the Department of Education, Bush expanded its power under the No Child Left Behind Act.

Conservatives were certain that the American people had not rejected their principles, but rather the devastating elections of 2006 and 2008 were lost because of the endemic corruption and incompetence that had taken hold of the Republican Party. According to this logic, conservatives didn't lose in 2008. Republicans, led by McCain, had.

Second, President Obama was their worst nightmare. This was a president with an exotic name, who was liberal, urban, and "pallin' around with terrorists,"[69] as Sarah Palin suggested. At the same time, Obama led a huge army, with an e-mail list of more than thirteen million followers, with a public appeal and private cool that made some on the right wonder if they would even be able to compete in the 2012 election.

Conservatives felt alone and insecure for the first time in nearly a decade. Suddenly in the minority, they were looking for a way to channel their anger. They wanted to fight the change that was occurring all around them, but had no means to do so.

Roger Ailes, having cultivated the conservative movement as his network's core audience for over a decade, must have been waiting for this moment. Seven years earlier, the president of Fox News had seen his network overtake CNN in the ratings, making it the most-watched cable news network. Now was his chance to lead a movement—not with his own voice, but, as he had done so effectively in the past, by channeling his political ambitions through others.

After more than a decade of Ailes's leadership, Fox News had been transformed into the ideal platform from which he could take advantage of this very situation. He was in control of the largest political megaphone on the right, speaking directly with more conservatives every day than any arm of the Republican Party. He had loyal lieutenants in his prime-time hosts Bill O'Reilly and Sean Hannity, and in executives such as Washington managing editor Bill Sammon and Michael Clemente. And, on the day before Barack Obama became commander in chief, Ailes added a new weapon to his arsenal: Glenn Beck.

Whenever confronted, even in a friendly environment, about the role Fox plays in American politics, Ailes does his best Gomer Pyle impression, giving his audience an aw-shucks response. "I'm not in politics anymore," he claimed in an April 26, 2010, speech at Ave Maria School of Law. "I don't do politics, I do the news."[70] One could presume this was as friendly an audience as Ailes could attract, considering conservative Domino's Pizza founder Tom

Monaghan was the primary source of funding for the school. In the same speech, showing his true colors, Ailes put his role as newsman aside, arguing that President Obama's health care bill was unconstitutional.

Throughout his political hiatus, there were hints of Roger Ailes's restlessness. Bob Woodward, in his book *Bush at War,* caused a stir by highlighting a message Ailes sent to Karl Rove following the September 11, 2001, terrorist attacks, which offered strategic political advice to the White House. Woodward wrote:

> Roger Ailes, former media guru for Bush's father, had a message, Rove told the president. It had to be confidential because Ailes, a flamboyant and irreverent media executive, was currently the head of FOX News, the conservative-leaning television cable network that was enjoying high ratings. In that position, Ailes was not supposed to be giving political advice. His back-channel message: The American public would tolerate waiting and would be patient, but only as long as they were convinced that Bush was using the harshest measures possible. Support would dissipate if the public did not see Bush acting harshly.[71]

Ailes did not deny he sent the message, but he protested the context. "Bob Woodward's characterization of my memo is incorrect," he shot back. "In the days following 9/11, our country came together in nonpartisan support of the president. During that time, I wrote a personal note to a White House staff member as a concerned American expressing my outrage about the attacks on our country. I did not give up my American citizenship to take this job."[72]

Ailes was doing the job of a political consultant, not acting as the head of a news network. Following its familiar pattern, Fox News responded by attacking CNN head Rick Kaplan and the host of NBC's *Meet the Press,* Tim Russert, for their supposedly close ties with Democrats. "Mr. Ailes said his letter was not comparable to Mr. Kaplan's 'sitting up all night in the White House' giving advice to Mr. Clinton," wrote Bill Carter and Jim Rutenberg in *The New York Times.* "He also said the letter was far less worthy of scrutiny than a meeting between the NBC anchor Tim Russert and Democratic senators last year in which Mr. Russert, who long worked in Democratic politics, offered what Mr. Ailes described as 'strategic tips and advice.' "[73] Both Kaplan and Russert denied giving advice to Bill Clinton or Senate Democrats.

Roger Ailes's political involvement did not stop at letters to political allies. An explosive charge was leveled in a 2007 lawsuit filed against News Corp. Court documents reveal that executives at the company attempted to coerce publisher Judith Regan to withhold information from federal investigators in order to protect the political ambitions of Ailes's former client Rudy Giuliani.

After working at the mayor's firm Giuliani Partners, former New York City police commissioner Bernard Kerik had been nominated by George W. Bush to head the Department of Homeland Security. Regan had been Kerik's lover, often meeting him for trysts in an apartment originally reserved for 9/11 rescue workers. According to the lawsuit, a "senior executive in the News Corp. organization told Regan that he believed she had information about Kerik that, if disclosed, would harm Giuliani's presidential campaign. This executive advised Regan to lie to, and to withhold information from, investigators concerning Kerik.... [D]efendants knew they would be protecting Giuliani if they could preemptively discredit her."[74]

Documents released as part of a subsequent suit between

Regan and her attorneys revealed that it was Roger Ailes whom Regan had accused of instructing her to lie about Kerik's misdeeds to protect the former mayor. According to an affidavit sworn by Seth Redniss, one of the attorneys who drafted Regan's suit, "a recorded telephone call between Roger Ailes, the chairman of Fox News (a News Corp. company), and Regan" took place, during which "Mr. Ailes discussed with Regan her responses to questions regarding her personal relationship with Bernard Kerik."[75]

A real news executive would strive to report on the misdeeds of those appointed to serve in or run for high federal office. Ailes instead used his perch to insulate future presidential candidate Rudy Giuliani from attacks.

While Roger Ailes refuses to take credit for his place in the political ecosystem, other Republicans openly tout his influence. In June 2010, conservative MSNBC host Joe Scarborough told his audience, "If you'd wanna win, seriously, Roger Ailes . . . is the most powerful voice in the Republican Party. He has set up something that—it is the only organizing institution for the GOP because everybody's let Republicans down in Washington, D.C."[76]

Because of Fox's standing as a "news" channel, Roger Ailes knew the network's reporting, unlike the rants of Rush Limbaugh or conservative radio host Michael Savage, would be taken seriously by others in the media. He might not have gone to the Columbia School of Journalism—in fact, Ailes mocked those who did—but he knew how professional journalists operated and would use that knowledge to manipulate them.

Even though he's now more than seventy years old, Ailes's current and former employees and colleagues still speak about him with a sense of fear. Nothing angers Ailes more than people leaking information about his network, and nobody wants to be the target of his wrath. A former Fox employee described Ailes's philosophy, stating, "When [Ailes] gets really crazy is when stuff leaks out the door. He goes mental on that. He can't stand that. He says in a dynamic enterprise like a network newsroom, there's going to be infighting and ego, but he says keep it in the house."[77]

Roger Ailes's intense paranoia extends beyond leaks from inside the Fox network. In his biography of Rupert Murdoch, Michael Wolff writes, "[Ailes] is a man of overriding obsessions, including his belief that he has been earmarked by Arab terrorists, which costs News Corp. a considerable premium for his 24/7 security apparatus." Wolff continues, "Delivering Ailes to work, his driver and bodyguard call from the SUV so that a second security team can fan out on the plaza in front of the News Corp. headquarters for Ailes' arrival."[78]

On one occasion, after seeing a man whom he "perceived" to be Muslim on the security monitor in his office, "Roger tore up the whole floor," a source close to Ailes told Tim Dickinson of *Rolling Stone*. "He has a personal paranoia about people who are Muslim—which is consistent with the ideology of his network." Ailes screamed, "This guy could be bombing me!"[79] The terrorist Roger Ailes thought was out to get him was a janitor.

Beyond a high level of personal security, Ailes has a penchant for contacting law enforcement from his weekend home in Putnam County, New York. According to the gossip website *Gawker*, "All told, according to police records we obtained from the Putnam County Sheriff's Department via New York's Freedom of Information Law, cops have been called to the Ailes' home 10 times since 2009." The report continued, "In eight of those calls, units were actually sent to the house. None of the calls resulted in an investigation, arrest, or determination that any criminal activity had taken place."[80]

Ailes has purchased two papers in upstate New York, the *Putnam County News and Recorder* and the *Putnam County Courier,* for his wife to run. True to form, he did not envision these as sleepy small-town papers. To run the venture, the Aileses hired former *Weekly Standard* staffer Joe Lindsley, who would move the political bent of the papers rightward. Lindsley resigned in April 2011. Afterward, according to *Gawker,* "he was driving to a deli in Cold Spring for lunch . . . when he noticed a black Lincoln Navigator that seemed to be following him, according to several sources familiar with the incident." Even more shocking, "Then he got a look at the driver, who was a News Corporation security staffer that Lindsley happened to know socially. Lindsley continued on his way and later called the driver to ask if he was following him. The answer was yes, at Ailes's direction."[81]

The Putnam papers were not News Corp. properties, yet Ailes was seemingly using the company's security to deal with a personal conflict. The surveillance was not limited to a single incident. According to *Gawker,* Ailes told three staff members, including Lindsley, that "he'd had them followed, and their private conversations surveilled, to catch them saying mean things about him."[82] These allegations were denied by Roger Ailes's wife, Elizabeth, in an e-mail to *Gawker:* "These rambling allegations are untrue and in fact not even reality based."[83]

Ailes's fights in Putnam County extend beyond his own employees. He also feuded with a rival newspaper owner, Don Hall. At a local business expo, Ailes confronted his eighty-year-old competitor and "pushed him in the chest and threatened to sue him"[84] for printing an unflattering story that had already appeared in *The New*

York Times. Ailes, of course, denies the incident occurred, stating, "There was no dispute with Don Hall—we had a joking conversation, but he may have missed the point—he's not exactly a barrel of laughs. As for suing Don, that would be fruitless because he's broke. I also never 'poked him in the chest'—if I did, he would have toppled over since he's only 60 pounds."[85]

Ailes's paranoid style and its resulting aggressive and over-the-top reactions create a climate of fear among current and former employees. Michael Wolff observed, "Everybody outside Fox News and inside News Corp. is afraid of Roger Ailes."[86]

Chapter 2

The Path to the Top

*You can produce a cable television network with people who talk nicely and are
articulate and are blonde and look good on television and say provocative things.
But it is not based on any discovery or intent to get to the bottom of something.*
— Michael Shanahan, George Washington
University School of Media and Public Affairs

Rupert Murdoch was steaming. Months earlier, at a news
conference in January 1996 announcing the creation of Fox News,
Roger Ailes had told assembled reporters, "[Fox News would] like
to be premier journalists. We'd like to restore objectivity where
we find it lacking. And certainly there could be that interpretation
because of my background. But I left politics a number of years
ago and run a news organization for the last two years. So we just
expect to do fine, balanced journalism."[1]

This was contradicted by Ailes's actions almost immediately
after he began at the company. Joe Peyronnin, who was president
of Fox News, recounted that the network boss asked some of the
staff "if they were liberal or not." He continued, "There was a
litmus test. He was going to figure out who was liberal or conservative when he came in, and try to get rid of the liberals."[2]

Now Murdoch's news network was weeks away from launch, and what was to be another jewel in his empire already looked as if it had been struck with a deathblow. Time Warner Cable in New York, with its millions of subscribers, announced it would not carry Fox News. MSNBC, another new arrival, would appear on the cable system's lineup instead.

Murdoch was not used to losing. Over forty years, he had built an empire, beginning with a single newspaper in Adelaide, a city on the southern coast of Australia. After acquiring numerous papers around the county, including Sydney's *Daily Mirror,* he founded Australia's first national daily in 1964. From there, he expanded to the United Kingdom and around the world. The year after he became a naturalized U.S. citizen in 1985, which legally permitted him to own broadcast stations, Murdoch founded the Fox Broadcasting Company. Along the way he had battled government regulators, politicians, unions, and, of course, rival newspapers, usually winding up on top, though sometimes after great expense. Few doubted Murdoch would fight to ensure that Fox News was broadcast in New York City.

Fox News was always a political operation at heart, and it had an ally in New York City's Republican mayor and former Ailes client Rudy Giuliani. At a party celebrating the network's launch, executives spoke with representatives from the mayor's office.[3] Shortly thereafter it was announced that New York City would grant Fox News one of the channels it owned on the cable system. The programming on these channels was supposed to carry public interest broadcasts. According to an article in *The New York Times* announcing the deal, "The News Corporation would pay the city for access to the channel and give unspecific support to other Crosswalks channels. In return, it would be allowed to carry commercials."[4]

This was an unprecedented and clearly illegal decision expressly prohibited by the Cable Communications Act of 1984, in which Congress forbade municipally owned channels to carry commercial programming. In order to attempt to make the decision more politically palatable, the Giuliani administration also granted a channel to another upstart network, Bloomberg Television.

It was clear why the Giuliani administration would take such an action. While some claimed the move "would bring jobs to the city," *The New York Times* reported that "aides told"[5] the paper, "Officials resented what they saw as a liberal bias in the news media, so by helping Mr. Murdoch, they were protecting what they believed was the only media conglomerate with a conservative voice."[6]

A little more than a week later, Federal District Judge Denise Cote issued an injunction prohibiting the city from broadcasting Fox News, writing in her decision, "The City's action violates long-standing First Amendment principles that are the foundation of our democracy. . . . The city has engaged in a pattern of conduct with the purpose of compelling Time Warner to alter its constitutionally protected editorial decision not to carry Fox News."[7]

Time Warner, of course, was no saint. Refusing to carry Fox News was a business decision made to protect its own interests. The media conglomerate owned CNN, and Ted Turner served as vice chairman of its board. News Corp. and Time Warner eventually settled their differences, and the cable company agreed to carry Fox News as part of an unrelated business transaction.

Fox's behavior throughout this episode was telling. Even prior to its launch, Republican politicians had recognized the network's potential—or at the least the political leanings of its owner. While purporting to be "fair and balanced," Fox had the ability to summon the assistance of leading political figures even before a single minute of programming aired. How would these efforts be repaid?

The ability of Fox News to beat the odds and become the highest-rated cable news channel is a testament to Roger Ailes's talent. At the time of Fox's launch, CNN was nearly twenty years old. It had grown from a scrappy cable network to the station of record. MSNBC launched around the same time as Fox News and was a partnership between NBC, with a newsgathering army of thousands at its disposal, and Microsoft, the untouchable technology king.

On the other hand, the Fox network had only a limited news department, and its programming centered on comedies such as *The Simpsons* and *Married . . . with Children.*[8] CNN and NBC already had correspondents around the world; they had studios, producers, and talent whose names were nationally known. Fox had none of these advantages.

Whenever big news broke—O.J.'s car chase or the bombing of the USS *Cole*—cable audiences turned to CNN. The network provided the best, most up-to-the-minute coverage of these events. But even with its early advantage, CNN quickly recognized the potent competition it would soon face. The network's ratings were already on the downswing, and now it had to contend with two new rivals. The channel needed a change.

Rick Kaplan, who left ABC to become the president of CNN in the fall of 1997, had a solution. Instead of following Fox's lead and creating its own opinion programming, CNN tried to reinvent the television news magazine. Shows like *60 Minutes* and *20/20* had the ability to draw huge audiences and revenue. Kaplan thought he could emulate this format on cable. This error in judgment proved to be nearly fatal.

CNN's first attempt at a magazine show, *Newsstand,* launched with a sensational story claiming that during the Vietnam War, American troops hunted down deserters in Laos and killed them with nerve gas. The story was immediately attacked, and the network's internal investigation concluded, "CNN should retract the story and apologize."[9]

Following the scandal's blowback, CNN was still the goliath of cable news. Fox was a fraction of the size, and its biggest names were unknown quantities—but Ailes had a knack for identifying and cultivating talent.

Bill O'Reilly, the star who would headline Fox's prime-time lineup, had worked his way up through the television news business, first at a string of local stations and eventually making the jump to become a correspondent at CBS and then ABC News. In his highest-profile role, O'Reilly was the anchor of the syndicated tabloid news program *Inside Edition*.

According to Scott Collins's book *Crazy Like a Fox,* "O'Reilly pitched the executives at King World (which distributed *Inside Edition*) a show that resembled an edgy, opinionated version of *Nightline*."[10] They declined, and O'Reilly left television to earn a master's degree from the Kennedy School of Government at Harvard. Ailes, however, brought the concept to Fox News, and when the show did not perform in its original 6 p.m. time slot, it was Ailes who took the risk of moving the show to 8 p.m.

The O'Reilly Factor's success now seems like a forgone conclusion. However, the show was revolutionary when it launched in 1996. Opinion programming was still dominated by the *Crossfire* format—the left and the right debating each other. Larry King, who hosted a nonideological political and celebrity schmooze-fest, owned prime-time cable news.

O'Reilly's acerbic style was an unknown quantity. Instead of conducting standard interviews, he was willing to throw red meat at his audience. And it worked. Fox's ratings began to climb, though it still lagged far behind CNN and MSNBC.

As the 2000 presidential race began to heat up, Fox found its niche. The network's average daily audience was still barely half of CNN's, but there were times—during the Republican National Convention, for example—when Fox News actually surpassed CNN in the ratings.[11]

To aid that year's election-night coverage, Fox hired journalist and media consultant John Ellis to help analyze the results. It was Ellis who determined that Fox News should call the state of Florida—and the election—for George W. Bush, leaving the rest of the networks playing catch-up. They would retract this prediction hours later, but the projection, while not carrying any official weight, set in motion the dynamic that Bush had already won and created the perception that Gore's attempts to get a recount made him a sore loser. Ellis was not an impartial observer; he was a Bush cousin who had been communicating with the campaign's headquarters all night.

As the recount election unfolded, Fox News offered its conservative audience a steady stream of coverage designed to reinforce their worldview. "I think what's going on is Democratic lawyers have flooded Florida. They are afraid of George W. Bush becoming president and instituting tort reform and their gravy train will be over," Fox News anchor John Gibson editorialized. "This is the trial association's full court press to make sure Bush does not win."[12]

Conservatives flocked to Fox as the place to get news during the hotly contested Florida recount, and it passed MSNBC in the ratings, averaging more than one million viewers per night in November 2000.[13]

That month also offered evidence that Fox was more than

simply a news channel to Republicans. When the network came under fire for Ellis's critical role on election night, the Bush team leapt to its defense. "The media is full of people who are very close to candidates," campaign spokesperson and future White House press secretary Ari Fleischer said. "The exception is to be close to a Republican. The norm is to be close to a Democrat."[14]

In the Congressional hearings that followed the election-night debacle, Roger Ailes began his testimony with a conciliatory note, admitting, "Fox News, along with all the other television networks, made errors on election night which cannot be repeated, the biggest of which occurred in Florida." Ailes continued, "Fox News acknowledges here that it failed the American public on Election Night and takes full responsibility for this failure."[15]

Ailes then eagerly defended his employee to the committee: "Mr. Ellis is the first cousin of President George W. Bush and Governor Jeb Bush. We at Fox News do not discriminate against people because of their family connections." Ailes, according to his testimony, saw an advantage in employing someone related to George W. Bush:

> I am aware that Mr. Ellis was speaking to then Governor George W. Bush and Jeb Bush on election night. Obviously, through his family connections, Mr. Ellis has very good sources. I do not see this as a fault or shortcoming of Mr. Ellis. Quite the contrary, I see this as a good journalist talking to his very high level sources on election night. Our investigation of election night 2000 found not one shred of evidence that Mr. Ellis revealed information to either or both of the Bush brothers which he should not have, or that he acted improperly or broke any rules or policies of either Fox News or VNS [Voter News Service, which provided polling data].[16]

Ailes made these remarks even after it was confirmed by Jane Mayer of *The New Yorker* that Ellis's communications with his family were not entirely professional in nature. In her accounting of election night at Fox News headquarters, she wrote:

> As the afternoon wore on, things weren't looking good for George W. Bush. At about 6 P.M., after two waves of exit polls, Fox News's chairman, Roger Ailes, called Ellis into his office for a private briefing. "What's your gut say?" Ailes asked him. Silently, Ellis slid his index finger across his throat.
>
> Soon afterward, Ellis received a telephone call from the Bush brothers. "They were, like, 'How we doin'?' " Ellis recalled. "I had to tell them it didn't look good."[17]

The Bush campaign was not a source for Ellis at Fox News; just the opposite was true. The network was supplying political data directly to George W. and Jeb Bush. These conversations took place throughout election night. "At 2 a.m., Ellis called his cousins and told them, 'Our projection shows that it is statistically impossible for Gore to win Florida.' They were elated. 'Their mood was up, big time,' Ellis recalled. 'It was just the three of us guys handing the phone back and forth—me with the numbers, one of them a governor, the other the president-elect. Now, that was cool.' "[18]

While Bill O'Reilly was regularly beating Larry King in the ratings by the spring of 2001, the network as a whole had yet to pass CNN. But that would soon change.

One of the most painful days in our nation's history, September 11, 2001, was the first national tragedy covered from start to finish on television. Nearly every network had cameras focused on the World Trade Center towers as the second plane hit. And Americans watched in horror for hours as those people in New York, Pennsylvania, and Washington, D.C., reacted to the plane crashes, culminating in the collapse of the towers.

Fox's strategy revolved around the theory that there was an audience of news consumers being underserved in the marketplace—people who lived in between New York and Los Angeles, who waved their flags with pride and saw the world through a prism of right and wrong. Fox built a dedicated audience, directly responding to this emotional chord. In their minds, Fox was biased—toward America. While other networks cared about fairness, Fox cared about winning, both as a network and as a country. Just as the attacks of September 11 gave the Republican Party a wedge issue to pound Democrats with, Ailes would use the event to pound CNN. As we moved further away from the September 11 tragedy, this "pro-American" position simply morphed into a pro-Bush position and a pro-Republican position. This is exactly what the network's conservative audience desired.

This is not to disparage the underlying brilliance of Fox News's marketing. The network's ideological clarity enabled it to innovate in ways that would leave the competition in the dust. In the wake of September 11, Fox News jumped on two opportunities to distinguish itself. One of these innovations was quickly emulated by the competition; the other has become a mark of brand distinction.

It is difficult to imagine cable news before the ticker existed, although there was nothing particularly novel about Fox News's decision to adopt it. Tickers had been used on the financial news networks for years to display information about the stock market. *The New York Times* had installed a news ticker on the outside of its headquarters in Times Square decades earlier.

On the morning of September 11, with terrorist attacks on two major U.S. cities and a hijacked plane in the air, news was coming in faster than ever before. The anchors struggled to keep up with the flow of information and provide their viewers with analysis at once. That morning, Fox News unveiled its ticker and CNN quickly followed suit. Acknowledging the competition, MSNBC launched its ticker a few hours later.

Fox's second innovation would come to define the network and build loyalty among its viewers. It was the simple addition of an American flag to the Fox News logo. In his book *Crazy Like a Fox,* Scott Collins tells the story of how the addition was made:

> With a wave of post-attack patriotism seizing the nation, Rich O'Brien, the network's celebrated graphics chief, toyed around on his computer and came up with an image of a waving Stars and Stripes alternating with the Fox logo. O'Brien showed the graphic to [Fox News executive John] Moody and asked if some viewers might find the image offensive.
>
> "Is it offensive?" Moody repeated. "Rich, I think it's one of the most beautiful things I've ever seen."
>
> "From there on," Moody says, the flag "became our trademark."[19]

By linking the American flag to the network, Fox declared, "We are America, and we're taking sides." Like a local sports anchor cheering on his team, Fox had made it clear where the network stood.

At the same time, other networks struggled with their place in the media landscape. A false report spread that "CNN had banned the use of the word 'terrorist' to describe"[20] the September 11 attackers on its airwaves. The story was absurd, but it spread like wildfire. Fox News was on the side of the American people; CNN was with the terrorists. Need evidence? Just turn on your television and see for yourself which network is waving the American flag.

The falsehood was spread so widely that on September 30, CNN released the following statement: "There have been false reports that CNN has not used the word 'terrorist' to refer to those who attacked the World Trade Center and Pentagon. In fact, CNN has consistently and repeatedly referred to the attackers and hijackers as terrorists, and it will continue to do so."[21]

In reality, it was Reuters—not CNN—that had instructed its reporters to avoid the word "terrorist." But as so often is the case, the damage of the lie could not be undone. The network that conservatives had derided as the Clinton News Network during the 1990s had been branded, in the minds of some, as a supporter of terrorism.

Fox emerged triumphant. After the September 11 attacks, ratings for all three news networks spiked. But throughout the fall, viewership of CNN and MSNBC receded while Fox's surged. According to the Associated Press, "During January [2002], Fox averaged 656,000 viewers while CNN had 596,000 viewers, according to Nielsen Media Research. MSNBC had 296,000 viewers. In Nielsen's cable measurements, a month ends on its last Sunday. In prime time, Fox averaged 1.1 million viewers, CNN was at 921,000 and MSNBC had 358,000. Fox beat CNN during two months last year in prime time, but by smaller margins. And it has never won in Nielsen's 24-hour average."[22]

In the Associated Press story announcing Fox's triumph, Ailes credited Murdoch: "He said that there's room and we can win, and nobody believed him." CNN responded defensively: "Fox and CNN do different things. If you watch CNN, we have a full day of smart, hard newscasts that cover the world and break news daily."[23]

Fox was not a news network; it was a place to which viewers could turn to cheer America on. In fact, the reporting of original stories was never a priority. "Fox does almost no original reporting, and they can do it on the cheap," says Michael Shanahan of George Washington University. "You can produce a cable television network with people who talk nicely and are articulate and are blonde and look good on television and say provocative things. But it is not based on any discovery or intent to get to the bottom of something."[24]

At a time when the country was collectively anxious about the future, Fox News was the confident coach rallying the team into battle, as opposed to just telling them what plays were being called on the field.

After taking the ratings lead in January 2002, Fox News never looked back. The network's cheerleading of the Iraq War only vaulted it forward. Murdoch and Ailes had accomplished their goal: Fox News was number one. With this victory, Ailes's influence inside News Corp. grew. The question was how he would use it.

Part II

Building the Movement

Chapter 3

A "Terrorist Fist Jab"?

It is true that Barack Obama is on the move. I don't know if it's true that
President Bush called Musharraf and said: "Why can't we catch this guy?"
—Roger Ailes

Rupert Murdoch had been flirting with the idea of endorsing
Barack Obama in the 2008 general election for months. The *New
York Post,* Murdoch's preferred vehicle for such an announce-
ment, had already supported Obama over Hillary Clinton in the
Democratic primary. Appearing at the All Things Digital confer-
ence in May 2008, Murdoch came close to publicly supporting
Obama, saying that "he was leaning toward it, but would know in
the next six months."[1]

Now, with the election pending, Murdoch was considering
announcing his support. This did not please Roger Ailes, who
went to his boss to complain about the potential endorsement and
"a book excerpt in *Vanity Fair*" that claimed the head of News
Corp. might be occasionally ashamed of Fox News. *The New York*

Times reported that during their encounter, "Mr. Ailes threatened to quit."[2] Ailes, for his part, denied making the threat.

When compared with the attacks on Obama launched by Fox News, The *New York Post*'s endorsement would have been insignificant.

From the moment Barack Obama took the stage at the Democratic National Convention in Boston in 2004, people knew he was a different kind of politician. "I have seen the first black president there," MSNBC host Chris Matthews declared. "And the reason I say that is because I think the immigrant experience combined with the African background, combined with the incredible education, combined with his beautiful speech, not every politician gets help with the speech, but that speech was a piece of work."[3]

As the young future senator faded into the background, Fox News would spend the next several weeks promoting the claims of the Swift Boat Veterans for Truth in its relentless battle against Democratic nominee and Vietnam veteran John Kerry. The impact of the Swift Boat Veterans' attacks was highlighted by anchor Brit Hume, who claimed in a post-election report, "Far more voters say the Swift Boat Veterans had the most impact than say that about any other [interest] group."[4]

Four years later, Fox would dust off this playbook when covering the Obama campaign, taking smears and distortions originating from marginal news sources and interest groups and repeating them ad nauseam until they became "fact" to a receptive segment of voters.

The first and most enduring lie of the 2008 campaign began with an article published on January 17, 2007, by InsightMag .com, a website affiliated with the conservative *Washington Times*.

The post claimed that "researchers connected to" Hillary Clinton had discovered that Barack Obama "spent at least four years in a so-called Madrassa, or Muslim seminary, in Indonesia." Furthermore, "sources close to [a] background check," which was "conducted by researchers connected to Senator Clinton," said that "the idea is to show Obama as deceptive." "These 'sources' also told InsightMag.com that 'the specific Madrassa Mr. Obama attended' might have taught 'a Wahhabi doctrine that denies the rights of non-Muslims.' "[5]

The story contained the elements Ailes loved to exploit as a campaign manager. Its message was not simply "Barack Obama is a Muslim"; it was "Barack Obama is not like you; he might even be connected to a foreign and dangerous religion." For Fox News, accusing the Clinton campaign of spreading the story was simply a bonus.

It is unclear if the "sources" behind the story even existed. On January 9, eight days before the InsightMag.com piece was published, Eric Zorn of the *Chicago Tribune* wrote, "The crazies are sending around an e-mail that attempts to establish that Barack Obama is actually a Muslim who masquerades as a Christian for political advantage."[6] This chain e-mail may have played a role in InsightMag.com's "scoop."

In spite of the story's thin sourcing and sensational allegations, on January 19, *Fox & Friends* reported on the madrassa story and solicited viewer comments. That afternoon, coverage on Fox News continued, with host John Gibson dedicating two segments of his show to the InsightMag.com article. That's not to say other conservative media outlets did not give airtime to the madrassa smear. The same day, numerous conservative talk radio hosts and media figures such as Rush Limbaugh and Michael Savage joined in spreading this lie.

The next day, on *Fox News Watch,* columnist Cal Thomas said that there are "[a] lot of questions" about whether Obama "spent two years in a Muslim school in Indonesia," and that "they start off these schools, if it was a madrassa, with a reference to God and his only prophet is Muhammad."[7]

Even neutral observers of Fox felt the network had gone too far. Howard Kurtz blasted John Gibson for not having "done the firsthand reporting" and noted that Obama wrote "in his autobiography that he spent two years at a Muslim school in Indonesia."[8] On January 22, Fox News finally clarified its story, with *Fox & Friends* cohost Steve Doocy acknowledging that "Mr. Obama's people called and they said that that is absolutely false."[9]

Kurtz returned to the topic in his *Washington Post* column on January 22, calling the InsightMag.com story "thinly sourced," adding: "These days, the time elapsed between a flimsy charge from some magazine or Web site and amplification by bigger media outlets is often close to zero."[10] That afternoon, Kurtz appeared on CNN's *The Situation Room* and commented that the smear "got a big boost from Rupert Murdoch's media empire."[11]

CNN made the effort to actually uncover the truth. International correspondent John Vause went to Indonesia to visit the elementary school Obama attended. Familiar with madrassas from his work in Pakistan, Vause determined the Indonesian school was "nothing like" one.[12] Vause's report was the first of several by media outlets discrediting the claim.

On January 24, the Associated Press reaffirmed CNN's story, reporting that "interviews by the Associated Press at the elementary school in Jakarta found that it's a public and secular institution that has been open to students of all faiths since before the White House hopeful attended in the late 1960s."[13]

The flurry of stories forced Fox executives to respond. On January 25, ABC quoted Fox News senior vice president of programming Bill Shine saying that "the hosts of *Fox & Friends* gave too much credence to the Insight magazine report and spent far too long discussing its premise on the air. Those remarks were clarified on the next *Fox & Friends* program." Shine continued, "When John Gibson focused on the item, he, like other news outlets, presented Senator Obama's statement on the subject. We consider the matter closed and believe the senator feels the same way."[14]

Shine, who had worked at the network from its first day on the air, delivered the company line. But Fox was not done with the madrassa story. Twelve days after the InsightMag.com story was published, one week after it was first debunked by CNN, and four days after the network's own executives called the veracity of the story into question, Fox News political analyst Dick Morris continued to speculate on the story. Appearing on *Hannity & Colmes,* Morris said, "I believe that that *Insight* magazine story that was inaccurate, that he went to a Muslim school, was indeed planted, as *Insight* magazine said, by somebody close to the Clinton war room."[15]

Almost two years after the madrassa smear was discredited, it was still being repeated on the Fox News Channel. On December 30, 2009, conservative pundit Ann Coulter told viewers of Glenn Beck's Fox show: "I think if you polled Americans after 9/11, they would have said drop the political correctness when it comes to boarding airplanes. And like I say, Obama can be doing more than Bush. He is specially situated that way, as having gone to madrassas as a child, not being a white male, which is, you know, the height of political incorrectness, but just the contrary, we're moving in exactly doing the—making—repeating the worst mistakes of the Bush administration."[16] These attacks from Fox on Obama's heritage and faith have continued throughout his presidency.

During the spring of 2007, questions about Barack Obama's personal story remained at the forefront of Fox News coverage. For example, on February 28, John Gibson devoted two segments of his show to a claim made in the British tabloid *Daily Mail*: that Barack Obama was not entirely truthful in his memoir *Dreams from My Father*.

Gibson suggested that Obama had lied when depicting his father, Barack Obama, Sr., as "a ray of hope" and "a great man," obscuring the fact that he was "a wife-beating alcoholic who didn't bother to get a divorce before marrying the next woman and having a few more kids."[17] Obama's religion also became a target. That same day, Sean Hannity stated that "many" call the Trinity United Church of Christ in Chicago "separatist . . . in some cases, even drawing comparisons to a cult."[18]

This line comes straight out of Roger Ailes's campaign textbook. Substance doesn't matter—not when there is a chance to stir up racial and ethnic animosities in order to convince voters that an opposing candidate doesn't share their values. The goal was never to show that Barack Obama was advocating the wrong policies for America. Ailes wanted to prove that Obama was not American.

It was no surprise when Roger Ailes, in the form of a misguided attempt at humor, joined in on the attacks. On March 8, while accepting a First Amendment Leadership Award from the Radio-Television News Directors Association, he joked: "It is true that Barack Obama is on the move. I don't know if it's true that President Bush called [Pakistani President Pervez] Musharraf and said: 'Why can't we catch this guy?' "[19]

As the attacks on candidate Obama escalated, they turned vulgar. On August 24, Sean Hannity aired footage of musician Ted Nugent "calling Barack Obama a 'piece of shit' and referring to" Hillary Clinton "as a 'worthless bitch.' " In the clip, Nugent held up assault rifles, telling Obama "to suck on my machine gun" and Clinton that " 'you might want to ride one of these into the sunset.' " After airing the clip, Hannity referred to Nugent as a " 'friend and frequent guest on the program' " and "asked Fox News contributor and former Democratic strategist Bob Beckel: 'What's more offensive to you? Is it Barack Obama's statement about our troops or Ted Nugent?' Beckel responded by asking Hannity if he was 'prepared to disavow this lowlife,' to which Hannity responded: 'No, I like Ted Nugent. He's a friend of mine.' "[20]

After Fidel Castro wrote about the U.S. election in a Cuban newspaper, Fox News jumped on the story. "Fidel Castro, of all people, endorses a Hillary Clinton–Barack Obama presidential

ticket,"[21] guest host Michelle Malkin said on *The O'Reilly Factor*. "What is that all about?" The next morning, *Fox & Friends* continued to push the story with an on-screen graphic reading, "CASTRO'S DREAM TEAM: WANTS CLINTON AND OBAMA IN '08."

Fox also displayed a graphic of Castro, Clinton, and Obama surrounded by a heart.[22] The only problem was, Castro never endorsed Clinton or Obama. He was actually critical of the Democratic candidates, writing, "Today, talk is about the seemingly invincible ticket that might be created with Hillary for President and Obama for Vice President. Both of them feel the sacred duty of demanding 'a democratic government in Cuba.' They are not making politics: they are playing a game of cards on a Sunday afternoon."[23]

Many of these incidents occurred when Obama was still considered an underdog. As it became clear he would win the Democratic nomination, the attacks began to resemble those that the network continued to lob in 2009 and 2010. "As more is learned about Barack Obama's positions, his past, and his affiliations, it seems that the 'change' candidate has all the same problems with race as those before him," Sean Hannity said on March 2, 2008. He added, "It's only fair to ask: Do the Obamas have a race problem of their own?"[24]

Hannity was discussing an award given to Louis Farrakhan by *Trumpet Newsmagazine,* a publication that was founded by Trinity Church. Hannity went on to claim that Obama's pastor, Jeremiah Wright, "honored Farrakhan for lifetime achievement, saying, quote, 'He truly epitomized greatness.' "[25] Wright never made the statement; it was the magazine's managing editor, Rhoda McKinney-Jones. Hannity also did not mention that Obama's campaign issued a statement disagreeing with the magazine's decision to give Farrakhan the award, condemning the Nation of Islam leader's anti-Semitic statements.

In the next segment, Hannity attacked Michelle Obama for what she wrote in her undergraduate thesis. "She wrote in her thesis," Hannity said, "that we see at Princeton, you know, the belief—'because of the belief that blacks must join in solidarity to combat a white oppressor.' "[26] Contrary to Hannity's assertion, Michelle Obama was describing views that black students who attended Princeton in the 1970s may have held, not asserting her own views. Hannity never acknowledged the distinction.

As the primary season came to a close, the Fox staple of comparing Barack Obama to Hitler and other genocidal dictators began. This was especially hypocritical, considering the outcry four years earlier when two members of the progressive organization MoveOn.org submitted ads to a contest comparing George W. Bush to Hitler. That year, Republican National Committee chairman Ed Gillespie went on *Fox News Sunday* to attack MoveOn.org, stating, "That's the kind of tactics we're seeing on the left today in support of these Democratic presidential candidates."[27] In 2008, these attacks would become par for the course on Fox.

In February 2008, a caller to Tom Sullivan's Fox News Radio show claimed that listening to Barack Obama speak "harkens back to when I was younger and I used to watch those deals with Hitler, how he would excite the crowd and they'd come to their feet and scream and yell." Sullivan then played a side-by-side comparison of Adolf Hitler and Barack Obama speaking.[28]

On April 3, Ann Coulter opened the floodgates on *Hannity & Colmes,* saying, "He's a dime store *Mein Kampf.*" Alan Colmes then asked the acerbic right-wing pundit whether Obama was "a two-bit Hitler," to which Coulter responded: "Yes."

"We should be as wary of Obama as they should have been of Hitler in Nazi Germany?" Colmes inquired.

"If only people had read *Mein Kampf*," Coulter answered.[29]

Of all the over-the-top attacks on Obama, the first one that caused Fox News to flinch came on June 6, when Fox host E. D. Hill teased a segment about Barack and Michelle Obama's fist-bumping by saying, "A fist bump? A pound? A terrorist fist jab? The gesture everyone seems to interpret differently."[30] On June 10, she was actually forced to apologize:

> Want to start the show by clarifying something I said on the show last Friday about an upcoming body language segment. Now, I mentioned various ways the Obamas' fist pump in St. Paul had been characterized in the media. I apologize because unfortunately, some thought I personally had characterized it inappropriately. I regret that. It was not my intention. And I certainly didn't mean to associate the word "terrorist" in any way with Senator Obama and his wife. Now, today, the senator is talking about the economy.[31]

Hill's show was canceled a week later, but her misfortune didn't dissuade other Fox News hosts from jumping deeper into the fray. On June 16, Brit Hume attempted to cast doubt about Barack Obama's Christian faith, based on a purported statement by the candidate's half brother. Hume reported, "Malik Obama tells *The Jerusalem Post* that 'if elected his brother will be a good president for the Jewish people, despite his Muslim background.' "[32]

However, as ABC's Jake Tapper pointed out, nowhere in the audio of the interview did Malik Obama assert that Obama would be "a good president for the Jewish people, despite his Muslim background." Additionally, Tapper's article indicated that Malik Obama did not speak with the *Post* but instead with Israel's Army Radio. Tapper concluded that the piece, cited by several conservative bloggers, "was a sloppy paraphrase that emerged as false evidence."[33]

Rupert Murdoch, normally accustomed to politicians courting him, had for months pursued a meeting with Obama. When it finally occurred in the early summer, he brought a guest along with him, Fox News chief Roger Ailes. "Obama lit into Ailes," according to Michael Wolff's biography of Murdoch. "He said he didn't want to waste his time talking to Ailes if Fox was just going to continue to abuse him and his wife, that Fox had relentlessly portrayed him as suspicious, foreign, fearsome—just short of a terrorist."[34]

Ailes shot back that "it might not have been this way if Obama had come on air instead of giving Fox the back of his hand. A tentative truce, which may or may not have historic significance, was thereupon agreed."[35] But this "truce" never seemed to affect the content on Fox News.

In July, Obama took a highly unusual trip for a candidate, leaving the campaign trail to travel abroad. The tour was viewed positively by the public and the media. Echoing the McCain campaign, Fox News seized on a false allegation to go on the attack. On July 29, Sean Hannity claimed that Obama had canceled a visit with wounded soldiers at Landstuhl Regional Medical Center in Germany because he was not allowed to bring cameras along on the visit. According to Hannity, Obama "abandoned the troop visit because the cameras weren't . . . allowed and the campaign wasn't allowed."[36]

This was simply false. As NBC correspondent Andrea Mitchell reported, "There was never any intention—let me be absolutely clear about this. The press was never going to go. The entourage was never going to go. There was never an intention to make this political."[37]

As the summer campaign season heated up, Democrats braced for a "swift boat" attack on Obama, and conservative author Jerome Corsi, who had worked with members of the Swift Boat Veterans for Truth to bring down the campaign of Senator John Kerry, obliged. His book *Unfit for Command* had been a bestseller and became the basis for the ad campaign that would help to sink Kerry's bid for the White House. Now he planned a repeat performance, and Fox News was willing to give Corsi its platform to smear Obama.

Corsi's promotional efforts began in earnest on *Hannity & Colmes.* "I do a great deal of analysis of [Obama's] autobiography," Corsi told viewers. Echoing John Gibson's comments from the previous year, Corsi gave his spin on the candidate's family history. "Obama first presents his father as a great hero, and the truth was, his father was a polygamist and an alcoholic. He had abandoned the family in Africa when he met Obama's mother in Hawaii [and] he married Obama's mother without disclosing that he had not divorced this African woman."[38]

Then, two weeks later on *Fox & Friends,* Corsi claimed Obama's campaign "has a false, fake birth certificate posted on their website." He continued, "The original birth certificate of Obama has never been released, and the campaign refuses to release it." As the interview continued, Corsi was allowed to expand on his conspiracy theory, claiming, "There's been good analysis of it on the Internet, and it's been shown to have watermarks from Photoshop. It's a fake document that's on the website right now."[39]

The allegation that Obama was not a natural-born citizen had already been widely discredited, but Fox News executives were not only happy to let Corsi spread his lies on air; they vouched for the author's credibility. On *Hannity & Colmes,* Fox News's Washington deputy managing editor, Bill Sammon, claimed, "Well, the nature of those inaccuracies [in Corsi's book], I think, is relatively innocuous," he said. "The first thing in that forty-page document that the Obama camp points out is that the author got their wedding date wrong—the year of their wedding wrong. Okay. Well, that's not a good thing, but it doesn't go to the ideology of Obama."[40]

Sammon was understating the extent of Corsi's smear campaign. In his book, Corsi spread numerous lies about the future president, ranging from the claim that Obama had "pledged to reduce the size of the military" to the claim that Obama "has yet to answer questions" concerning whether "he stopped using marijuana and cocaine completely in college, or whether his drug use extended into his law school days or beyond."[41]

Unlike what had occurred in 2004, other networks simply did not allow Corsi to spread his falsehoods on their airwaves, or they were prepared to challenge him, limiting his ability to repeat his performance. Fox gave Corsi free reign to spread his lies in the name of book promotion.

As the summer came to an end, Fox's coverage of the election was as unbalanced as ever. Consider the network's reporting during the five-day period that followed the Republican convention—from September 5 to September 9, 2008. Of the total time Fox News devoted to candidates or campaign surrogates speaking directly to the camera, 78 percent went to Republicans and 22 percent went to Democrats.[42]

With McCain trailing Obama as the election drew closer, the attacks became more and more desperate. One frequent perpetrator was Dick Morris, who served the dual role of Fox News

contributor and consultant to political action committees airing
attack ads against the Democratic nominee.

Morris was a political mercenary. He had begun his career
managing future congressman Jerry Nadler's campaign for student
government secretary at Stuyvesant High School in New York
City.[43] As a political consultant, he had worked for right-wing
senators Trent Lott and Jesse Helms before signing on to work
with Bill Clinton in late 1994. After resigning from the campaign
during the Democratic convention because of a prostitution scandal, Morris turned vehemently anti-Clinton and became a favorite
Fox News guest and eventual paid contributor.

On October 6, Morris claimed that Bill Ayers, a former member
of the 1970s radical left-wing group Weather Underground, had
"hired" Barack Obama as chairman of the board for the Chicago
Annenberg Challenge, a public school reform project, "to distribute
the $50 million that Ayers raised"[44] for the organization. *The New
York Times* reported that, in reality, "according to several people
involved, Mr. Ayers played no role in Mr. Obama's appointment."[45]

Morris's wild attacks on the future president did not let up. On
October 13, he claimed that "Obama served as 'general counsel'
to ACORN." "Obama was never 'general counsel' to ACORN;
he was part of a team of attorneys from the law firm Miner, Barn-
hill & Galland who represented ACORN in a lawsuit against the
State of Illinois."[46] The ACORN tie was significant only because
Fox had spent weeks attacking ACORN. They were so successful at branding the organization that in interviews at campaign
rallies, McCain supporters would talk directly about ACORN's
nonexistent voter fraud operation that would supposedly steal the
election for Obama.

"Between October 27 and October 31, Morris touted an ad by

the National Republican Trust Political Action Committee attacking [Obama's] association with his" by-then "former pastor Jeremiah Wright—three times on *Fox & Friends* and once on *Hannity & Colmes*. Each time, Morris solicited viewers to go to GOPTrust .com—National Republican Trust PAC's website—and make contributions."[47] Morris, of course, was being paid by the PAC, a fact Fox viewers were never informed of.

On October 27, Morris told Fox's audience that GOPTrust .com "is an independent expenditure accepting contributions, if you know what I mean, folks, who are running the world's best anti–Reverend Wright ad." Morris continued, "It's a thirty-second spot. It includes all the stuff that needs to be done in battleground states. They only have a million bucks for this right now. If they had two million, they could do a huge amount to swing this election. Let's win this election despite John McCain."[48]

Morris made similar comments on October 30, claiming that GOPTrust.com was "raising money right now for the next twelve hours, and they're hoping to come up with another two million. They are going to saturate all of the swing states and the networks with the ad you just saw." Morris added, "I hope your viewers go online to GOPTrust.com and make it possible to run this ad all over the United States."[49]

On October 31, Morris was at it again. "One of the things that I think McCain should—or the McCain supporters should do, is there are still about two hours to contribute to GOPTrust.com, which is the independent expenditure group that is running the Reverend Wright advertisement," he said. "I hope people give funds to GOPTrust.com to get that issue out."[50]

No other network had a paid contributor on air promoting his political work without noting any financial ties. Fox was paying

Morris to promote his outside political work attacking the president and raising funds for attack ads.

Despite all the attacks, smears, and attempted "swiftboating," the unthinkable happened: Obama won. At Fox News, Election Day was a stoic affair. Barring another cataclysmic polling error, the entire political establishment knew Barack Obama would be the next president of the United States—all that was left was the actual voting.

For the most part, Fox played election night straight. There were no delays in calling states for Obama, no early calls for McCain. The only oddity was the network "endlessly repeating some footage of a surly-looking fellow outside a polling place in Philadelphia who apparently represented the leading edge of a massive 'Black Panther' conspiracy to intimidate white voters."[51]

One interesting aspect of Fox's election coverage was who was *not* mentioned—George W. Bush. Although he was still president and leader of the Republican Party, Bush had already disappeared from the scene. The only time his name came up was in a slip of the tongue, when Chris Wallace mistakenly called Texas for Bush and quickly corrected himself.[52]

At approximately 11 p.m., Brit Hume informed the Fox audience that Barack Obama would be the next president of the United States. Karl Rove was surprisingly apolitical, telling viewers that the election of our first African-American president, who "was aspirational and inspirational, who appealed to the better angels of our nature, is very powerful. It's a night for our country to celebrate, and for the world to celebrate."[53]

Chapter 4

A Stalin-esque Mouthpiece

Some are wondering if the honeymoon is already over.
—Fox News's Bret Baier, on President Obama's
seventeenth day in office

J ust as George W. Bush disappeared from Fox News's election-night coverage, the legacy of his presidency seemed to vanish from the network the next day. It was as if the eight-year period that had seen two major wars, a massive financial crisis, and budget numbers that had swung from an inherited $236 billion surplus to a $1.3 trillion deficit had never happened. Before Barack Obama had been president-elect for a single week, Fox hosts were already blaming him for the state of the economy.

On November 6, Dick Morris and Sean Hannity pinned the stock market declines that followed Election Day on Obama. "Now, the other thing that I predicted in *Fleeced* is that the stock market would go crazy after he [Obama] was elected," said Morris. "Not just because he's a radical, not just because he's a Democrat, but because he's going to raise the capital gains tax."

Hannity replied, "If he doesn't come out and say 'I'm not going to, you know, raise the capital gains tax, I'm not going to raise taxes,' but heading into an economic slowdown, you're predicting the stock market is going to—it's the Obama tanking?"[1]

A week after the election, Hannity was not only trying to stick stock market declines on the newly elected president: in a conversation with conservative radio host Hugh Hewitt, Hannity attempted to claim the recession was Obama's fault. "This is really the Obama recession in this sense: that people that have money are looking at this, 'Look, if—if he is true to his word, you know what? I'm getting out now.' "[2]

Fox News acted as if "history did not go back before the inauguration, as if this was Obama's crisis," says Tom Fiedler, dean of the College of Communication at Boston University and former executive editor of *The Miami Herald*. "It was the prism through which Fox reported on the 2010 election that had that skewed point of view, that the economic crisis was all a result of Obama's failed economic policies, with no recognition that not only did the problem emulate from regulatory positions under George W. Bush, but the bailout that led to the deficit was also started under Henry Paulson and Bush."[3]

Fox also could not resist linking Obama to the scandal brewing in Illinois following the arrest on federal corruption charges of Governor Rod Blagojevich and the fraud and bribery conviction of Democratic donor and fund-raiser Tony Rezko. On December 9, while discussing the criminal complaint against Blagojevich, Sean Hannity said, "I think the Tony Rezko issue is going to be a big problem for [Obama], especially because he's all over this document. The pres—the word 'president-elect' is mentioned forty-four times in the document. Pretty troubling."[4] The truth was, "president-elect" was used in the documents primarily to suggest that Obama and his advisers were unwilling to conspire with Blagojevich, while other mentions simply were descriptions of the Senate seat vacated by Obama or references to his forthcoming presidential administration.

Since its founding, Fox News has been in a constant state of transition. A former employee described the fluid nature of the network this way:

> For the first few years, it was, "Let's take the conservative take on things." And then after a few years, it evolved into, "Well, it's not just the conservative take on things, we're going to take the Republican take on things," which is not necessarily in lock step with the conservative point of view. And then two, three, five years into that, it was, "We're taking the Bush line on things," which was different than the GOP. So we were parroting the White House. We were a Stalin-esque mouthpiece.[5]

Now, with the country in transition, Fox News would undergo major personnel changes that put Roger Ailes at the top of the GOP food chain. Fox had always been a conservative news operation, but Ailes would remake it into a political one as well.

The transition began with a simple lineup change. Since Fox News's founding, *Hannity & Colmes* had been the network's left-versus-right show. While hardly a fair fight between the milquetoast Alan Colmes and the bullying style of Sean Hannity, at least Colmes always was a token liberal in Fox News's prime-time lineup.

Sean Hannity's career as a right-wing talker began in college, when he first appeared on KCSB-FM at the University of California, Santa Barbara. His show was canceled within months, after featuring *The AIDS Cover-Up? The Real and Alarming Facts About AIDS,* a book widely condemned by the scientific and medical community, which made numerous false claims, such as "that AIDS could be spread by kissing and mosquito bites."[6]

C. Everett Koop, surgeon general under Ronald Reagan and George H. W. Bush, criticized the book and its promotion by radio host and Focus on the Family head James Dobson, causing the evangelical leader to backpedal. Dobson claimed through a spokesperson, "We gave careful consideration to the feedback we subsequently received from members of the medical community and made the decision to discontinue it."[7]

During one show, Hannity told a lesbian caller, "I feel sorry for your child."[8] The UCSB campus paper also reported that Hannity said, "Anyone listening to this show that believes homosexuality is a normal lifestyle has been brainwashed. It's very dangerous if we start accepting lower and lower forms of behavior as the normal."[9] The ACLU fought the station, and Hannity was offered a return to his position in the lineup, but he declined. Hannity then marketed himself as "the most talked-about college radio host in America"[10] and was hired by the Alabama station WVNN.

He was a host in Atlanta when Roger Ailes brought him to New York to host a show on Fox News with the working title *Hannity & LTBD*—"Liberal to Be Determined." [11]From there his popularity and stature as both a Fox host and now a national radio host grew.

Following the 2008 elections, Alan Colmes would be gone and Hannity would host the 9 p.m. hour alone. Instead of debating a liberal foil, Hannity would have the hour all to himself to promote the causes and candidates he believed in.

Left untouched was Greta Van Susteren's 10 p.m. show. Van

Susteren began her television career appearing on CNN during the O. J. Simpson trial as a legal expert. When the media circus concluded, CNN brought her aboard as a host. She moved to Fox in 2002 and joined its prime-time lineup. After the 2008 election, her husband, John Coale, became a close friend of Sarah Palin, advising the former vice presidential candidate on certain legal matters.

With Van Susteren's close ties to the Alaska governor and O'Reilly's traditional conservative views, Fox now did not have a single mainstream Democrat in its evening schedule.

While the small shift in the network's lineup had this seismic effect, the network's biggest on-air change was weeks away. Roger Ailes, with his keen eye for talent, recruited Glenn Beck from CNN Headline News to host a show in the 5 p.m. hour. According to Beck's version of events, Ailes told him, "I see this as the Alamo . . . If I just had somebody who was willing to sit on the other side of the camera until the last shot is fired, we'd be fine."[12]

Beck was a former morning zoo DJ who had worked at a myriad of stations. His outrageous and offensive stunts often caused an uproar in the local markets where he was broadcast. While Beck was on the air in Phoenix, for instance, he called the wife of a rival station's morning host to ridicule the couple over a recent miscarriage. In Hamden, Connecticut, his show was protested after he and cohost Pat Gray insulted an Asian caller on air.

According to Beck, as he bounced from city to city, much of his paycheck went "up [his] nose."[13] After meeting his second wife, Beck cleaned up, converted to Mormonism, and began to take his show in a more political direction. In 2000, *The Glenn Beck Program* launched on WFLA in Tampa, Florida, and Premiere Radio Networks began syndicating the show in 2002.

In 2006, Beck launched his CNN Headline News program. While the show was a success, Beck was clearly held back, producing a far milder program than what was to come at Fox. With Beck on board, Roger Ailes landed a key piece of conservative talent at the network—one who could not only draw viewers, but also generate controversy across the media.

An even more significant change at Fox took place when Brit Hume, who had been Fox News's Washington, D.C., managing editor since the founding of the network, retired at the end of 2008. Though he would make controversial remarks from time to time, Hume was at heart a journalist who had made his way up the ladder in the mainstream news industry. He began as a print reporter working for *The Hartford Times,* UPI, and Baltimore's *Evening Sun.* Hume then moved to ABC News in 1973 and rose to become White House correspondent during the George H. W. Bush and Clinton presidencies.

When Hume stepped down, Ailes replaced him with former *Washington Times* White House correspondent Bill Sammon, a conservative who, after beginning his career at *The Plain Dealer* in Cleveland, had risen through the ranks at right-wing news sources such as *The Washington Examiner.*

In addition to his reporting duties at *The Washington Times,* Sammon was the author of four hagiographies of George Bush, who had nicknamed him "Big Stretch": *Fighting Back: The War on Terrorism—from Inside the Bush White House; Misunderestimated: The President Battles Terrorism, Media Bias, and the Bush Haters; Strategery: How George W. Bush Is Defeating Terrorists, Outwitting Democrats, and Confounding the Mainstream Media;* and *The Evangelical President: George Bush's Struggle to Spread a Moral Democracy Throughout the World.* The title of his first book, *At Any Cost: How Al Gore Tried to Steal the Election,* gives a hint as to why the Bush White House rewarded

Sammon with excellent access and why Sammon's publisher was able to state in promotional materials for his 2006 book, *Strategery,* "No other journalist has interviewed the president more times."[14]

Having joined Fox's management as Washington, D.C., deputy managing editor in the summer of 2008, Bill Sammon was promoted to Hume's job overseeing "editorial content in the Washington bureau"[15] in February 2009. It was a behind-the-scenes change that would dramatically affect Fox's coverage of politics.

Numerous Fox employees say that during his tenure, Bill Sammon has consciously tilted coverage rightward. Sources suggest that Roger Ailes often calls the Washington bureau with requests to cover certain stories with a conservative bent. Hume, because of his stature, was able to resist these entreaties. Sammon, on the other hand, happily relays these orders, which are often journalistically questionable, directly to the bureau's reporters.

"[There is] more pressure from Sammon to slant news to the right or to tell people how to report news, doing it in a more brutish way," said a source with knowledge of the situation. "There is a point at which it is no longer reporting, but distorting things."[16]

Things had been different under Hume's leadership. According to this source, Hume believed that the mainstream media had been ignoring conservative points of view, and he worked to include them in his coverage. But he remained dedicated to a journalistic ethic that didn't allow Fox News journalists to "ignore points of view and ignore facts." To do this would just be repeating the sins that Fox News, in Hume's eyes, was created to address, and would be "straying away from being a legitimate news reporter."[17]

The network has paid a price for Sammon's leadership, as other seasoned journalists have departed from the increasingly partisan network. When previously attacked for journalistic malpractice, Fox had often cited White House correspondent Major Garrett as an example of a hard-nosed, incorruptible journalist—and most members of the Beltway media agreed. But in the summer of 2010, just as Fox inherited a front-row seat in the White House Press Briefing Room, Garrett took a pay cut to leave the network for a job at *National Journal,* acknowledging that he had been a "conscientious objector" in the bitter war between the White House and his former network.[18]

Tom Fiedler cites the blurring of the line between opinion and news at Fox as a liability for its reporters. "The problem that they labor under is that Fox itself doesn't respect the line between Fox News and Fox, the broader commentariat. You end up with the anchors on the Fox morning program, for instance, who traffic entirely in commentary and opinion. They are lumped in the same general stew [with reporters]. The result is that their credibility is greatly damaged."[19]

Sammon's desire to alter Fox's news reporting to match his ideology was demonstrated in another series of leaked e-mails, outlining his directions to producers during the politically contentious health care debate in the fall of 2009. In a memo with the subject lines "friendly reminder: let's not slip back into calling it the 'public option,' " Sammon provided the following list of instructions:

1. Please use the term "government-run health insurance" or, when brevity is a concern, "government option," whenever possible.

2. When it is necessary to use the term "public option" (which is, after all, firmly ensconced in the nation's lexicon), use the qualifier "so-called," as in "the so-called public option."

3. Here's another way to phrase it: "The public option, which is the government-run plan."

4. When newsmakers and sources use the term "public option" in our stories, there's not a lot we can do about it, since quotes are of course sacrosanct.[20]

The guidelines provided by Sammon match the recommendations of Republican pollster Frank Luntz, who had told Sean Hannity on Fox two months earlier that "if you call it a 'public option,' the American people are split," but "if you call it the 'government option,' the public is overwhelmingly against it."[21] For health care professionals and journalists, "public option," of course, had been widely accepted as the term to describe this component of Barack Obama's proposal for health care reform since before his election.

The impact of the e-mail can clearly be seen in Fox's coverage at the time. On October 27, not a single journalist on Fox's highest-rated news show, *Special Report,* made reference to the health care legislation without following Sammon's orders. Host Bret Baier spoke about the public option three times, calling it "government-run health insurance"[22] or a "government-run health insurance option."[23] Baier had previously used the term "public option"[24] on air several times in the weeks leading up to Sammon's order.

In contrast, during George W. Bush's administration, Fox aggressively adopted any euphemism—however Orwellian—dictated by the White House. "Suicide bombers" became "homicide bombers," and the warrantless wiretapping of U.S. citizens became the "Terrorist Surveillance Program." Of course, with President Obama in office, the network no longer found it necessary to parrot the White House's preferred expressions. As another leaked memo from Sam-

mon shows, Fox News staffers were now encouraged to be highly
skeptical of White House language:

From: Sammon, Bill
Sent: Thursday, January 14, 2010 10:04 AM
To: 169 -SPECIAL REPORT; 069 -Politics; 036 -FOX.WHU;
      054 -FNSunday; 030 -Root (FoxNews.Com);
      050 -Senior Producers; 051 -Producers
Subject: It's a bank tax, not a "financial crisis
responsibility fee"

Just as we refrained from adopting such administration
euphemisms as "man-caused disaster" and "overseas con-
tingency operation," so too should we resist parroting the
phrase du jour, "financial crisis responsibility fee." As far as
I can tell, this is a bank tax, plain and simple. It appears to
have little if anything to do with the repayment of TARP
loans, despite Valerie Jarrett's assertion to the contrary on
Fox and Friends this morning:

"What we're saying is every single penny of TARP money that
was put out and lent out to the taxpayers will be paid back
by the financial institutions. That's what the law provides. If
you go and look at the actual law that was passed, it says that
the financial institutions will be responsible for paying back
the TARP money. And they should honor that commitment."

Consider these facts:
• The banking industry has repaid two-thirds of the TARP
  loans, with interest, and has four more years to repay the
  rest.

- As Major Garrett rightly points out, most of the current TARP deficit is linked to taxpayer bailouts of GM, Chrysler, Fannie and Freddie, all of which ARE EXEMPT FROM THE NEW BANK TAX.

- In other words, the two institutions that are arguably the most responsible for triggering the recession in the first place, Fannie and Freddie, are exempt from the "financial crisis responsibility fee."

- Even after all TARP monies are repaid in full, the bank tax will remain in place, costing banks billions for the indefinite future.

- The administration says it would be "unseemly" for the banks to pass along these taxes to consumers (rather than cut bonuses), but does not PREVENT the banks from doing so.

If the administration wants to try and conflate the repayment of TARP loans with the imposition of a bank tax, that's their political prerogative. As journalists, we must be careful to factually parse these important issues. Words mean things.

Discuss.

Bill Sammon's orders were clear—language offered by the administration was not to be repeated on air. That day, reporting on President Obama's proposal, Bret Baier told his audience, "One Republican's reaction to the financial crisis responsibility fee. Most people are calling it the bank tax."[25]

By Sunday, "Financial Crisis Responsibility Fee" had been eliminated from the Fox lexicon, with Brit Hume, who retained some hosting duties at the network, artfully expounding during an interview with Senate Republican Leader Mitch McConnell, "Let me turn, if I can, quickly to the proposal that the president made this week in which the banks that received TARP funds, rescue funds, whether they paid them back with interest or not, and some banks that didn't receive TARP funds, would pay a new fee called—which is being labeled a bank tax by some."[26]

Sammon's e-mails were not the first time Fox News's partisan bias had been exposed in leaked internal memorandums. In 2004, a series of e-mails from John Moody, then Fox News's senior vice president for news, were given to the filmmaker Robert Greenwald and became central to his film *Outfoxed*. The Moody memos consisted of daily talking points and directions for Fox News hosts and producers to follow.

On May 9, 2003, Moody weighed in on the fight over judicial nominees, writing, "Nominees who both sides admit are [qu]alified are being held up because of their POSSIBLE, not demonstrated, views [on] one issue—abortion. This should be a trademark issue for FNC today and in [th]e days to come."

On April 6, 2004, Moody directed journalists covering the Iraq War to "not fall into the easy trap of mourning the loss of US lives and asking out loud why are we there?"

On June 3, 2003, Moody pressed Fox employees to praise George W. Bush, writing, "[Th]e president is doing something that few of his predecessors dared undertake: [pu]tting the US case for mideast peace to an Arab summit. It's a distinctly [sk]eptical crowd that Bush faces. His political courage and tactical cunning ar[e] [wo]rth noting in our reporting through the day."

On April 26, 2004, Moody expressed the opposite sentiment about presumptive Democratic presidential nominee John Kerry, writing, "Ribbons or medals? Which did John Kerry throw away after he returned from Vietnam? This may become an issue for him today. His perceived disrespect for the military could be more damaging to the candidate than questions about his actions in uniform."[27]

In all, more than thirty leaked memos laid out a pattern of conduct by network executives forcing their political views on reporters. Moody, responding in *The Washington Post,* dismissed "the implication that" he was "controlling the news coverage" and claimed that "people are free to call me or message me and say, 'I think you're off base.' Sometimes I take the advice, sometimes I don't."[28]

In 2009, with a straight Republican lineup in prime time and Bill Sammon and Glenn Beck ensconced within the network, Ailes could set out to fundamentally alter Fox's role in American politics. No longer would it simply be infotainment for the conservative base. Fox could now become a political vehicle designed to advance an ideological agenda.

On March 4, 1933, Franklin Delano Roosevelt was sworn into office during a time of incomparable economic chaos. Three and a half years earlier, Black Tuesday had sent the economy spiraling into depression, and there was no end in sight. Unemployment was high, banks were failing, mines were closing, and farmland had dried up.

The country was demanding action, and Roosevelt entered the White House with an unparalleled level of political capital. In his first hundred days, Congress passed every law that Roosevelt asked for in order to get the nation back on track. Every president's first hundred days in office since have been measured against FDR's.

Barack Obama was inaugurated amid the worst economic downturn since the Great Depression and had a similar mandate for change. Many in the media alluded to Roosevelt's first hundred days, suggesting that the beginning of the Obama presidency might bring a similar period of reform, or, at the very least, the customary "honeymoon period" that usually immediately followed an election. But Obama's first hundred days would be different. Rush Limbaugh made headlines when he declared, days before Obama's inauguration, "I hope he fails,"[29] and Fox News was determined to make the radio host's desire a reality.

On the day of Obama's swearing in, Glenn Beck, in his second day on Fox News, was ready to pass judgment on the new president. "Mr. President, I want to believe. I want to trust, I want to hope for change," Beck said. "But I am really failing to see how this is any different."[30]

On day two, Sean Hannity reached his own verdict on the Obama administration. "He's not going to succeed," Hannity proclaimed. "Socialism has failed."[31]

On day three, Fox News contributor and conservative radio host Laura Ingraham informed Fox News viewers that, under Obama, "our country is less safe today."[32]

On day four, Beck lied to his audience, telling them that "Obama declared the end to the war on terror."[33]

Fox News's coverage of the Obama administration's first weekend was not any better. On Saturday, former Arkansas Governor, presidential candidate, and Fox News host Mike Huckabee asked, "Is this the change America voted for?"[34] On Sunday, Brit Hume remarked, "You can't break all your campaign promises."[35]

The examples above are just a small sample of the dozens of attacks leveled at President Obama during his first week in office. Over the next hundred days, the rhetoric would heat up steadily.

On day eight, Beck asked Fox's audience, "Do you want socialism or not?"[36] And by day eleven, he had concluded that the country was, in fact, on a march toward socialism.[37] Not to be outdone, Sean Hannity declared that Obama's presidency represented the end of capitalism.[38]

On the seventeenth day of the president's term, Bret Baier mused, "Some are wondering if the honeymoon is already over."[39] On Fox News, it never began.

As the first months of Obama's presidency progressed, the differences in coverage between Fox News and other networks continued to emerge. Fox became a breeding ground for Republican talking points. This link grew so tight that Fox began airing Republican press releases verbatim, presenting them as original reporting with no citation.

On the February 10 edition of *Happening Now,* host Jon Scott decided to "take a look back at the [stimulus] bill, how it was born,

and how it grew, and grew, and grew."[40] As part of his presentation, Scott cited seven news reports using on-screen graphics. Each of the articles he cited, as well as the on-screen text, came directly from a Senate Republican Communications Center press release. If this coincidence was not enough evidence to prove that Scott had lifted his work from GOP sources, one of the graphics indicated that a *Wall Street Journal* report that the stimulus package could reach "$775 billion over two years" was published on December 19, *2009*. This obvious error—December 19, 2009, would not arrive for another nine months—was also contained in the GOP release Scott had taken his report from.

Then, in early April, as Scott was interviewing Republican Congressman Paul Ryan of Wisconsin, seven on-screen graphics labeled "FOXfact" were lifted straight from an op-ed Ryan had published in that day's *Wall Street Journal*:

1. Ryan op-ed: "The Republican budget achieves lower deficits than the Democratic plan in every year."

   FOXfact: "GOP Budget: Achieves lower deficits than Dem plan in every year."

2. Ryan op-ed: "Under our plan, debt held by the public is $3.6 trillion less during the budget period."

   FOXfact: "GOP Budget: Debt held by public $3.6 trill less during budget period."

3. Ryan op-ed: "Our budget gives priority to national defense and veterans' health care."

   FOXfact: "GOP budget gives priority to natl defense & vet health care."

4. Ryan op-ed: "We do these things by rejecting the president's cap-and-trade scheme."

   FOXfact: "GOP budget rejects President's cap-and-trade scheme."

5. Ryan op-ed: "Our budget does not raise taxes, and makes permanent the 2001 and 2003 tax laws."

   FOXfact: "GOP budget doesn't raise taxes; makes permanent '01 and '03 tax laws."

6. Ryan op-ed: "Capital gains and dividends are taxed at 15%, and the death tax is repealed."

   FOXfact: "GOP Budget: Capital gains & dividends taxed at 15% & death tax repealed."

7. Ryan op-ed: "The budget permanently cuts the uncompetitive corporate income tax rate."

   FOXfact: "GOP budget permanently cuts corporate income tax rate."[41]

Not only were these "FOXfacts" essentially a transcription of an opinion piece written by the Republican leader, but Fox News didn't even bother to remove the slanted language—like "president's cap-and-trade scheme" or a reference to the "death tax"—from their list of "facts."

Again in April, during an interview with Republican Congressman Mike Pence of Indiana, Fox host Bill Hemmer mentioned four supposedly "wasteful" projects funded by the stimulus bill. At the conclusion of the segment, Hemmer seemed to take credit for the research that uncovered the projects. "We told our viewers we're keeping track of the stimulus money," he said. "And that's what the intention of this was."[42]

Hemmer was "keeping track of the stimulus money" with the help of House Minority Whip Eric Cantor's website, where each of the examples he mentioned was prominently displayed. At no point did Hemmer acknowledge that the research he cited came from an unambiguously partisan source.

As a veteran of three successful presidential campaigns, Roger Ailes understood that the beginning of the Obama administration was critical to the long-term success of the president's agenda. The network needed to make a stand against Obama's first signature piece of legislation, a stimulus package designed to boost the economy.

There was widespread agreement on the need for action to get the economy moving again, and the president even crafted his plan in a way that should have satisfied conservatives—with an $800 billion cap on its cost and a significant portion of the stimulus coming in the form of tax cuts. In fact, many liberal economists publicly argued that the package was too small.

But the attacks coming from Fox News were rarely based on reality. For example, Dick Morris told viewers of *The O'Reilly Factor* that the stimulus bill "won't work" because "two hundred billion of it is just money to the state. That just stops taxes from going up, but it doesn't stimulate anything."[43] Economist Mark Zandi contradicted these claims, telling Congress that "aid to financially-pressed state governments" is "an economically potent stimulus." Furthermore, the Congressional Budget Office noted that cash infusions to states can produce a greater "cumulative impact on GDP"[44] than tax cuts, the preferred policy of Morris and O'Reilly.

Lies about the stimulus package that had been debunked by other outlets could still find a home on Fox News. On January 29, correspondent Carl Cameron and Laura Ingraham reported that the stimulus would allow "illegal aliens" to claim "tax credits of five hundred dollars per person or one thousand dollars per couple."[45] This distortion was first reported in an Associated Press article that cited a single GOP aide as its source. A revised version of the AP article, which was available before Cameron and Ingraham went on the air, made clear that the stimulus limited tax credits to people with Social Security numbers, ruling out undocumented immigrants.

Fox News also attempted to link the stimulus bill to other liberal bogeymen that were targeted on the network. On January 29, *Fox & Friends* host Steve Doocy claimed: "They are spending $4.19 billion for neighborhood stabilization activities—ACORN. Four billion for ACORN. Let me get this straight. So we're giving four billion dollars for ACORN."[46]

The bill did not mention ACORN at all, and, of course, the organization never received the $4 billion. ACORN had received tens of millions of dollars in total from the federal government over the course of more than a decade. To suddenly suggest the organization would now be eligible to receive billions in a single year was completely disingenuous.

Meanwhile, Glenn Beck seized on the stimulus debate to whip his audience into a McCarthyite frenzy, alleging that Obama was on par with some of the past's greatest monsters, informing viewers on February 4 that he would show them how the president's policies "line[d] up with some of the goings-on in history's worst socialist, fascist countries."[47]

Appearing on *The O'Reilly Factor* two days later, Beck told guest host Laura Ingraham, "We are really truly stepping beyond socialism and starting to look at fascism." Ingraham had opened the interview by comparing Obama's policies to the Soviet Union and asking, "Which five-year plan is this more like, the first one in 1928 or the last one?"[48]

Beck continued his Red Scare tour on the February 10 episode of *Fox & Friends*. "It's the nanny state. They're going to tell us what we can eat, they can tell us what our temperature needs to be in our homes, they can tell us what kind of car to drive, they can tell businesses how to run their businesses," he declared. "It's slavery. It is slavery."[49]

The next day, on his own program, Beck went even further. "You know what this president is doing right now?" Beck said. "He is addicting this country to heroin—the heroin that is government slavery."[50]

Fox News jumped on every story, no matter how specious, that might turn viewers against the stimulus bill. Perhaps the most far-fetched claim was that the legislation allocated $30 million to protect the salt marsh harvest mouse in then-Speaker Nancy Pelosi's district. On the February 11 edition of *Your World with Neil Cavuto*, Mike Huckabee stated that the legislation included "thirty million dollars to save the malt—excuse me, the salt marsh mouse in Nancy Pelosi's district. Thirty million dollars for a mouse."[51] Huckabee, the former governor of Arkansas, was given a weekend program on Fox News after leaving the 2008 presidential campaign trail. Additionally, he serves as a political commentator on the network.

The next morning on *Fox & Friends,* correspondent Caroline Shively continued to report on the false story without checking any of the facts.[52] Fox created such a buzz that Greg Sargent of *The Washington Post* investigated the claim and found no evidence to

support it. Rather, House Republicans and Fox News appeared to
have created a talking point based on nothing more than hearsay:

> How did this one get going? Yesterday a House Republi-
> can leadership staffer circulated a background email, which
> I obtained, charging that GOP staffers had been told by an
> unnamed Federal agency that if it got money from the stim
> package, it would spend "thirty million dollars for wetland
> restoration in the San Francisco Bay Area—including work to
> protect the Salt Marsh Harvest Mouse."
>
> The GOP staffer's email didn't say what agency it was. It
> didn't say the money was actually in the package—just that an
> unnamed agency had said they *would* spend it on that if they
> got it. . . .
>
> But I just contacted the House GOP staffer who wrote the
> initial email laying out this talking point, and he conceded that
> the claim by conservative media that the mouse money is cur-
> rently in the bill is a misstatement. "There is not specific lan-
> guage in the legislation for this project," he said.[53]

Of course, being proved wrong didn't change the way Fox
News covered the story. Just hours after Sargent's report debunk-
ing the lie was published online, Beck announced, "Nancy Pelosi
put twenty million dollars into the stimulus package to preserve
the salt marsh mouse."[54]

Fox's misleading stimulus coverage was capped off with a
three-day special hosted by Bret Baier that aired February 14–16
and repeatedly misrepresented the content of the bill. Among
other falsehoods, the network aired claims that the bill would lead
to "the government deciding which procedures you can have and

which ones you can't"[55] and that it would prohibit any religious activity in facilities receiving money.

In addition to painting the president as a reckless liberal spender, Fox News continued its quest to portray him as un-American. Obama's first trip outside of North America as commander in chief in April, to attend the G-20 and the Summit of the Americas, offered a perfect opportunity to do just that.

During a speech in Europe, Obama stated: "In America, there's a failure to appreciate Europe's leading role in the world. Instead of celebrating your dynamic union and seeking to partner with you to meet common challenges, there have been times where America has shown arrogance and been dismissive, even derisive."[56]

On Fox News, Obama's remarks were evidence that he was "blam[ing]" America. The next two sentences Obama uttered did not fit into the network's prescribed narrative, so they were simply omitted. "But in Europe, there is an anti-Americanism that is at once casual but can also be insidious," Obama had said. "Instead of recognizing the good that America so often does in the world, there have been times where Europeans choose to blame America for much of what's bad."[57]

Sean Hannity, in particular, continued to make false claims about what Obama said in Europe. When the president told the Turkish parliament that "the United States is not . . . at war with Islam," Hannity accused Obama of "seemingly apologizing for our engagement in the war on terror." In those same remarks Obama had stated that "Iraq, Turkey, and the United States face a common threat from terrorism" and that "we are committed to a more focused effort to disrupt, dismantle, and defeat Al Qaeda."[58]

Fox News commentators also criticized Obama for saying that "we do not consider ourselves a Christian nation" during an April 6 press availability with the president of Turkey. For instance, Karl Rove said it was "very strange" for Obama to deny that "we have historically had, you know, a robust presence of faith in our public square."[59]

Of course, the president was making a broader point about the nature of American values. After acknowledging earlier in the speech that the United States was "a predominantly Christian nation," Obama added that "one of the great strengths of the United States is—although as I mentioned, we have a very large Christian population, we do not consider ourselves a Christian nation or a Jewish nation or a Muslim nation; we consider ourselves a nation of citizens who are bound by ideals and a set of values."[60]

The attacks continued during Obama's trip to the Summit of the Americas. Fox News personalities condemned the president for shaking hands with and accepting a book from Venezuelan president Hugo Chavez, and for listening to a speech by Nicaraguan president Daniel Ortega. The frequent criticism of Barack Obama's handshake with Chavez was especially absurd, as Fox never denounced George W. Bush for shaking hands with brutal dictators, such as Uzbekistani president Islam Karimov.

Liz Peek, a financial columnist for FoxNews.com, even wrote a column titled "Chavez Handshake May Cost the U.S. Billions" because it signified that Obama would "buy Chavez' friendship."[61]

These same attacks continued well after the president's first hundred days ended. In June, Barack Obama spoke at Cairo University. His address was well received even by those who had differences with the president on foreign affairs. Senator Joe Lieberman, who had endorsed John McCain in the presidential election, was effusive with praise, declaring that "Obama is off to a very, very good start in a very difficult time in our nation's history."[62] Republican senator Richard Lugar called the speech a "signal achievement."[63]

Fox News had a different opinion. Several hours after the speech, Bill Sammon wrote to the network staff, "My cursory check of Obama's 6,000-word speech to the Muslim world did not turn up the words 'terror,' 'terrorist' or 'terrorism.' "[64]

Bill Sammon's e-mail quickly became the guide for Fox News's coverage of the event. Ten minutes after sending the e-mail, he appeared on *America's Newsroom* with anchors Megyn Kelly and Bill Hemmer to inform the audience, "Well, I make of it that he has taken us off a war footing as a nation. And it's now clear—when you give a six-thousand-plus-word speech to the Muslim world and you don't mention 'terror,' 'terrorist,' or 'terrorism,' you know, that's not an accident."[65]

On *Special Report* that day, host Bret Baier reported on Obama's speech, claiming, "The address from Cairo, Egypt, featured references to both the nine-eleven attacks and the war in Iraq, but did not use the words 'terror,' 'terrorist,' or 'terrorism.' "[66] Later that night, on *The O'Reilly Factor,* Karl Rove claimed, "He talked about confronting extremism but could never bring himself to say 'terrorism.' "[67] In the next hour, Sean Hannity took the criticism of the president's remarks a step further, claiming, "Mr. Obama refused to use these words—'terror,' 'terrorism,' 'terrorist'—or even that term 'manmade disasters.' But he repeatedly quoted the Quran and even accused Americans of overreacting to the nine-eleven terror attacks."[68] The theme continued on *Fox & Friends* the next day, with Steve Doocy saying, "President Obama was at Cairo University, he had a six-thousand-word speech, and yet, of those six thousand words, not once did he use the word 'terrorist,' 'terrorism,' or 'terror,' 'war on terror,' or any of that stuff."[69]

Fox's analysis was incredibly misleading. The president had devoted nine paragraphs of his speech to Al-Qaeda and "violent extremists who pose a grave threat to our security."[70] Experts praised the president's word choice as a way to alleviate some anti-American hostility that had accumulated in the region due to the overuse of the word "terrorist." Either no one at Fox News had actually read the speech, or a major part of its content was deliberately ignored in order to paint the president as soft on fighting terrorism.

The facts did not matter. At Fox News, the start of Obama's presidency was about establishing the narrative that he was a weak, big-spending liberal who would ruin the country. By denying the president a honeymoon, Ailes had set the tone for the rest of Obama's term. Instead of bringing America together, as Obama had promised, Fox would work to ensure that we were torn apart. Steve Doocy appropriately closed out the president's first hundred days on *Fox & Friends* by proclaiming, "It was only a hundred days. It seems longer, doesn't it?"[71]

Chapter 5

Time for a Tea Party

You can hang [a teabag] from your mirror, too, like fuzzy dice.
—*Fox & Friends* host Gretchen Carlson

On February 19, 2009, in the midst of a rant against the stimulus bill making its way through Congress, CNBC reporter Rick Santelli announced, "We're thinking of having a Chicago Tea Party in July. All you capitalists that want to show up to Lake Michigan, I'm gonna start organizing."[1]

Santelli's pronouncement on the floor of the Chicago Mercantile Exchange was a call to arms to those who had already benefited from the bailouts previously doled out by the Bush administration and Congress. The cry of "It's a moral hazard"[2] from a trader on the floor, was not directed toward the banks that had lost trillions of dollars betting on bad mortgages, crashing the economy in the process. And Santelli's fury certainly was not directed at those in the exchange cheering him on. Their markets had benefited from the easy flow of credit supplied during the boom years, lining investors' pockets and driving up CNBC's ratings.

Santelli was ranting against government assistance for individual homeowners, some of whom were victims of fraud, caught up in the middle of a crashing market. This pseudo-populist ranting became a touchstone for Tea Party activists as they railed against the government, yet happily enjoyed the benefits of a variety of programs. While cheers erupted on the floor of the exchange, the anchors in the studio seemed a bit surprised by the political outburst from the "on-air editor," whose job was analyzing the movements of the market—not leading an angry mob of traders.

The network was caught off guard as well. Despite advocating a pro-business point of view, CNBC was no place for rowdy activists. Indeed, it depended on its reputation as a high-minded business network to maintain its elevated ad rates based on catering to an elite market. Investors who were often glued to CNBC did not want bombastic political commentary mixed into the news while the market was open. In 2009, the network was also under the microscope for its bullish cheerleading of the real-estate bubble, best exemplified by host Jim Cramer telling investors to ignore warnings about Bear Stearns a few days before the bank went under. Cramer later claimed he was merely advising depositors that their funds were safe.

CNBC quickly shut down Santelli's organizing efforts, relinquishing any role the network had in the Tea Party protests. Ironically, CNBC's abandonment of the Tea Parties probably helped build a larger movement. With its niche audience of investors, the station did not have the ability to compel activists into action and organize with the same gusto as Fox.

When CNBC quashed Santelli's activism, Fox was ready to

pounce. As conservative activists and political consultants began to schedule Tea Parties around the country, the network became their primary organizing and promotional agent. In the months following Santelli's original rant, Fox News aired scores of promos and segments on the movement, and even graphics declaring the events "FNC Tax Day Tea Parties."[3]

Using its false platform as a news organization, Fox News was able to bring the Tea Party into prominence in a way that clearly partisan organizations such as the Republican National Committee or the fiscally conservative Club for Growth could only dream of. Roger Ailes didn't just embrace the message of the Tea Parties—he took Santelli's faux populism and morphed it into a direct attack on President Obama. The Tea Party movement followed Fox's lead, converting itself from a neo-populist, antigovernment movement into an army for the Republican Party.

Much of the network's coverage was based on the constant

claim that the Tea Party movement was nonpartisan. However, polls consistently showed that the overwhelming majority of Tea Party members were Republicans and were primarily angry with the president. As *The New York Times* reported in April 2010, "The 18 percent of Americans who identify themselves as Tea Party supporters tend to be Republican, white, male, married and older than 45."[4]

Furthermore, the activities of the variety of local organizations and PACs affiliated with the Tea Parties, in addition to the party of the candidates the Tea Parties endorsed, contradicted the notion of a nonpartisan movement. By portraying the Tea Party as a nonpartisan movement, Fox could essentially back a Republican campaign vehicle without technically crossing the line into partisan politics.

Fox News provided wall-to-wall coverage of Tea Party gatherings. While only four years earlier, network personalities attacked attendees at antiwar marches attended by hundreds of thousands in New York and Washington, D.C., as "anti-American," "morally vacuous," and "stupid,"[5] Fox now rewarded meetings attended by as few as a dozen people with hours of air time and live satellite feeds.

"They latched on to the people who came to be known as the Tea Party people very early on," says Tom Fiedler, dean of the College of Communication at Boston University. "Then they covered them as news events that came to be known through natural events. It was a self-fulfilling situation."[6]

On February 27, 2009, Greta Van Susteren informed her audience: "Tea Party protests are erupting across the country. Angry taxpayers, or at least some of them, are taking to the streets in the spirit of the Boston Tea Party. People are protesting President Obama's massive $787 billion stimulus bill, his $3.55 trillion budget, and a federal government that has been ballooning by the day since the president took office."[7]

As the coverage progressed, the message evolved. On the March 25 edition of *Special Report*, anchor Bret Baier described the Tea Parties as "protests of wasteful government spending in general and of President Obama's stimulus package and his budget in particular."[8]

By April 6, the network's coverage of the Tea Parties had begun to take a decidedly different tone, shifting from an attack on progressive policies to a direct attack on President Obama. On *America's Newsroom*, contributor Andrea Tantaros proclaimed: "People are fighting against Barack Obama's radical shift to turn us into Europe."[9]

As the April 15 Tea Party rallies approached, Fox's promotional efforts increased. The network announced that four of its hosts would broadcast live from Tea Parties around the country—Greta Van Susteren in Washington, D.C.; Sean Hannity in Atlanta; Neil Cavuto in Sacramento, California; and Glenn Beck from the Alamo in San Antonio.

Fox's participation in these events became a key part of its coverage. Nightly in the weeks leading up to the Tea Parties, Sean Hannity and Glenn Beck promoted their attendance on Fox News, telling their audiences as Beck did on April 6 that they could "celebrate with Fox News"[10] by either attending a protest or watching one on TV. The network was now a part of the news story, not just covering it. During the same show, Beck made sure to also promote his Fox colleagues, exclaiming, "If you can't make the one in San Antonio, please go to the one with Neil or with Sean in Atlanta. That's supposed to be great. Greta is in Washington, D.C. Just get out and let your face be seen and connect with other people."[11]

Hannity was even more direct on April 2, telling his audience, "And don't forget to log on to our website to get all the details about our special 'Tax Day Tea Party' show. That's live in Atlanta. It's on April fifteenth. John Rich will be there and many more; details coming up." Hannity later said: "On April fifteenth, we'll be broadcasting from a Tea Party in Atlanta. I will be there in Atlanta, where one of the dozens of Tea Parties around the country will be going on. And we hope you'll be watching."[12]

In addition to Fox's own publicity efforts on behalf of the Tea Parties, organizers used Fox and appearances by its stars as a promotional tool, as well. The Sacramento Tea Party wrote on its Facebook page, "We've just received notice that Fox News will be broadcasting the *Your World with Neil Cavuto* show live from the Sacramento Tea Party. Now we really have a chance to let the whole nation hear our voices in Sacramento. Bring your friends, family and everyone you know!"[13]

AtlantaTeaParty.net shared the same level of enthusiasm about Sean Hannity's planned attendance: "Moments ago, Sean Hannity, of *Hannity* on Fox News, announced that he is going to broadcast LIVE from the ATLANTA TEA PARTY!!!! Fox will also have news crews in other cities around the country at their Tea Parties. This is huge and exciting news for the Atlanta event and also for the Tea Party movement in general."[14]

In Texas, *San Antonio Express-News* media columnist Jeanne Jakle wrote, "Eric Adam, the media correspondent for the San Antonio Tea Party, said he's expecting thousands to attend the event now that Beck and his national forum are involved."[15]

Back at Fox News, *America's Newsroom*'s website displayed a link to "Upcoming 'Tea Party' protests"[16] with a list of scheduled rallies, telling visitors that "protests over big government spending and bailouts are popping up all over the country."[17]

Fox hyped the events across its platforms. Bill Hemmer repeat-edly promoted Tea Party developments on air. For example, on March 24, Hemmer mentioned protests in Florida and Ohio and directed viewers to learn more about the protests on his pro-gram's website. "There's a list of the nationwide Tax Day Tea Party events coming up on the fifteenth of April," Hemmer told his audience. "[The events] will be a huge deal for those organiza-tions. So check it out online right now."[18]

As Hemmer spoke, the on-screen text encouraged viewers to visit his website for a listing of the Tea Party protests.

Overexcited hosts were not the only source of Tea Party hype on Fox. The network itself pushed the Tea Parties in ten- and thirty-second promotional spots. Between April 6 and April 15, Fox News aired at least 107 commercials for its coverage of the April 15 Tea Parties.[19] The spots were thinly disguised as net-work promotions but were clearly crafted to advance the message of and plug the Tea Parties. For instance, here is the script of a thirty-second spot promoting Fox News' coverage of the protests:

ANNOUNCER: April fifteenth, all across the country, Americans are making their voices heard. In California, Texas, Georgia, Washington, D.C., citizens are standing up, saying "no" to more taxes and demanding real economic solutions.

April fifteenth: As Tea Parties sweep the nation on Tax Day, we're there with total fair-and-balanced network coverage—live. What is the fate of our nation? We report. You decide.[20]

And the script of a ten-second spot promoting Glenn Beck's coverage of the Tea Parties:

Taking a stand at the Alamo: Citizens revolt against more taxes and demand change now. Plus, Ted Nugent fires back at the government. Glenn is live at the Tea Party in Texas.[21]

The morning of April 15, Fox News began with a discussion of how viewers could show their support for the movement. *Fox & Friends*'s Gretchen Carlson recommended, "You can hang [a teabag] from your mirror, too, like fuzzy dice."[22] If you couldn't attend a protest in person, Fox News anchor Megyn Kelly told her audience, "You can join the Tea Party action from your home if you go to TheFoxNation.com . . . a virtual Tax Day Tea Party."[23]

As the events began, Fox's coverage heated up. Covering one rally, Fox Business anchor Cody Willard played the role of team mascot, howling to the camera, "Guys, when are we going to wake up and start fighting the fascism that seems to be permeating this country?" And when it came time to interview participants, Willard's question to a child summed up his performance that day: "Are you worried about me taking these dollars from you . . . or destroying those dollars? I mean that's what the government does, anyway."[24]

During the prime-time lineup, the network's "opinion" hosts analyzed the day's events. The battle lines had been drawn. Far from participants in a simple political fight, the Tea Party protesters, comprising primarily Fox viewers,[25] were heroes in the ultimate battle of good versus evil.

Others in the media took notice of Fox News's role in the Tea Parties. During an interview on CNN, Howard Kurtz observed that Fox "practically seems to be a cosponsor" of the Tea Party protests. Kurtz pointed out that Fox contributors Newt Gingrich and Michelle Malkin were supporting the protests, commenting that "Fox News, whose new online slogan is 'Just say no to biased media,' began publicizing the protests. And, soon, some hosts were signing on." Kurtz later added, "These hosts said little or nothing about the huge deficits run up by President Bush, but Barack Obama's budget and tax plans have driven them to tea." While Beck and Hannity "and the gang" were "paid for their opinions," Kurtz said, "the question is whether Rupert Murdoch's network wants to be so closely identified with what has become an anti-Obama protest movement."[26]

Los Angeles Times media critic James Rainey followed Kurtz, writing, "Fox has been building up to the protests with Super Bowl–style intensity. Promos promise 'powerful' coverage of an event that will 'sweep the nation.' " According to Rainey, Fox News gave "relentless support" to the protests. "You'd expect conservative commentators like Glenn Beck and Sean Hannity to be hyping today's wave of anti-tax 'tea parties.' But Fox per-

sonalities labeled 'news' anchors are right there with their bless-
ings too," he wrote.[27]

As the year progressed and more Tea Parties were held
throughout the nation, Fox continued to act as promoter, organizer, and cheerleader. This massive effort didn't appear to have
the approval of the boss's boss. At a 2010 forum hosted by former *Meet the Press* host Marvin Kalb, News Corp. chairman Rupert
Murdoch distanced himself from the movement when questioned
on the network's role in the events: "No, I don't think we should
be promoting the Tea Party or any other party."[28]

Something was clearly amiss. How was Fox's active role in the
Tea Party movement possible, considering Rupert Murdoch's
directive? Less than a week later, this contradiction came to a head
inside Fox.

Sean Hannity was scheduled to tape his April 15, 2010, show
at the Cincinnati Tea Party's 2010 Tax Day Tea Party. The event
required paid admission, and, according to the group, "All pro-
ceeds benefit the Cincinnati Tea Party."[29] The *Cincinnati Enquirer*
even reported that the twenty-dollar premium seats would give
attendees "a chance to be on TV,"[30] linking the fund-raising for
the Tea Party to Fox.

Fox News quickly responded. According to the *Los Angeles
Times*:

> Senior Fox News executives said they were not aware Han-
> nity was being billed as the centerpiece of the event or that
> Tea Party organizers were charging for admission to Hannity's
> show as part of the rally. They first learned of it Thursday morn-
> ing from John Finley, Hannity's executive producer, who was
> in Cincinnati to produce Hannity's show. Furious, top officials

recalled Hannity back to New York to do his show in his regular studio. The network plans to do an extensive post-mortem about the incident with Finley and Hannity's staff.[31]

The Tea Parties—and the coverage they received—created a sense that the president was not invincible and that his agenda could be stopped. Perhaps most important, this conservative uprising made President Obama's grassroots operation, Organizing for America, seem impotent. The strength of the grassroots on both sides was on the minds of many political observers in Washington as Congress began fighting over President Obama's health care and climate bills. With the Tea Party movement looming large, Democrats in swing districts watched the Tea Parties fearfully.

In January 2009, it looked as if Obama could buck history—as Bush did after 9/11—and win seats in Congress during the midterm election. But the Tea Parties flipped the conventional wisdom on its head. Ever the political strategist, Roger Ailes knew this would be the case, which is why Fox News put so much effort into promoting the Tea Party.

"In 2010, the coverage was certainly aimed at taking advantage of doubts that were arising about Obama from a lot of different quarters," says Michael Shanahan, former reporter for the Associated Press and assistant director of the School of Media and Public Affairs at George Washington University. "When the Tea Party got going and the suspicions about the health care bill got out and started showing up, Fox ran with those stories and got them out there. In that way, they contributed to some of the political shift in the country. [Fox News] certainly exploited it and tilted their coverage to take advantage of the attitude."[32]

The bigger and more powerful the opposition movement

seemed, the less likely the president's legislation was to pass Congress. The movement's actual size didn't matter, only its perceived power according to the media. And for those watching Fox News on Capitol Hill at that moment, no movement was more powerful than the Tea Party.

During his first year in office, President Obama set his sights on several major policy goals, in addition to rebuilding the economy. When it became clear early on that the administration and congressional Democrats would prioritize health care and climate change, Fox News led the charge against needed reforms, using a barrage of falsehoods and misleading stories with one goal in mind: weakening the president of the United States.

Ultimately, it would not have mattered what legislation President Obama was attempting to pass into law. If his agenda had included "The Fox News Must Be on TV in Every Home Act," the network would have opposed it. Preventing a liberal president from appearing to succeed was more important than the popularity or effectiveness of any particular piece of legislation. Since health care reform and clean energy were issues that had strong support from the American people, it would be an uphill climb.

For decades, reforming the nation's health care system has been the preeminent progressive cause. Numerous times, most recently in 1993, the hope existed of actually achieving this goal, only to be thwarted by conservative and industry lobbying and grassroots efforts. Not only had the election of Barack Obama increased faith among progressives that health care reform would pass, but state reforms such as the Massachusetts plan stewarded by former and current presidential candidate Mitt Romney also seemed to demonstrate than even Republicans had recognized reforming our health care system as a national priority. Nevertheless, conservatives, led by Fox News, decided it was not to be—they would fight President Obama's reforms, many of which where taken directly from conservative Heritage Foundation experts.

First, Fox News personalities claimed that there was no health care crisis in need of a solution. As Steve Doocy told the audience of *Fox & Friends* in July 2009, "Currently, ninety percent of all Americans have got some sort of health care coverage, which means they are effectively blowing up the system for five percent."[33]

But denying the problem wasn't enough. Fox News needed to terrify its viewers about the consequences of reforming the health care system. "We're gonna have a government rationing body that tells women with breast cancer, 'You're dead,'" Sean Hannity told his audience. "It's a death sentence."[34]

Meanwhile, after watching the deficit balloon for years under President Bush with little comment, Fox News hosts and contributors suddenly became concerned with the fiscal impact of health care reform. Karl Rove, who helped shape many of the Bush administration's policies that added trillions to the national debt, warned Fox viewers that Obama was "planning on a 1-trillion, 420-billion—420-million-dollar price tag of additional spending over the next ten years."[35]

And, of course, Fox would repeatedly promote the conservative nightmare that Obama was going to impose a nationalized "single-payer" system like Canada's or the United Kingdom's. Anchor Bret Baier reported, "President Obama spent a good deal of time at that news conference [on June 23] talking about health care reform, and Canada's medical system has been cited as a possible model."[36] In reality, Obama, as president, had never proposed a single-payer system—something many progressives would have cheered.

Sean Hannity went a step further, claiming the bill would ban private insurance. "The one thing that we do know in the health care bill is that . . . the bill says that if you don't have your insurance the year this legislation is implemented, you can't have a private insurance company," said Hannity. "So that will end—hang on—that will end private insurance."[37]

Quite the opposite. The Obama plan relied on the private market as the primary provider of insurance, much to the consternation of many in the progressive movement.

"They were selecting out the information available that was going to appeal to the people who had an opinion about health care, but no facts," according to Bill Kovach, founder of the Committee of Concerned Journalists. "It was an opinion they chose to reinforce, an opinion not based on facts."[38]

While each of these distortions made an impact, none was more damaging than the idea that health care reform would create "death panels" with the power to decide who receives treatment and who is left to die. The "death panel" lie became impossible to kill and drove the national conversation about health care reform for months. It was no surprise that the debate was taken over by a single falsehood—in the era before Fox News, conservatives had used the same tactic to kill the last major push for health care reform.

In 1994, just days before President Clinton was scheduled to deliver the State of the Union address, Betsy McCaughey, then a fellow at the conservative Manhattan Institute, published a factually challenged article in *The New Republic* claiming that Clinton's health care bill would ration care and prevent patients from making their own medical decisions. As Tom Wolfe wrote in the *New York Post,* "that one article shot down the entire blimp."[39]

It turned out that McCaughey was not acting on her own but working inside a network of conservatives funding efforts to defeat the bill. An internal Philip Morris memo titled "Tobacco Strategy" states that company staff "worked off the record with Betsy McCaughey as part of the input to the three-part expose in *The New Republic* on what the Clinton Plan means to you."[40]

Roger Ailes, while at CNBC, was also moonlighting for the tobacco industry's campaign against health care reform. He had maintained a consulting relationship with the tobacco industry dating back to the late 1980s. While working for George H. W. Bush's presidential campaign in 1988, Ailes also fought to oppose a twenty-five-cent-a-pack tax increase on cigarettes in California. "The antismoking zealots tried first to throw water in everybody's face," commented Ailes at the time. "Now, they're throwing legislation."[41] His $20 million ad campaign failed to win over voters, but in a memo recapping the campaign, Ailes Communications boasted, "Although we were not successful, the CAUTI [Californians Against Unfair Tax Increases] campaign moved an extremely large number of voters to our position."[42]

One of the proposed funding mechanisms for the 1993 health care plan was a significant increase in the federal tax on a pack of cigarettes. The tobacco companies lined up to oppose the proposal.

At the time according to a February 1993 Philip Morris budget memo, Roger Ailes was receiving $15,000 per month for "general media strategy."[43]

In May, a memo from Philip Morris spokesperson Craig Fuller detailed some of Ailes's efforts: "Roger Ailes and I have talked about running ads with a coalition we will form ... one name 'Coalition for Fair Funding of Health Care.' "[44] Another memo from July 6, 1993, tasked Ailes to "develop ad copy for review, testing and approval by senior management." It notes, next to Ailes's name, "Real people affected by taxes."[45] On a subsequent page, Roger Ailes and two colleagues are charged with finding "shows where we can deliver our message" in addition to creating "counter talking points."[46]

Ailes joined CNBC in August 1993. As head of a financial news network that was covering the issue of health care reform and its impact on businesses and the stock market, he should have ceased his consulting activities. However, according to tobacco company documents, Ailes continued to work for the industry. A document titled "Tobacco Strategy Review," dated March 22, 1994, reads, "We have developed ads on FET [federal excise tax] developed by Ailes Communications. Only a couple were run and they were run under the name of a tax organization as focus groups showed this was most effective."[47] Then, in June 1994, Philip Morris vice president Thomas Collamore sent a memo to Craig Fuller noting, "We pay [Roger Ailes] 5k a month to be available."[48] Even as head of the preeminent financial news network, Ailes would not cease his political activities.

Almost immediately following the publication of her article, Betsy McCaughey became a star in the conservative movement. Bob Dole used elements of her piece in his response to the State of the Union address, and conservative groups were soon broadcasting ads across the country based on her work. Then, after a brief tenure as lieutenant governor of New York under Governor George Pataki, McCaughey faded from the spotlight. President Obama's push to improve the country's health care system was the perfect opportunity for McCaughey's return to the fray.

On July 16, 2009, McCaughey told radio host, former senator, and failed presidential candidate Fred Thompson that health
care reform "would make it mandatory—absolutely require—that
every five years people on Medicare have a required counseling
session that will tell them how to end their life sooner." These sessions, according to McCaughey, would teach seniors to "decline
nutrition, how to decline being hydrated, how to go into hospice
care . . . all to do what's in society's best interest or in your family's
best interest and cut your life short."[49]

The nonpartisan, Pulitzer Prize–winning website PolitiFact
.com jumped on McCaughey's statement, rating it "Pants on
Fire," a designation reserved for the most dishonest claims. "For
our ruling on this one, there's really no gray area here," Politi-
Fact explained. "McCaughey incorrectly states that the bill would
require Medicare patients to have these counseling sessions and
she is suggesting that the government is somehow trying to interfere with a very personal decision. And her claim that the sessions
would 'tell [seniors] how to end their life sooner' is an outright
distortion. Rather, the sessions are an option for elderly patients
who want to learn more about living wills, health care proxies and
other forms of end-of-life planning. McCaughey isn't just wrong,
she's spreading a ridiculous falsehood."[50]

McCaughey's lie attracted one important follower. In August,
former vice presidential candidate Sarah Palin wrote on her Facebook page, "And who will suffer the most when they ration care?
The sick, the elderly, and the disabled, of course. The America I
know and love is not one in which my parents or my baby with
Down Syndrome will have to stand in front of Obama's 'death
panel' so his bureaucrats can decide, based on a subjective judgment of their 'level of productivity in society,' whether they are
worthy of health care. Such a system is downright evil."[51]

With that posting, the "death panel" debate was born. Palin's proclamation was given wall-to-wall coverage, especially on Fox News, where the former governor's lies went unchecked. The morning after Palin published her post, *Fox & Friends* cohost Brian Kilmeade asked, "Are seniors going to be in front of the death panel?" Responding to his own question, Kilmeade continued, "And then just as you think, 'Okay, that's ridiculous,' then you realize there's provisions in there that seniors in the last lap of their life will be sitting there going to a panel possibly discussing what the best thing for them is."[52]

Other Fox News personalities, from Glenn Beck to Andrew Napolitano, a libertarian former New Jersey state judge, echoed Palin's distortion, never stopping to question whether or not it was true. And it wasn't just Fox's "opinion" hosts who were giving "death panels" credence. "Former Republican vice presidential nominee Sarah Palin says President Obama is misleading the public about what she has called 'death panels' in health care reform," reported Bret Baier. "Palin contends advanced care planning consultations, which are an element in the House reform legislation, would not be voluntary, as the president says. She lays out a detailed rebuttal on her Facebook page. The White House has named Palin as a person spreading wrong information about reform plans."[53]

Over the next week, more than forty separate media outlets, including the Associated Press, debunked Palin's outrageous claim. The lie stuck anyway. A week later, Fox News was still using the "death panel" charade to scare its viewers about health care reform. For instance, on August 19, *Fox & Friends* hosted network contributor Dick Morris to discuss his *New York Post* column from two days earlier, in which he alleged that Democratic reform proposals amounted to "one giant death panel." During the segment, on-screen text read: "DEFACTO [*sic*] DEATH PANELS? OBAMA PLAN COULD RESULT IN RATIONING."[54]

Palin's false claims had a tremendous impact on the public's perception. In a CNN/Opinion Research poll conducted on September 11–13, 2009, 41 percent of respondents believed that "death panels" were part of Obama's health care bill.[55] In December, PolitiFact singled out "death panels" as the "Lie of the Year." A few weeks later, Sarah Palin was hired as a contributor to Fox News. More than a year later, Fox was still keeping the "death panel" rumor alive. On January 3, 2011, Andrew Napolitano, who was filling in for Glenn Beck, declared that there were now panels that would "tell Grandma and Grandpa . . . how and when to die."[56]

As the fight over health care reform unfolded, Fox News hosts such as Beck, Hannity, and Mike Huckabee openly advocated against Democratic efforts and implored viewers to help defeat the bill. Beck warned that the health care bill would bring on "the end of America as you know it,"[57] while Hannity called it "the most irresponsible piece of domestic legislation in our lifetime."[58]

Even more revealing, Fox itself declared victory each time Democrats suffered a setback. After Democrats removed the provision that started the cries of "death panels," a headline on the Fox Nation website read: "Fox Nation Victory! Senate Removes 'End of Life' Provision."[59] When the White House gave up on the public option, the website proclaimed: "Fox Nation Victory! Obama backs down from Gov't-Run Health Care!"[60] And when a vote on the bill was stalled, the headline boasted: "Fox Nation Victory! Congress delays health care rationing bill."[61]

As the summer began, strategists in both parties understood that August would be critical in setting the tone for the fall debate on President Obama's health care legislation. Coming into the

congressional recess, Democrats had the momentum. The House had passed president Obama's climate bill, and health care reform was making its way through Congress. If conservatives were going to succeed, they needed a shift in public perception. In April, Fox News had demonstrated that there was a viable movement to carry on the fight against the Obama agenda. The next test was to find out whether that movement could actually scare Democratic members of Congress away from the president.

In early August, Fox News aired footage from a string of unruly town hall events. The video didn't show the orderly debate typically associated with town hall meetings, but rather lawmakers being shouted at and intimidated by their constituents.

Sean Hannity explained the strategy to his radio audience on July 29, saying, "There's going to be no floor vote immediately [on health care reform], so members have time to go home and read the bill, which, by the way, creates the best opportunity for people to go like they did to [Democratic Senator] Claire McCaskill's

town hall meeting or go to [Democratic Congressman Russ] Car-
nahan's town hall meeting or go show up wherever there's any
representative. This is your moment, your opportunity to stop
this thing."[62]

Local town hall meetings, which allow citizens to speak to their
elected representatives face-to-face, are at the core of American
democracy. Conservative strategists decided that the town halls
of August 2009 would be different. Rather than engaging in civil
discourse about the best way to move the nation forward, they
would create disruptions, attempting to silence anyone who disagreed with them.

Although progressives had launched town hall protests in
response to George W. Bush's plan to privatize Social Security, their efforts did not receive overwhelming media coverage
or control the national narrative, as the actions of conservatives
would in August 2009. Of course, the left did not have a national
news network at their disposal to shape the dialogue.

On June 30, the tone was set for the period to follow. Republican congressman Mike Castle of Delaware, one of the few
remaining centrists in the GOP, was the presumptive Republican senatorial nominee and a strong bet to win the seat formerly
held by Vice President Joe Biden. During a town hall meeting in
Georgetown, Delaware, an enraged woman held up what she said
was her birth certificate and asked why Castle and other members
of Congress were ignoring questions about the president's citizenship. Castle answered that Obama was a U.S. citizen and fully
qualified to be president, which led to a rousing chorus of boos
from the crowd. The woman proceeded to grab the microphone
and started reciting the Pledge of Allegiance.

Fox News soon began encouraging town hall outbursts on the
air. On August 3, *Fox & Friends* analyst Peter Johnson, Jr., com-

mented on a raucous town hall meeting held by Pennsylvania senator Arlen Specter, who had recently defected from the Republican
Party to the Democrats, proclaiming, "We need to have this every
day throughout August."[63] According to one report on the event,
which Secretary of Health and Human Services Kathleen Sebel-
ius also attended, protesters "shouted and booed to drown out
remarks from both officials and questions from the audience."[64]

Later that morning, Steve Doocy announced that viewers
could use Fox as a tool to contact members of Congress. "If you
want to contact your Congress members and sound off, go to
FoxNation.com," he said. "It is a great interactive website where
you can sound off, and you'll also find your lawmakers' phone
numbers and e-mail there. Hmm, very handy."[65] This was the call
to action of an advocacy organization, not the reporting of an
impartial news outlet.

The promotion continued the next day on *Fox & Friends,* with
Gretchen Carlson calling the audience to action. "You probably
have a lot on your mind for your respective members of Congress when they come home from recess," Carlson said. "Are
you gonna call them up and tell them how you really feel, or are
you going to go to one of these receptions where they're actually
there in person?" Peter Johnson concluded the segment by telling
a town hall protester, "We thank you for representing Americans,
and we hope that other Americans get out there."[66]

Hannity touted the town hall outbursts on his show, proclaiming to Dick Morris that a forum held by Senator Specter "sounded
more like a Philadelphia Eagles game or a Flyers game than a town
hall."

"It sure is. We got to sign that lady up,"[67] Morris replied, referring to a woman who had confronted the senator.

As the month wore on, Fox injected new controversy into the

town hall protests to keep the story fresh. In an August 10 op-ed in *USA Today,* Democratic leaders Nancy Pelosi and Steny Hoyer wrote that "it is now evident that an ugly campaign is underway not merely to misrepresent the health insurance reform legislation, but to disrupt public meetings and prevent members of Congress and constituents from conducting a civil dialogue," adding that "drowning out opposing views is simply un-American."[68] Predictably, Fox News went on the attack.

Gretchen Carlson blatantly distorted the op-ed, stating, "Nancy Pelosi says anyone who speaks out is un-American."[69] Similarly, Steve Doocy falsely claimed, "Pelosi [said] that apparently the opposing view to her is un-American."[70]

As usual, Sean Hannity escalated the rhetoric. "Now, we've had hardworking Americans called Nazis and brownshirts and un-American by Nancy Pelosi."[71] The Nazi claim was a reference to Pelosi's answer days earlier, when she was asked whether she believed the town hall disruptions were evidence of "legitimate grassroots opposition." Pelosi said, "I think they're astroturf; you be the judge. They're carrying swastikas and symbols like that to a town meeting on health care."[72]

Contrary to Hannity's claim, Pelosi had not called anyone "brownshirts," but had merely stated a fact. In the previous week, numerous pictures had emerged showing town hall protesters using Nazi imagery to communicate their message. For the Tea Party movement, this was par for the course.

A week later, *Fox & Friends* illustrated Pelosi's point by airing footage of a town hall meeting held by Democratic Congressman Brian Baird of Washington. "If Nancy Pelosi wants to find a swastika," one attendee declared, "maybe the first place she should look is the sleeve of her own arm."[73]

Fox's reporting painted even the most extreme protesters in a positive light. On August 19, Steve Doocy criticized Democratic congressman Barney Frank of Massachusetts for being rude to a constituent who confronted him at a town hall meeting:

> DOOCY: Well, give him credit for showing up. But let's face it: he was downright rude. Somebody asked him a question—
>
> BRIAN KILMEADE: Smug.
>
> DOOCY: Okay, somebody asked him a question, then he said, "On what planet do you spend most of your time?" And then to somebody else he said, "Trying to have a conversation with you would be like arguing with a dining room table." Barney, they showed up at the senior center in Dartmouth last night for some answers. Give them some answers, don't give them attitude.[74]

Doocy never mentioned the outrageous question that induced Frank's ire: "Why do you continue to support a Nazi policy, as Obama has expressly supported this policy?"[75]

During the last week of August, Fox News repeatedly claimed that New Hampshire Democratic congresswoman Carol Shea-Porter had a constituent who opposed health care reform "ejected" from a meeting on the grounds that "he did not have the correct ticket to speak."[76] This was a lie.

The conservative *New Hampshire Union Leader* reported a statement from the local sheriff's office: "Towards the end of the meeting, [the constituent] was escorted out of the meeting. Mr. Tomanelli was very disruptive throughout the meeting and was told repeatedly to quiet down. He continuously interrupted people who were asking questions or making statements that he didn't agree with."[77]

The coverage on Fox News left the impression that every single speaker at town halls across the country was furiously opposed to Obama's health care plan—and that was the point. "In fact, after the president convened a low-key town hall in New Hampshire, press secretary Robert Gibbs told reporters: 'I think some of you were disappointed yesterday that the president didn't get yelled at.' There was a grain of truth in that," Howard Kurtz recounted. "As Fox broke away from the meeting, anchor Trace Gallagher said, 'Any contentious questions, anybody yelling, we'll bring it to you.' "[78]

During the week of August 24 alone, Fox News broadcast twenty-two clips of town hall attendees speaking out against health care reform and showed not a single example of people expressing support for reform. Five times that week, Fox aired a single sound bite from an August 25 town hall meeting, where an attendee implored John McCain not to waver in his commitment to stopping the bill. "No compromises!" the constituent said. "Senator, nuke it now."[79]

Fox News also gave airtime to comments such as:

- "Have you ever, or any of your family members, lived under so-called socialized medicine, as I call it? I have, and I've had relatives living on it. And trust me, it ain't working."[80]
- "I'd like to know why illegal aliens—illegal—not members of this country, don't belong here, are gonna be insured under this . . . I have taken the time to look at certain provisions of the bill on the Internet. I can quote the—what is it?—the section and the page, and it definitely says that they will be insured. They don't even belong here, and I'm paying for it."[81]
- "There will be rationing health care . . . and, in addition, the Cystic Fibrosis Foundation, through, with the help of pharmaceuti-

cal companies, do a lot of research and they have made great strides in helping people like Maya live normal, productive, longer lives. I'm afraid when this government option is passed, Maya's life will not be worth anything to the government."[82]

There were plenty of examples of Americans speaking out in favor of health care reform, but Fox News simply ignored them. For instance, Congressman Baird was asked why Congress was not considering a more progressive proposal for reform. "Could you please help us understand why this single-payer option is not on the table, for one?" the constituent said. "And two, could you then lead us into some understanding as to why even a public option seems to be in doubt?"[83]

In another case, a town hall attendee said to McCain, "I believe you have had access to government-provided health care for most of your life, and, you know, I would imagine that most of us here are on Medicare, and there may be some who would like to give up their Medicare. No, none of us do. So what is so wrong with government-provided health care?"[84]

"Please support real national health care, also called universal single-payer,"[85] one Minnesota resident said to Republican Congresswoman Michele Bachmann, a Tea Party favorite.

Of course, Fox News would never give any airtime to the attendee at Virginia Democratic congressman Jim Moran's town hall meeting who decried the overheated discourse the network was glorifying. "I'm very concerned about the quality of the debate," the constituent said. "You know, not only the screaming of misrepresentations, but also the fact that the press really doesn't seem to want to cover policy. You know, they want to cover gossip, and I'm very disappointed, and I would like all of you press to start covering the policy."[86]

The coverage of this particular town hall meeting epitomized Fox's entire August campaign. Host Gregg Jarrett surmised that there "seemed to be more jeers than cheers at that town hall meeting." Bret Baier claimed, "Virginia Democratic congressman Jim Moran was greeted by boos Tuesday in Reston, and the crowd frequently interrupted him."[87]

Other media outlets told a different story. According to *Congressional Quarterly,* conservative protesters "were overmatched by supporters of Moran and Obama, who had their own signs—or were provided them by Organizing for America, Obama's grass-roots support group—and who were able to yell the loudest."[88] Similarly, *The Washington Post* reported, "Unlike at many town hall meetings that have received attention across the country, the crowd in the Democratic-leaning district was dominated by reform proponents, many carrying signs distributed by President Obama's political action group Organizing for America."[89]

Fox News continued to inflate the level of anger at these events. During an August 25 segment on a town hall meeting held by Missouri Democratic senator Claire McCaskill, Fox aired on-screen text that read, "TOWN HALL TEMPERS: SENATOR MCCASKILL GETS BOOED,"[90] along with footage of the audience booing. As the Associated Press reported, the booing wasn't representative of the mood at the town hall: "A couple of shouts and a few boos punctuated Sen. Claire McCaskill's health care forum in Hannibal, but mostly the crowd crammed into a grade school auditorium offered polite, if mixed, feedback."[91]

By the time August ended, Fox News had successfully put Democrats on the defensive. The goal of its one-sided coverage was simple: paint a picture of the world where Democratic members of Congress, the president, and supporters of his agenda were on the defensive. It is an understatement to say that Fox succeeded. The network's persistent coverage of town hall meetings and amplification of Tea Party anger had shifted the national dialogue and taken the momentum away from Obama's agenda. This would prove critical as Congress returned to work in January and the final sprint to pass health care and climate bills began.

Early in the process, President Obama and congressional leaders made unpopular compromises on the health care bill. While many progressives in Congress and the activist community wanted single-payer health care, Obama and the Democrats decided the political reality was such that that kind of a plan was not a possibility. Instead, they agreed to leave the private insurance system intact while giving Americans the option of purchasing their health care plans from the federal government.

This "public option" quickly became the object of relentless attacks from Fox News and conservatives across the country. As previously noted, during the summer, Republican pollster Frank Luntz told Sean Hannity that opponents of the president's plan should refer to the "government option" instead of the "public option" to make it sound less appealing. A few weeks later, Bill Sammon decreed that Fox News employees should use Luntz's language and refrain from saying "public option" on the air.

As the debate picked up, conservatives demonized the public option, accusing Obama of supporting what they called "socialized medicine." The House of Representatives was able to pass a bill that included the public option, but conservative Democrats in the Senate eventually demanded the provision's removal. At Fox News, the elimination of the public option was a double-edged sword. When the hated policy disappeared, so did one of the network's favorite talking points and reasons for opposing the bill.

With that in mind, Bill Sammon drafted another e-mail to producers, suggesting that Fox's fight was not over:

From: Sammon, Bill
Sent: Thursday, December 10, 2009 4:02 PM
To: 169 -SPECIAL REPORT; 069 -Politics; 036 -FOX.WHU;
    054 -FNSunday; 030 -Root (FoxNews.Com);
    050 -Senior Producers; 051 -Producers
Cc: Clemente, Michael; Stack, John; Wallace, Jay;
Smith, Sean
Subject: Was the public option really removed? Or instead
replaced with the "mother of all public options"?

After copying and pasting several quotes praising the tentative compromise to replace the public option with a provision allowing individuals over the age of fifty-five to buy into Medicare, Sammon wrote:

Remember, single payer was always portrayed as the ideal that
liberals dared not dream was within their reach. Instead, they
were going to settle for a robust public option. Now comes the
spin that the public option has been dropped from the Senate compromise, as reached by the Gang of 10. But that spin,
which was quickly accepted as conventional wisdom, is contradicted by the above quotes.

Allowing more Americans to opt into Medicare would have made the system more financially solvent and provided care to millions of Americans. There was no backdoor public option, but Fox News continued to attack the compromise proposal to help

Republicans stop the bill. This idea, too, was eventually taken off the table.

Following Republican Scott Brown's surprising victory in the race for the late Ted Kennedy's Massachusetts Senate seat, the media were ready to declare health care reform dead. However, with a few deft political moves, Obama, House Speaker Nancy Pelosi, and Senate Majority Leader Harry Reid brought it back to life. The centerpiece of the president's push to resuscitate the bill was a bipartisan summit with leaders from both chambers of Congress that would take place at the end of February. With the showdown looming, Fox's activism intensified.

To understand why killing health care reform was so crucial to Fox News and conservatives in general, one needed only to look back to 1993–94 and a memo written by the Republican strategist—and Fox News contributor—William Kristol. As conservatives were formulating their opposition to President Clinton's plan, Kristol sent a memo to Republican leaders titled "Defeating President Clinton's Health Care Proposal." In the memo, Kristol wrote:

> Any Republican urge to negotiate a "least bad" compromise with the Democrats, and thereby gain momentary public credit for helping the president "do something" about health care, should also be resisted. Passage of the Clinton health care plan, in any form, would guarantee and likely make permanent an unprecedented federal intrusion into and disruption of the American economy—and the establishment of the largest federal entitlement program since Social Security. Its success would signal a rebirth of centralized welfare-state policy at the very moment we have begun rolling back that idea in other

areas. And, not least, it would destroy the present breadth and quality of the American health care system, still the world's finest. On grounds of national policy alone, the plan should not be amended; it should be erased.[92]

For Republicans, the same rationale still applied fifteen years later. An Obama victory on health care reform could potentially help restore America's faith in government, something conservatives had been working for more than five decades to destroy. "Obamacare" needed to be stopped at all costs. A bipartisan summit designed to bring the parties together was simply unacceptable.

On February 8, Rush Limbaugh spoke out against the summit. "This is no time for bipartisanship," Limbaugh declared. "This is a setup because Obama wants to be able to blame this on the Republicans when in fact it is his own party that's been saying 'no' to itself."[93]

Fox News was quick to echo Limbaugh's disapproval. The next morning on *Fox & Friends*, Peter Johnson, Jr., said, "Rush is right. Of course it's a trap. There's such a deep chasm and wide chasm over the goals and the objectives of health care reform in this country."[94]

The theme continued throughout the week. "The only thing you can do with the Republicans is make them look bad," Andrew Napolitano said. "I am in full accord with Rush Limbaugh on this, that this is a trap that he's setting for the Republicans. He will look presidential and open-minded, and they will look narrow."[95]

The truth was, Republicans had no choice but to fall into Obama's "trap" and attend the summit. The night before the meeting, Fox escalated its attacks on the Democratic plan. Karl Rove got the ball rolling during an appearance on *The O'Reilly Fac-*

tor. "There is a trillion dollars' worth of additional money being spent over the next ten years," Rove said. "It's got to come from somebody, and it's not just tanning salons. Remember, it's going to come from everybody who has an insurance policy, because the Congressional Budget Office says everybody's health care premiums are going to be higher than they would be otherwise."[96] This was a blatant distortion of the Congressional Budget Office's report, which actually found that most people's premiums would stay the same or decrease under health care reform.

Later, Dick Morris continued the onslaught by reviving Palin's award-winning lie. "What is major about this bill," he said, "is that it gives the federal government the power to tell people, 'No, you can't have this bypass surgery. You have to die.' "[97] Morris's claim was absurd on its face.

Fox News was equally unimpressed by the actual content of the summit. Bill O'Reilly called the meeting "boring,"[98] while Glenn Beck dubbed it "Snorefest 2010."[99] Others on Fox decided that it was embarrassing for the president to sit down with leaders of the opposing party. For example, *Washington Post* columnist and Fox News contributor Charles Krauthammer claimed that Obama had "given up the aura of the presidency—which is half king, half prime minister—and he's now at the level of prime minister, toe-to-toe with members of Congress."[100] And after O'Reilly conceded that Obama "did a good job as moderator," Laura Ingraham responded, "He's the president of the United States, he's not a moderator . . . He lowered himself."[101]

Additionally, Fox aired clear falsehoods from Republican lawmakers during the summit without making any effort to correct the record. For example, Major Garrett's report on the summit included this exchange between the president and Republican Senator Lamar Alexander:

ALEXANDER: Premiums will go up, and they will also go up
    because of the government mandates.

OBAMA: It's not factually accurate. The cost for families for
    the same type of coverage as they're currently receiving
    would go down fourteen to twenty percent.

ALEXANDER: I believe, with respect, you're wrong.[102]

Alexander's assertion had been contradicted by the Congressional Budget Office, but Fox let it stand unchallenged. Garrett
also aired Congressman Paul Ryan's claim that the bill "does not
reduce deficits"[103] without noting the CBO's estimate that the legislation would reduce the deficit by $130 billion over ten years.

Following the summit, the momentum toward passage
increased. When conservatives recognized that they could not
defeat the bill on substance, they turned to attacking the process
by which it would pass Congress.

The House of Representatives and the Senate operate on
an arcane set of rules that are incomprehensible to most casual
observers. Even reporters who cover Congress day in and day
out are often confused by these procedures. In order to pass
the health care bill, Democrats considered using two procedural
maneuvers known as "deem and pass" and budget reconciliation.
On Fox News, these mundane tactical moves were portrayed as
subversions of democracy, even though Republicans had adopted
similar tactics in recent years when attempting to pass the Bush
tax cuts and a bill permitting drilling for oil in the Arctic National
Wildlife Refuge.

In March, Fox started claiming that Democrats planned to
pass the bill through the House without ever holding a vote. Steve
Doocy told the audience of *Fox & Friends* that, by using the deem

and pass procedure, "they can pass the health care bill without actually voting on it."[104]

Contrary to Doocy's suggestion, the procedural measure still required a majority vote in the House of Representatives. Nevertheless, the maneuver was renamed "Demon Pass," an epithet that was soon adopted by the entire conservative movement.

The second procedure that Fox News vilified was budget reconciliation. Under this procedure, Senate Democrats could pass the health care bill with fifty-one votes instead of the sixty required to break a filibuster. The attacks on reconciliation were particularly ironic given the network's coverage of the 2005 fight over the obstruction of President Bush's judicial nominations. At that time, many Fox commentators had proclaimed that the filibuster itself was unconstitutional.

Far from an unprecedented ploy, budget reconciliation is a process codified in U.S. law. Major adjustments in health care policy had been enacted under reconciliation in the past. Many Americans who were left unemployed as a result of the recession were receiving health insurance through COBRA, which allows workers to keep their employer-sponsored insurance for up to eighteen months after losing their jobs. COBRA is an acronym for the Consolidated Omnibus Budget Reconciliation Act of 1985.

George W. Bush had used reconciliation five times to usher major policy changes through Congress, including both of his signature tax-cut bills. But now that Obama wanted to play by the same rules, Fox News was up in arms. Moreover, the health care reform bill had already passed both the House and the Senate under normal rules. The only thing left to do was resolve the differences between the two legislative bodies.

During the fight over judicial filibusters in 2005, Republicans threatened to use a process that Senator Trent Lott termed the "nuclear option," whereby the Senate president would rule on a point of order declaring the use of the filibuster for judicial nominations unconstitutional. Realizing that the "nuclear option" wouldn't go over so well with the public, Republicans eventually tried to rebrand the procedure as the "constitutional option."

In 2010, Fox News's Sean Hannity, Greta Van Susteren, Bret Baier, Dick Morris, and Bill Sammon all mislabeled the budget reconciliation process the "nuclear option." For example, Baier declared that reconciliation "was once called the nuclear option" before airing clips of what he claimed were Democrats criticizing the procedure "when Republicans were using it."[105] But that wasn't the case at all. The video showed Democrats criticizing Lott's "nuclear option," which was an unprecedented attempt to change the Senate rules without a vote. Budget reconciliation was a tool, codified in law, that had been used dozens of times since the 1980s.

Predictably, newly minted Fox contributor Sarah Palin joined in the attacks, inarticulately claiming that Democrats were trying to "cram through via reconciliation, this scheme, this government growth takeover of too many aspects of our health care." Palin added, "The risk is this one-sixth of our economy being so controlled and one-sixth of our society being so controlled by government with this takeover of health care."[106]

The truth was, the Senate was using reconciliation only to alter aspects of the bill to gain final approval in the House. The total changes comprised fewer than a hundred pages, amending the legislation that was more than a thousand pages long.

Of course, Fox wasn't interested in the intricacies of Senate procedure. Led by Glenn Beck, who had declared in November that the bill's passage would mean "the end of America as you know it," the network had spent thousands of hours trying to kill health care reform. And with the bill on the verge of passage, the rhetoric became even more unhinged.

On March 16, Beck stated, "You know and I know in this twenty-three-hundred-page bill that includes education now, the control that this government has is endless. They will—if this passes, they will control every aspect of your life." Moments later, Beck added, "They will be able to—there is places in here that if you can be deemed someone who maybe shouldn't have a baby, they can have their people come in. The government is in our homes on this."[107] Three days later, Beck added to his bizarre rant by asking, "If this passes, don't we lose, really, the Democratic Party to the socialists?"[108]

Meanwhile, Bill Hemmer suggested that Americans could be thrown in jail because of the bill's requirements. "The mandate would tell Americans you've got to buy health insurance, if not you could be fined, and I guess eventually that could lead to prison," he said. "I mean, this—the way you understand it right now, could people be going to jail for not owning health insur-

DON'T DO IT!

CLEAR WEAPONS TREATY... ON FRI, CLINTON W   MIL   64/41

ance?"[109] There was no provision in the bill establishing criminal penalties for noncompliance with the individual mandate; the consequence was a fine from the IRS.

Fox & Friends was even more shameless in its advocacy. While the show's hosts teased a segment about the health care bill on March 18, an on-screen graphic superimposed the words "DON'T DO IT"[110] over an image of President Obama exiting Air Force One. Later that day on Twitter, Laura Ingraham announced, "I'll be hosting the O'Reilly Factor on Friday, 8pm eastern. Let's kill the bill!"[111] Ingraham seemed to be echoing the sentiment of the full-time host, who declared that "Obamacare is a huge risk for the country, and at this point, I believe the risk is not worth taking."[112]

Once again, Fox shed the pretense of objective journalism by repeatedly encouraging viewers to contact members of Congress to express their opposition to the bill. On March 19, FoxNation.com reported what it judged to be the "breaking news" that Rush Limbaugh was urging Americans to "Keep Calling Congress."[113] The website touted Limbaugh's criticism of the bill and provided the phone number for the congressional switchboard so readers could take action.

Glenn Beck also boosted Limbaugh's effort, saying, "Rush Limbaugh, for only the second time in his career, told his audience yesterday to flood the switchboards of Congress and, boy, did they ever. He's right. He said yesterday that this is the endgame. This is it. The fundamental transformation of America is here, America."[114]

Mike Huckabee told his show's viewers, "Obama and House Speaker Nancy Pelosi are attempting to ram their massive health care bill through Congress . . . We must stop this bill." Huckabee

LIVE

FOX NEWS .COM

HUCKABEE: CALL CONGRESS; TELL THEM VOTE NO ON HEALTH CARE

NOW

MBENTS IN CONGRESS, COMPARED TO JUST 2(NASDAQ ▼ 16.87

urged those watching to "call, e-mail, write" to lawmakers and repeated his call to action while appearing on *Your World with Neil Cavuto,* aided by on-screen text reading "HUCKABEE: CALL CONGRESS; TELL THEM VOTE NO ON HEALTH CARE."

When last-minute protests against the bill were scheduled to take place outside of Congress, Fox News assumed its role as lead promoter. On March 18, Beck hosted Republican Congressman Steve King, telling him, "I hope people show up on Saturday at noon there at the Capitol and plan on just staying there. I mean, you know, camp out if you have to."[115]

Thousands did show up at the Capitol, and Fox gave the protesters wall-to-wall coverage. Nearly every speaker, including several Republican members of Congress, repeated lies about the health care reform legislation that had been prominently featured on Fox News.

The network's presence could also be felt throughout the crowd. Protestors carried signs supporting and promoting the network. Invariably, those who attended believed the misinformation Fox spread about the health care bill. They claimed it would add a trillion dollars to the deficit, that patients would no longer be able to choose their doctors, and, of course, months after its being called the lie of the year, that the bill included death panels.

"[Fox News] certainly changed the attitude about Obama's health care plan and made people believe big government was coming to get them, that they were somehow going to be controlled by a government, that your health care would be controlled by government bureaucrats," said George Washington University's Michael Shanahan. "What they do is not journalism. It is propaganda."[116]

Despite Fox's efforts, President Obama signed the Patient Protection and Affordable Care Act into law. But victory was fleeting, and Fox's fight against health care reform was not over. As conservatives launched efforts to repeal, defund, and overturn the law in court, Fox News was more than ready to lend a helping hand.

Chapter 6
Violent Rhetoric

If you come out and say that a guy's a commie, fag bastard, the public turns you off, not him.

—Roger Ailes

On the morning of July 28, 2009, appearing on *Fox & Friends,* Glenn Beck declared, "This president, I think, has exposed himself as a guy, over and over and over again, who has a deep-seated hatred for white people or the white culture."[1]

When Brian Kilmeade seemed to disagree, pointing out that President Obama was surrounded by white advisers such as David Axelrod, Robert Gibbs, and Rahm Emanuel, Beck responded, "I'm not saying that he doesn't like white people, I'm saying he has a problem . . . He has a—this guy is, I believe, a racist."[2]

Beck, who had cut his teeth in broadcasting by testing the limits of acceptable behavior on morning-zoo radio programs, had pushed the envelope before as a political pundit. On CNN Headline News, for instance, Beck opened an interview with Congressman Keith Ellison, the first Muslim elected to the House of

Representatives, by saying, "I have been nervous about this interview with you, because what I feel like saying is, 'Sir, prove to me that you are not working with our enemies.'" Beck added: "I'm not accusing you of being an enemy, but that's the way I feel, and I think a lot of Americans will feel that way."[3]

At Fox, Roger Ailes was willing to defend the host's most extreme behavior. "I don't think that he's nuts. I think that what he's doing is, he's half history professor and half Shakespearean actor," Ailes told *Esquire* magazine. "He admits that he's kind of off-the-wall. If he didn't, that would be a problem for that show. But because he's willing to say, 'Don't listen to me, look it up, I'm a rodeo clown, I'm just saying this is what it looks like.' And because there's a lot of truth in what he says and it probably mirrors what over half of the country believes, he's successful."[4]

Ailes had recognized decades earlier that incendiary attacks have the potential to backfire when used by political campaigns. "If you come out and say that a guy's a commie, fag bastard, the public turns you off, not him,"[5] he told *The Washington Post* in 1972. A news network, playing to a polarized conservative base, not seeking votes in the center, was under no such restrictions.

From the paranoid rants about the creeping threats of communism to odd comparisons between mainstream political leaders and Nazis, Beck gave voice to some of Ailes's deepest fears about the Obama presidency. In October 2009, Obama adviser David Axelrod was interviewed during the First Draft of History conference, hosted by *The Atlantic* magazine. Addressing the polarization that was infecting political discourse, Axelrod mentioned a conversation he had once with a "significant figure on the right"— later revealed to be Roger Ailes—who tried to explain to him why conservatives were suspicious of the president.

Ailes told Axelrod he believed Obama wanted to form a national police force, based on a twenty-one-second clip from a speech where the president proposed a civilian force that would complement the military in providing humanitarian aid around the world. Axelrod quoted Ailes telling him, "You can understand why that has people very nervous. This has shades of Nazism."[6]

Glenn Beck brought Roger Ailes's theory to Fox's audience, claiming that President Obama's proposal of creating a civilian humanitarian force was "about building some kind of thugocracy."[7] Later in the program Beck went a step further to claim, "This is what Hitler did with the SS. He had his own people. He had the brownshirts and then the SS."[8]

The kinship between Roger Ailes and Glenn Beck would become more evident in the spring of 2010, when the host attacked criticism of him by Jewish Funds for Justice president and CEO Simon Greer. Greer had written in a *Washington Post* op-ed, "If we all attended houses of worship that put government last, humankind would be last, and God would be last too." Greer continued, "From where I stand, the house of worship you desire—where God is divorced from human dignity—is not a house of worship at all. When churches, synagogues, mosques, and other houses of worship across this country advocate for social justice, advocate for the common good, advocate for America, they, and we, walk in God's path."[9]

Beck claimed on his radio program that Greer's comments about putting "humankind and the common good" first were "exactly the kind of talk that led to the death camps in Germany," adding, "a Jew, of all people, should know that."[10]

In previous eras, a statement like that would have been grounds for immediate termination. But not at Fox. Glenn Beck and conservative pundits such as Ann Coulter had shifted the boundary of acceptable attacks on political opponents. What would have been a major scandal just four years earlier was now par for the course.

In response to Beck's taunting of Simon Greer, a group of politically mainstream rabbis and prominent Jewish figures led by Steve Gutow, president of the Jewish Council for Public Affairs, wrote Rupert Murdoch a private letter:

> Mr. Beck has, for quite some time, invoked the Holocaust and Nazi fascism on air in support of political arguments on a variety of subjects. He has compared public officials to Nazi party figures and characterized legitimate policy positions as akin to murderous Nazi policies . . . We appeal to you to consider the impact of Mr. Beck's words; in our community, for the global understanding of the Holocaust, and for the reputation and standing of the business you have built and nurtured. You are providing him with a platform to reach millions. We believe he has been abusing that platform . . . With respect and friendship we request an opportunity to discuss these concerns directly with you. We are confident that you, like us, having fully considered the power of Mr. Beck's words and the hurt and damage they are causing, will wish to work with us to rectify this situation in a responsible and productive manner."[11]

It was a simple request for reasoned and calm discourse. Nowhere did the rabbis ask Murdoch to alter the political positions or leanings of the network or its hosts. Instead, they merely asked him to respect the historic horror that was the Holocaust. The letter was forwarded to Roger Ailes, who made Fox News's position clear. "I do not agree with your characterization of Mr. Beck or our program. In the specific language you point out, I've reviewed the program and Mr. Beck is talking about dictators who use 'social justice' language to accomplish political goals," Ailes wrote the rabbis. "Of course social justice means different things to different audiences, however it has been used in situations leading to fascism, socialism, and communism as well."[12] The letter was an acknowledgement that, while his words were his own, Beck was speaking for the network, or at least its president.

Like Beck, Roger Ailes is not afraid to use Nazi imagery to score points against opponents. In the wake of National Public Radio's firing of NPR and Fox News contributor Juan Williams (for comments he made on *The O'Reilly Factor* about his fears of flying with men wearing "Muslim garb"), Ailes described the radio network in the following way: "They are, of course, Nazis. They have a kind of Nazi attitude. They are the left wing of Nazism."[13]

In an awkward coincidence, these comments came just weeks after Rupert Murdoch had received a major award from the Anti-Defamation League, which was now forced to condemn Ailes's remarks.

He apologized but was hardly contrite. In a letter to Anti-Defamation League president Abe Foxman, Ailes vented that "the rabbis used us in an unscrupulous manner. Instead of quietly working with us to solve the problem internally, they put out a cheap press release to say Glenn Beck was out of line, Fox was out of line and they of course came in and told us what we could do. None of that happened. I was and still am insulted by their behavior."[14] According to his own logic, Roger Ailes should be permitted to call others Nazis because of a perceived slight by a group of rabbis.

The only defect Roger Ailes saw in Beck's broadcast was that he attacked Republicans too much of the time. According to Ailes, "[Beck] and I have had conversations and lunches where I say, 'What the hell are you doing, man?' . . . Beck trashes Republicans every night. I've said to him, 'Where the hell are you going to get your audience if you keep this up? You're trashing everyone.' "[15]

Glenn Beck's declaration that the president was a racist marked a turning point. Color of Change, an online group that works to give African-Americans a stronger political voice, sent an e-mail to supporters demanding consequences for Beck's comments. "Together we can stop Glenn Beck," the e-mail stated. "Starting today we're calling Beck's advertisers, asking them if they want to be associated with this kind of racist hate and fear-mongering. When they see tens of thousands of people signing on behind that question, we believe they'll move their advertising dollars elsewhere, damaging the viability of his show and possibly putting him out of business."[16]

By the end of August, approximately seventy companies had ceased advertising on Beck's program. Although he claimed not to care, the loss of advertisers clearly angered the host, who spoke about the action repeatedly on the air. He previously had attacked Barack Obama's Green Jobs adviser, Van Jones. In August, Beck became obsessed with him.

Jones was a progressive activist and Yale-educated attorney from the Bay Area, where he founded the Ella Baker Center for Human Rights, which works to strengthen communities in the inner city. Jones had helped launch Color of Change in 2005, and then started the group Green For All in 2007 to promote a new green economy, which he believed could provide well-paying jobs to those who had been economically left behind.

In a move widely cheered by the left, Obama chose Jones to be the White House Council on Environmental Quality's Special

Advisor for Green Jobs, a position some on the right termed the "green jobs czar." As an activist, Jones had a history of controversial statements, which Glenn Beck would use to wage a smear campaign against him.

In 1992, Jones was arrested while protesting the acquittal of the police officers who brutally attacked Rodney King. The experience had a profound impact on Jones's political philosophy. According to a profile of Jones in the *East Bay Express*:

> Jones had planned to move to Washington, DC, and had already landed a job and an apartment there. But in jail, he said, "I met all these young radical people of color—I mean really radical, communists and anarchists. And it was, like, 'This is what I need to be a part of.'" Although he already had a plane ticket, he decided to stay in San Francisco. "I spent the next ten years of my life working with a lot of those people I met in jail, trying to be a revolutionary." In the months that followed, he let go of any lingering thoughts that he might fit in with the status quo. "I was a rowdy nationalist on April 28th, and then the verdicts came down on April 29th," he said. "By August, I was a communist."[17]

Aaron Klein of the conservative *WorldNetDaily* wrote about the *East Bay Express* story in April, but it did not receive any real coverage until July 23, when Beck declared on Fox News, "This is a guy who is a self-avowed communist and he is in the Obama administration . . . This guy wasn't a radical, and then was arrested. He spent six months in jail, came out a communist."[18]

As Dave Weigel reported in *The Washington Independent*, "Beck took a shot at the 'avowed communist' Jones again on July 28, again on Aug. 4, again on Aug. 11 ('this is a convicted felon, a guy who spent, I think, six months in prison after the Rodney King beating'), again on Aug. 13, and again on Aug. 21."[19]

On August 25, Beck began airing what Weigel called "a week-long special series, 'The New Republic: America's Future,'" in which Jones became Exhibit A of the "radical leftists currently advising the president of the United States."[20]

Beck's obsession with Jones spread to other hosts on Fox News. "This guy reminds me of Reverend Wright," commented Bill O'Reilly. "He's an anti-American guy, we think. And they don't—the Obama administration doesn't seem to have a problem with that."[21]

Meanwhile, Beck continued his onslaught. On September 1, he ranted, "Do we want communists in the United States government as special advisers to the president?"[22]

What ultimately doomed Jones's tenure at the White House was the charge that he signed a petition distributed by conspiracy theorists claiming our government was involved in the September 11 terrorist attack. In an op-ed in *The New York Times,* Jones would state that the accusation was false.[23] He had never accused the Bush administration of plotting the attacks. At worst, Jones carelessly added his name to a petition from a dubious source, but that didn't matter to Beck and the conservatives who were committed to bringing him down.

Congressional Republicans began echoing Beck's charges. In a statement, Congressman Mike Pence called on Jones to resign, saying, "His extremist views and coarse rhetoric have no place in this administration or the public debate."[24] In an open letter, Senator Kit Bond asked, "Can the American people trust a senior White House official that is so cavalier in his association with such radical and repugnant sentiments?"[25] And Senator John Cornyn, the chairman of the National Republican Senatorial Committee, took his message to the social networking site Twitter: "Van Jones has to go."[26]

Jones resigned on September 5, proclaiming, "On the eve of historic fights for health care and clean energy, opponents of reform have mounted a vicious smear campaign against me. They are using lies and distortions to distract and divide." Jones added, "I have been inundated with calls—from across the political spectrum—urging me to 'stay and fight.' But I came here to fight for others, not for myself. I cannot in good conscience ask my colleagues to expend precious time and energy defending or explaining my past. We need all hands on deck, fighting for the future."[27]

After the Van Jones episode, Glenn Beck was no longer just a host; he had taken a scalp. This did not go unnoticed in the conservative movement or in the media. On September 6, *Politico* reporters Ben Smith and Nia-Malika Henderson wrote that Beck had "rocketed to a status as de facto leader of the opposition" and that Jones's resignation had "confirmed Beck's stature as the administration's most potent foe."[28]

The most dangerous element of Beck's successful scalping of Van Jones was that journalists now felt compelled to pay attention to his wild and untrue claims. As *The Washington Post*'s Chris Cillizza explained on CNN, "I think when you have someone like Glenn Beck, with the ratings that Glenn Beck gets or Sean Hannity with the ratings that Sean Hannity gets, if they are every single night highlighting this you are starting as a reporter to . . . you're paying more attention to it than if they ignored it. I mean, to me, the Van Jones story and this story suggest that we better pay attention because they have power. There is clearly no debate about that."[29]

·   ·   ·

While Glenn Beck's influence was growing, his message to view-ers, that the Obama administration and the Democratic Congress were destroying the United States, had dangerous consequences. In April 2009, Richard Poplawski allegedly killed three Pittsburgh police officers after stockpiling guns and ammunition, fearing that President Obama would take away his Second Amendment rights. In an interview with *Philadelphia Daily News* reporter and Media Matters senior fellow Will Bunch, one of Poplawski's best friends made it clear who his inspiration was:

> "Rich, like myself, loved Glenn Beck," [said] Poplawski's
> best friend Eddie Perkovic . . . For months Poplawski had
> been obsessed with an idea—frequently discussed by Beck,
> including in ads for his sponsor Food Insurance—of the need
> to stockpile food and even toilet paper for a societal break-
> down. Poplawski was also convinced that paper money would
> become worthless—another claim given credence by the Fox
> News Channel host, particularly in close connection with his
> frequent shilling for the now-under-investigation gold-coin
> peddler Goldline International.[30]

This wasn't the only instance in which Beck's rhetoric was linked to violent acts. Charles Wilson, a Washington State resident, was sent to prison for repeatedly threatening to kill Washington sena-tor Patty Murray after her vote in favor of heath care reform. A cousin wrote the presiding judge, requesting leniency for Wilson:

> I found Glenn Beck about the same time Charlie did. I under-
> stand how his fears were grown and fostered by Mr. Beck's
> persuasive personality. The same thing happened to me but I
> went in a different direction with what I was seeing. Rather

than blame politicians for the current issues, I simply got prepared for what Glenn said was coming. I slowly filled our pantry as Glenn fed fear into me . . . While his actions were undeniably wrong and his choices were terrible, in part they were the actions of others played out by a very gullible Charlie. He was under the spell that Glenn Beck cast, aided by the turbulent times in our economy.[31]

Perhaps the most spectacular incident of Beck-inspired violence occurred when Byron Williams engaged in an eleven-minute gun battle with California Highway Patrol officers in Oakland. Williams was on his way to kill employees of the ACLU and the Tides Foundation, a progressive nonprofit organization. Williams believed Tides was part of a plot orchestrated by the billionaire George Soros—one of Beck's favorite villains—that culminated in the sinking of the Deepwater Horizon oil rig in the Gulf of Mexico. Williams constructed his conspiracy theory in part based on a series of shows Beck aired in June 2010, saying Beck was "like a schoolteacher on TV . . . He's got that big chalkboard and those little stickers, the decals. I like the way he does it."[32]

On March 13, several months before Van Jones's resignation, Beck announced the launch of his 9/12 Project, a purportedly nonpartisan movement designed to "bring us all back to the place we were on September 12, 2001," when we "were united as Americans, standing together to protect the values and the principles of the greatest nation ever created."[33]

Leading up to the 9/12 Project's signature event, a rally in Washington, D.C., on September 12, 2009, Beck frequently touted the initiative's effectiveness in organizing followers. During his August 12 Fox News show, he claimed the 9/12 Project would give "an outlet, a voice to connect, because you needed to community organize . . . Well, you have already done it. There are Nine/Twelve Projects and rallies happening all over. The biggest one seems to be in Washington, D.C., on September twelfth."[34]

On August 27, Beck said, "A few months ago, I told you, you got to know you're not alone. You've got to know. You got to unite. Talk to people. Make sure you know you're not alone, through the Nine/Twelve Project. We started that. Millions now involved across the country and the Nine/Twelve Project and other organizations like it. I knew we needed to connect with one another."[35]

The next day, Beck described his "March on Washington" as something "worth standing up for," adding, "I hope to see you in Washington. I will make sure you're seen all over the country."[36]

Predictably, Beck's rally received heavy promotion on Fox News, the Fox Business network, FoxNation.com, and FoxNews .com. On the afternoon of Saturday, September 12, Beck broadcast a two-hour special edition of his show.

The media rewarded Beck's crusade against Van Jones with extensive coverage of the rally on 9/12. According to Howard Kurtz in *The Washington Post*, "The other networks indeed covered the protest, which—like similar demonstrations across the country—were heavily promoted by Fox, especially talk show host Glenn Beck . . . ABC, for instance, covered it Saturday and Sunday on *Good Morning America* and Sunday on *World News,* along with extensive reports by ABC Radio and the network's website. NBC covered it Saturday on *Nightly News* and the next morning on *Today*. CBS covered it on the *Evening News*. CNN covered the Saturday protests during the 10 a.m., 11 a.m., 5 p.m. and 7 p.m. hours, as well as on other programs afterward. Correspondents such as NBC's Tom Costello, ABC's Kate Snow and CBS's Nancy Cordes were involved in the coverage."[37]

With Beck's influence on the rise in the wake of Jones's ouster, Fox News began targeting other Obama administration staffers whom they labeled "czars." Although the term "czar" has been used for decades to describe certain positions in the executive branch, Beck and others on Fox applied the term loosely and used it rhetorically to link Obama to Soviet communism. Of course, Russia had czars only in the prerevolutionary period.

One day before Jones resigned, Beck announced his next targets on Twitter: "Watch Dogs: FIND EVERYTHING YOU CAN ON CASS SUNSTEIN, MARK LLOYD AND CAROL BROWNER. Do not link before burning to disc."[38] Sunstein and Browner both worked in the Obama White House, while Mark Lloyd was the Federal Communication Commission's Chief Diversity Officer.

Fox Business host Eric Bolling echoed Beck, writing: "Van Jones resigns amid controversial past. How about J Holdren Science Czar (mass sterilizations) and Cass Sunstein . . ."[39]

At a rally in West Virginia, Sean Hannity gloated about Jones's resignation and declared that "my job starting tomorrow night is to get rid of every other [czar]. I promise you that!"[40]

 @glennbeck
Glenn Beck ✔

Watch Dogs: FIND EVERYTHING YOU CAN ON CASS SUNSTEIN, MARK LLOYD AND CAROL BROWNER. Do not link before burning to disc.

3 Sep 09 via web

@ericbolling
ericbolling ✪

Van Jones resigns amid controversial past.
How about J Holdren Science Czar (mass
sterilizations) and Cass Susstein...
http://bit.ly/qlBYi

6 Sep 09 via Facebook

On September 8, Megyn Kelly reported that "more of President Obama's special advisers are now under scrutiny after the resignation of his green jobs czar."[41] This scrutiny, of course, was coming from her own network.

That evening, Hannity launched his promised witch hunt, telling viewers that White House science and technology adviser John Holdren "advocated compulsory abortion."[42] This claim was not true. PolitiFact.com had fact-checked this allegation months earlier, stating, "We think it's irresponsible to pluck a few lines from a 1,000-page, 30-year-old textbook, and then present them out of context."[43]

Meanwhile, on Glenn Beck's show, Michelle Malkin targeted yet another member of the Obama administration. "I have been warning about energy czar Carol Browner since December," she said. "I followed her career, her subversion of transparency."[44] Beck had previously called Browner a "socialist."[45]

The race for the next scalp was on. Anyone associated with the Obama administration could come under attack. Past statements, no matter how innocuous, would be taken out of context and blared across Fox News Channel and other network properties. Fox's next success, though, did not involve an Obama administration figure, but a decades-old foil of the conservative movement.

Chapter 7

Six Steps

They were in search of these points of friction real or imagined. And most of them were imagined or fabricated. You always have to seem to be under siege. You always have to seem like your values are under attack.

—a former Fox News employee

The conservative movement had long been obsessed with the Association of Community Organizations for Reform Now, or ACORN, a membership organization designed to serve the needs of low-income Americans. There was perhaps no progressive group that could arouse the visceral reaction among conservatives that ACORN provoked. From conservative elites to grassroots activists, they might not have known exactly what ACORN did, but they knew it was evil. This was evident in videos that appeared on YouTube in October 2008. When approached by videographers outside of rallies, McCain supporters would direct some of their ire toward the organization.

What made this antipoverty group the object of so much derision? The answer was as straightforward as it was offensive. ACORN's registration drives and ballot initiatives had helped

bring out millions of voters all over the country—1.3 million
in 2008 alone. These voters, as a result of the constituency that
ACORN served, were often African-American and poor, and
therefore demographically linked to the Democratic Party, and
so the organization needed to be stopped. It was political racism,
plain and simple.

Wade Rathke founded ACORN in Little Rock, Arkansas, in
1970. Rathke had worked as an organizer for the National Welfare
Rights Organization and wanted to broaden his efforts beyond
welfare recipients. Early on, the organization promoted Vietnam
veterans' rights and helped people living in poverty obtain clothing and furniture.

The group became involved in politics for the first time in
1972, endorsing two of its members for the school board in Little
Rock. From there, the group expanded nationally, serving communities in need across the country.

In 1986, ACORN created a subsidiary, the ACORN Housing
Corporation (AHC). According to its website, "Since its inception, AHC has assisted over 45,000 families to become first time
homeowners, and has rehabilitated over 750 vacant and abandoned housing units. Virtually all of ACORN Housing's work
takes place in areas that have been seriously disinvested and forgotten."[1]

ACORN was not without controversies of its own making. In 2000, Wade Rathke's brother, Dale, was caught embez-
zling close to one million dollars from the organization. When
the alleged embezzlement was discovered, the Rathkes returned
the money but did not report the incident to ACORN's board
or law-enforcement agencies. Further complicating the situation, although Wade Rathke resigned his position on the board
after the embezzlement became public, he was allowed to remain

on the payroll of the organization. While the scandal damaged ACORN's reputation, it continued to thrive, registering more and more low-income voters.

In 2008, ACORN presented a tempting political target for the right, due to its loose ties to Barack Obama. In 1992, he had organized an ACORN-affiliated get-out-the-vote campaign in Chicago, which helped elect Carol Moseley Braun as only the second African-American senator since Reconstruction. Additionally, Obama later worked as part of a team of lawyers who helped sue the governor of Illinois on behalf of ACORN, and he spoke at two ACORN training sessions in the 1990s. These were tenuous connections, but they were enough for Fox News and the conservative movement to accuse Obama of being deeply involved with what they deemed a criminal organization.

In Fox News's reporting during the presidential race, ACORN was targeted first for voter registration irregularities and then over accusations that its dealings with mortgage lenders had helped cause the housing crisis.

The allegations of voter fraud stemmed from the fact that voter registration in the United States is a difficult business, with complicated rules that often vary from location to location. ACORN would collect hundreds of thousands of registrations, some of which contained fraudulent or funny names. In several localities the organization was essentially defrauded by its own paid canvassers, who filled out these phony registrations in order to collect paychecks without doing the work. While this proved embarrassing for ACORN and time-consuming for election officials, there was no chance that anyone using these fake names would end up casting illegal votes.

Rather than automatically discarding such registrations, many state laws required ACORN to submit them to local boards of elections, who would judge their validity. Instead of crediting the organization for its efforts to expand the electorate, Fox News mocked ACORN for following the law.

On October 14, 2008, Megyn Kelly derided ACORN's statement that it was required by Florida law to submit a voter registration form filed under the name "Mickey Mouse" to the Orange County board of elections. When Bill Hemmer noted that the form in question had been rejected, and that "ACORN says they are required to turn in every application that is filled out, even if it says Mickey Mouse," Kelly replied: "I love that, they've got the obligation to submit it no matter what it says. Mickey Mouse, Jive Turkey, which we saw yesterday. How are we to know?"[2]

Despite Kelly's scorn, ACORN was telling the truth—under Florida law, the organization could be fined up to a thousand dollars for every registration form withheld.[3] The organization had to either submit registrations it thought might be fraudulent or face penalties. And yet, by obeying the law, ACORN opened itself up to attacks from Fox News and other conservative media organizations.

ACORN's involvement in increasing home ownership among minorities also gave Fox News commentators an opening to claim the group was responsible for the housing crisis. Reporting from the White House on October 5, Bret Baier said, "And the risks kept rising over the years, in part because the federal government wanted it that way. In particular there was the Community Reinvestment Act, or CRA, passed in 1977 during Jimmy Carter's first year in office. The law increased oversight of financial institutions to ensure that they were giving credit to low-income families so that more people would have the chance to own homes."[4]

Later in the segment, Baier said, "Indeed, ACORN, the Association of Community Organizers for Reform Now, would before long come up with a new tactic: challenging a thrift merger in Illinois, claiming they didn't make the kind of loans that ACORN felt were required under the CRA. The bank complained that such loans would be financially irresponsible." He then attempted to link the problem to Obama, saying, "A young community organizer named Barack Obama worked closely with the ACORN activists behind the new strategy. And that strategy worked. ACORN prevailed in court, and soon credit standards were being lowered across the country."[5]

These accusations were patently false. Soon after the election, Federal Reserve chairman Ben Bernanke wrote: "Our own experience with CRA over more than 30 years and recent analysis of available data, including data on subprime loan performance, runs counter to the charge that CRA was at the root of, or otherwise contributed in any substantive way to, the current mortgage difficulties."[6] Furthermore, Obama's work with ACORN had nothing to do with the CRA or the housing crisis that coincided with his presidential campaign.

After Barack Obama's inauguration, Fox News's fictitious attacks on ACORN continued. Glenn Beck, in particular, spent an inordinate amount of time talking about the organization, devoting dozens of segments to supposed "connections" between ACORN and AmeriCorps, the AARP, Supreme Court Justice Sonia Sotomayor, the Puerto Rican Legal Defense and Education Fund, and the Service Employees International Union. While most of these ties were uncontroversial or tangential, Beck consistently used ACORN as a bludgeon to bash the Obama administration and its policies.

The straw that finally broke ACORN's back was a videotaped stunt conducted by conservative activists James O'Keefe and Hannah Giles. O'Keefe's patron, Andrew Breitbart, published heavily edited versions of the tapes that supported false charges against ACORN on his website. Fox News then parroted the allegations on the air.

Andrew Breitbart worked alongside Matt Drudge, aggregating content for the popular conservative-leaning website *Drudge Report.* He emailed Drudge in 1995, asking him, "Are you 50 people? A hundred people? Is there a building?"[7] Quite the opposite, "Drudge was at that time writing, editing and maintaining his site by himself."[8] This was several years before he broke the Monica Lewinsky story.

When he emailed Drudge, Breitbart previously worked on digital content in the early days of the Internet at E! Entertainment Television. He soon began working at the *Drudge Report.* In a 2005 interview, Breitbart reminisced, "I thought what he was doing was by far the coolest thing on the Internet. And I still do."[9]

Arianna Huffington approached Breitbart in 2005, and he helped her launch *The Huffington Post.* Leaving after a few months, he went on to found *Breitbart.com,* which primarily served as a news aggregator. The *Drudge Report* would often link to newswire articles posted on the site, ballooning its traffic. He launched *Breitbart.tv* in 2007 to serve as a video aggregator. While the site was well trafficked, Breitbart had not made much of a mark with a site of his own. That would soon change.

In September 2009, Breitbart used James O'Keefe's videos to launch his new website, *BigGovernment.com.* Glenn Beck previewed the tapes on September 9, saying, "Tomorrow—tomorrow, things change. I think things change a lot for those in power. The tides are about to turn, and that will be on tomorrow's broadcast. Trust me. Everybody now says they're going to be talking about health care. I don't think so. Tomorrow you will see an exclusive—stuff on tomorrow's program. Don't miss it."[10]

The next morning the first set of videos were posted on *Big Government.com*. O'Keefe exclaimed: "Hannah Giles and I took advantage of ACORN's regard for thug criminality by posing the most ridiculous criminal scenario we could think of and seeing if they would comply—which they did without hesitation."[11] This was far from the truth. What actually occurred was that O'Keefe and Giles had visited ACORN offices around the country, supposedly posing as a pimp and a prostitute. Their goal was simple: try to entrap low-level employees on video.

By the next day at 7 p.m. Eastern Time, Fox News had aired more than seventeen segments on the videos. "I am just asking you this—please, take a stand," Glenn Beck implored his audience a week later. "Take a stand. This is clear-cut, unadulterated, taxpayer-funded corruption. You love your children. You love your country just like I do. You must understand that what you've been seeing from ACORN on these tapes this past week isn't compassion, it's corruption!"[12]

Good government had nothing to do with Fox's interest in the story. Fox News's hypocrisy is clear when one compares its coverage of ACORN with its coverage of real examples of corruption. Between May 8, 2006 (Glenn Beck's first show on CNN Headline News), and September 18, 2009, Beck and Sean Hannity's show mentioned ACORN 1,502 times. Over the same period, they mentioned Jack Abramoff or Bob Ney a combined sixty-two times. The shows mentioned Halliburton just forty-three times and Blackwater/Xe just four times, even though those scandals cost taxpayers far more money. Beck had individually aired 1,045 segments on ACORN in his career, with the vast majority, 1,002, coming in less than a single year at Fox News.[13]

A Fox source explains why the network would repeat these seemingly non-newsworthy controversies ad nauseam: "It was relentless and it never went away. If one controversy faded, god-damn it, they would find another one. They were in search of these points of friction, real or imagined. And most of them were imagined or fabricated. You always have to seem to be under siege. You always have to seem like your values are under attack. The brain trust just knew instinctively which stories to do, like the War on Christmas."[14]

The War on Christmas was a particularly egregious example of Fox's creating a story where none existed. Each year, as the holiday season began, the network would search for examples of individuals, corporations, or municipalities removing Christmas from the public square.

This fight was personal to Roger Ailes, who had engaged in his own pro-Christmas activism. "The first time I ever went over there [to his son's school], they wouldn't put up a Christmas tree. They had a friendship tree," said Ailes. "I said to the headmas-ter, 'What the hell's a friendship tree?' 'Oh, we can't say the word Merry Christmas.' So I wrote 'Merry Christmas' on the wall in crayon and left. My wife said, 'You're fricking five years old. What the hell are you doing writing on the school wall with a crayon?' I said, 'Oh, screw 'em.' "[15]

Following Ailes's lead, Fox blows up these typically insignifi-cant local incidents into nationwide controversies. For example, in December 2010, Fox claimed that an elementary school in Heathrow, Florida, had banned "traditional Christmas colors."[16] *Fox & Friends* breathlessly covered the story, and *Fox Nation,* the network's *Huffington Post*–like website launched in March 2009, prominently featured the "ban" on its homepage.

Fox, however, never called the school district. When asked to comment, the district revealed that the entire story had been a lie, simply stating that there was "no ban on the colors red and green at Heathrow Elementary."[17] This was typical of Fox's War on Christmas: lots of bluster and outrage, backed by dubious facts, repeated year after year.

The hidden-camera videos promoted by Fox did not prove the institutional corruption at ACORN that they purported to expose. According to Breitbart, the tapes showed conclusive evidence of ACORN employees helping O'Keefe and Giles with an underage prostitution scheme. To make this case, O'Keefe was forced to heavily edit the videos. For instance, while O'Keefe often appeared in a pimp costume outside of ACORN offices, it was later revealed that he did not wear it inside.

Some of the most damning evidence of Breitbart's deception came in a video taken at the ACORN office in San Bernardino, California, where an employee, Tresa Kaelke, recognizing that O'Keefe was engaged in an absurd stunt of some kind, decided to play along with his act. During her conversation with O'Keefe and Giles, Kaelke claimed that she had murdered her husband before giving the duo fake instructions for setting up a brothel.

Fox News saw the tape and went wild. A few hours after James O'Keefe posted the video, Glenn Beck went on the air and announced, "Tonight—a special program with tape from *BigGovernment.com* that is so explosive it's going to peel the skin right off of your face. ACORN yet again caught on hidden camera showing their true colors. This is much more than anything you've seen yet."[18]

"This is twisted, bizarre, macabre," Beck said after playing the video. "I mean, is this theater? I'm not a lawyer. I'm not a jury. But, gosh, even to me, it seems like this is a potential admission of murder. And the way she was describing doing some groundwork beforehand, you know, so everybody in town knew exactly what was going on, a case might be made for premeditated murder." He added, "We haven't been even able to confirm from the state of California whether Tresa's husband from ten years ago was killed, or if he's dead, or if she even had a husband. Did she make the story up? I don't know. Nobody's asking questions."[19]

In the 6 p.m. hour, correspondent Molly Hennenberg showed portions of the San Bernardino tape. At 8 p.m., Bill O'Reilly devoted his opening monologue to the video, stating, "So there you have an ACORN employee having a conversation about setting up a house full of child prostitutes. It doesn't get much worse than that."[20] The 9 p.m. hour was no different. Sean Hannity gave Hannah Giles star treatment in an interview. When he asked whether anyone had "checked to see if in fact she had a husband that was killed," Giles answered, "We've—we're working on that." Hannity went on to claim, "So she's on tape admitting that she plotted to kill and had her husband killed, but we don't know if it's true yet."[21]

Fox's wall-to-wall coverage continued at 10 p.m., when contributor Karl Rove told Greta Van Susteren that Kaelke "claimed to have killed her husband because she thought he was going to abuse her at some point. So, she's claimed that she shot him in the head." Rove added, "I mean, this is an organization that really must have a terrific human relations—human resources department to hire people like that."[22]

Contrary to Beck's earlier assertion, the San Bernardino Police Department was in fact asking questions. That same day they put out a release stating, "From the initial investigation conducted, the claims do not appear to be factual. Investigators have been in contact with the involved party's known former husbands, who are alive and well."[23]

Kaelke had recognized that O'Keefe and Giles were putting on a show, she explained, and "decided to shock them as much as they were shocking me. Like Stephen Colbert does—saying the most outrageous things with a straight face."[24]

The next morning, on *Fox & Friends,* Gretchen Carlson exclaimed, "She killed somebody?" But an hour later, the Fox hosts explained that Kaelke had not "killed somebody,"[25] in the following exchange between Carlson, Brian Kilmeade, and Steve Doocy:

> CARLSON: Well, yeah, basically that she was playing along in a game after the fact. We are not really sure about the details yet, including whether or not she actually did kill her husband. That is still unknown at this time.
>
> KILMEADE: I believe she didn't. The husband is still around.
>
> CARLSON: OK.
>
> DOOCY: Right, he's alive and living in Barstow.[26]

In two other ACORN offices, employees contacted the police following O'Keefe and Giles' visit—an obvious sign that they had no intention of helping set up a prostitution business.[27] And in Los Angeles, an ACORN employee flatly refused to assist the duo with their scheme—a fact that Breitbart, O'Keefe, and Giles hid from the public until more than two months after the story broke.[28] (Even that didn't stop Breitbart from falsely suggesting that ACORN employees had helped "set up a prostitution ring in every single office.")[29]

In the end, not a single investigation revealed widespread wrongdoing by the organization. An investigation led by former Massachusetts attorney general Scott Harshbarger found "no evidence that any action, illegal or otherwise, was taken by ACORN employees on behalf of the videographers."[30] According to the Office of the Attorney General in California, "The evidence illustrates that things are not always as partisan zealots portray them through highly selective editing of reality. Sometimes a fuller truth is found on the cutting room floor."[31] Additionally, the New York *Daily News* quoted "a law enforcement source" saying that O'Keefe and Giles had "edited the tape to meet their agenda."[32]

But the truth did not matter. Within a week of the first video's release, the Democratic-led House of Representatives voted 345–75 to defund ACORN, and the Senate followed suit, voting 85–15 to bar the organization from receiving federal funds. By the spring of 2010, ACORN's national operation had dissolved. Although state chapters continued with their work, Fox News had succeeded in shutting down one of the largest and most active progressive organizations in the country.

The ACORN saga also provided a perfect example of how Fox News helps conservatives stir up national controversies:

- **STEP 1: Conservative activists introduce the lie.** It's important to note that often the source doesn't matter. O'Keefe and Giles were unknown quantities, and Breitbart was primarily a news aggregator. There was no reason for their work to be trusted without verification, but Fox still relied on it, turning a fringe story into a national scandal.

- **STEP 2: Fox News devotes massive coverage to the story.** In the twenty-four hours after Breitbart and O'Keefe posted the first ACORN video on *BigGovernment.com,* Fox News ran more than a dozen segments about the controversy.

- **STEP 3: Fox attacks other outlets for ignoring the controversy.** The day after the first round of tapes was released, Glenn Beck was already complaining about the lack of media coverage: "This story was so huge, so huge, I wondered last night, how many in the media are going to cover it? Well, we watched. Let's take a look here. Let's just take this story by the numbers. Since yesterday morning until about noon today, how many times did the mainstream media outlets cover the ACORN story? What a surprise! Coming in at number one, FOX, nineteen times, at least nineteen times. CNN, how many times? Whoa! Three, three, wow . . . How about MSNBC, how much did they cover the ACORN scandal? Zero. ABC, how many times did ABC cover it? Zero. What do you say, CBS? Oh, zero. NBC, how many times did they cover this story? *New York Times*, this is a good one, huh? You could get a Pulitzer Prize."[33]

- **STEP 4: Mainstream outlets begin reporting on the story.** *The New York Times* and CBS News began reporting on the ACORN story on September 15, 2009. NBC's *Nightly News* and ABC's *World News* followed with reports the next day.

- **STEP 5: Media critics, pundits praise Fox News's coverage.** On September 20, Howard Kurtz asked, "Were the rest of the media late to this burgeoning scandal?" *Washington Post* ombudsman Andy Alexander clearly believed so, writing: "It's tempting to dismiss such gimmicks. Fox News, joined by right-leaning talk radio and bloggers, often hypes stories to apocalyptic proportions while casting competitors as too liberal or too lazy to report the truth. But they're also occasionally pumping legitimate stories. I thought that was the case with ACORN and, before it, the Fox-fueled controversy that led to the resignation of White House environmental adviser Van Jones."[34]

- **STEP 6: The story falls apart once the damage has been done.** None of the investigations that cleared ACORN of wrongdoing received the same breathless coverage as Breitbart and O'Keefe's misleading videos.

This pattern holds true not just for attacks against ideological foes, but for attacks on issues as well. As the network was smearing a progressive group, it was simultaneously battling President Obama's proposal to address climate change. To combat the plethora of data proving the need for legislation, Fox News hosts touted false studies and data emanating from conservative think tanks such as the Heritage Foundation. These institutions were often funded by companies whose profits would suffer from the decreased use of fossil fuels resulting from the passage of climate legislation.

When the House of Representatives took up the American Clean Energy and Security Act, Sean Hannity declared: "Most Americans don't know that we're going to lose two and a half million new jobs and that your electricity bills, as a result of this vote tonight, will go up maybe as high as three thousand dollars per family."[35]

But the three-thousand-dollar figure was based on a false extrapolation of a 2007 study by the Massachusetts Institute of Technology that had already been discredited by one of the study's own authors.

In contrast to Hannity's assertion, the nonpartisan Congressional Budget Office estimated that climate legislation would have an average annual cost of $175 per family. Similarly, the EPA found that the average annual cost to households of legislation to solve the climate crisis would be between $80 and $111 from 2010 to 2050.

FactCheck.org explained that "the $3,100 figure is a misrepresentation of both Obama's proposal and the study from which the number is derived."[36]

In addition to spreading false statistics about the Democratic bill, Fox News helped conservatives promote the trumped-up scandal that became known as "Climategate." Thousands of stolen e-mails from scientists at the University of East Anglia's Climatic Research Unit (CRU) in the UK appeared online days before negotiations were set to begin at an international climate summit in Copenhagen. Fox News and other conservative outlets gleefully seized on the e-mails in an attempt to undermine the overwhelming scientific consensus that human activities are contributing to global warming.

Sean Hannity cited the e-mails as a reason to believe the decades of data proving global warming was fraudulent. "This climate change hoax," he exclaimed, "now we find out that this institute, in fact, was hiding from the people of Great Britain and the world that, in fact, climate change is a hoax, something I've been saying for a long time."[37]

Experts at NASA had a different opinion of the Climategate fiasco. As one climate scientist at NASA's Goddard Institute for Space Studies explained, "There's nothing in the e-mails that shows that global warming is a hoax."[38]

But Fox's misguided interpretation of the e-mails was not an accident. Climate skepticism was network policy, enforced by Washington managing editor Bill Sammon. At the outset of the international climate talks in Copenhagen, Sammon sent an e-mail to producers with instructions on how to cover climate change:

From: Sammon, Bill

To: 169 -SPECIAL REPORT; 036 -FOX.WHU; 054 -FNSunday; 030 -Root (FoxNews.Com); 050 -Senior Producers; 051 -Producers; 069 -Politics; 005 -Washington

Cc: Clemente, Michael; Stack, John; Wallace, Jay; Smith, Sean

Sent: Tue Dec 08 12:49:51 2009

Subject: Given the controversy over the veracity of climate change data . . .

. . . we should refrain from asserting that the planet has warmed (or cooled) in any given period without IMMEDI-ATELY pointing out that such theories are based upon data that critics have called into question. It is not our place as journalists to assert such notions as facts, especially as this debate intensifies.[39]

Fifteen minutes before the e-mail was sent, Fox correspondent Wendell Goler reported from Copenhagen that the 2000s were "expected to turn out to be the warmest decade on record," following a "trend that has scientists concerned because 2000–2009 [was] warmer than the 1990s, which were warmer than the 1980s." When anchor Jon Scott asked about the Climategate e-mails, Goler replied that "the data also comes from the National Oceanic and Atmospheric Administration and from NASA. And scientists say the data of course across all three sources is pretty consistent."[40]

Indeed, Sammon's take on Climategate had been widely debunked by the scientific community. Four days before Sammon's memo, twenty-nine scientists sent a letter to Congress stating: "The body of evidence that human activity is the dominant cause of global warming is overwhelming. The content of the stolen emails has no impact whatsoever on our overall understanding that human activity is driving dangerous levels of global warming."[41]

Additionally, the American Meteorological Society explained, "For climate change research, the body of research in the literature is very large and the dependence on any one set of research results to the comprehensive understanding of the climate system is very, very small. Even if some of the charges of improper behavior in this particular case turn out to be true—which is not yet clearly the case—the impact on the science of climate change would be very limited."[42]

Climategate was a fabricated controversy that did nothing to undermine the veracity of climate research. That fact did not matter to Sammon, who was intent on crafting his own narrative about global warming—one that fit perfectly into the conservative movement's alternate reality.

Climate change is one of the issues that exposed the divisions between Rupert Murdoch and Fox News, underscoring Roger Ailes's power inside the network. In 2007, Murdoch delivered a speech to News Corp. employees, announcing that the company would become carbon neutral by 2010:

> As many of you know, I grew up in Melbourne, Australia, and the last few months and years have brought some changes there:
>
> In Melbourne, 2006 was the tenth consecutive year with below-average rainfall. And 2005 was the hottest year on record throughout Australia.
>
> Australia is suffering its worst drought in one hundred years.
>
> Now, I realize we can't take just one year in one city or even one continent as proof that something unusual is happening. And I am no scientist.
>
> But there are signs around the world, and I do know how to assess a risk.
>
> Climate change poses clear, catastrophic threats. We may not agree on the extent, but we certainly can't afford the risk of inaction.
>
> We must transform the way we use energy.[43]

In an interview with *Grist* magazine, Murdoch added, "I think when people see that 99 percent of scientists agree about the serious extent of global warming, it's going to become a fact of life."[44]

News Corp. even commissioned pollster Frank Luntz to help determine the best way to communicate with voters about climate change issues. Luntz found that "Americans want their leaders to act on climate change" and that a "clear majority of Americans believe climate change is happening. This is true of McCain voters and Obama voters alike. And even those that don't still believe it is essential for America to pursue policies that promote energy independence and a cleaner, healthier environment."[45]

But Murdoch's own views would be considered liberal lies on Fox News. Sean Hannity, for example, has called carbon offsets a "sham"[46] and a "fraud,"[47] despite Murdoch's intention to use carbon offsets to make the company more environmentally responsible.

Furthermore, Fox has attacked others for their work outside of the government to combat global warming. In the case of former vice president Al Gore, Fox distorted his comments to create the appearance that he was personally profiting from his climate activism. "It seems that being green does pay big time—just ask Al Gore," Laura Ingraham said while guest hosting *The O'Reilly Factor*. "Mr. Global Warming was worth about two million dollars or so when he left office in 2001, but after eight years of tirelessly working to save the world, the planet, he's now reportedly—get this—worth a whopping hundred million dollars. His financial windfall came up at last week's Capitol Hill hearing."[48] She then broadcast a portion of the congressional hearing:

REP. MARSHA BLACKBURN (R-TN): Is the legislation that we are discussing here today, is that something that you are going to personally benefit from?

[Ingraham's cut]

GORE: If you believe that the reason I have been working on this issue for thirty years is because of greed, you don't know me.

[Ingraham's cut]

GORE: I've been willing to put my money where my mouth is. Do you think there's something wrong with being active in business in this country?

BLACKBURN: I am simply asking for clarification—

GORE: I'm proud of it.

BLACKBURN:—of the relationship.

GORE: I'm proud of it.[49]

In the edited clip Ingraham aired, Gore appeared to acknowledge that he would financially benefit from climate legislation. However, the full exchange told a much different story. Here it is with the portions of the segment Ingraham broadcasted in italics, with Gore's responses, left off the air, in boldface:

BLACKBURN: So you're a partner in Kleiner Perkins. Okay. Now, they have invested about a billion dollars in forty companies that are going to benefit from cap-and-trade legislation. So *is the legislation that we are discussing here today, is that something that you are going to personally benefit from?*

GORE: I believe that the transition to a green economy is good for our economy and good for all of us, and I have invested in it. **But every penny that I have made, I have put**

**right into a nonprofit, the Alliance for Climate Pro-
tection, to spread awareness of why we have to take
on this challenge.**

And Congresswoman, if you're—*if you believe that
the reason I have been working on this issue for thirty years is
because of greed, you don't know me.*

BLACKBURN: Sir, I'm not making accusations, I'm asking questions
that have been asked of me and individuals—constituents
that were seeking a point of clarity, so I am asking you
for that point of—point of clarity.

GORE: I understand exactly what you're doing, Congresswoman. Everybody here does.

BLACKBURN: And, well—you know, are you willing to divest
yourself of any profit? **Does all of it go to a not-for-profit
that is an educational not-for-profit—**

GORE: **Every penny that I have made—**

BLACKBURN: **Every penny—**

GORE:—**has gone to it. Every penny from the movie,
from the book, from any investments in renewable
energy.** *I've been willing to put my money where my mouth is.
Do you think there's something wrong with being active in business in this country?*

BLACKBURN: *I am simply asking for clarification—*

GORE: *I'm proud of it.*

BLACKBURN: *—of the relationship.*

GORE: *I'm proud of it.*[50]

While Ingraham painted the former vice president as a profi-
teer, Gore testified that he had given all of his earnings from green
investments to nonprofits. Even after these false attacks on Gore

were noted by many in the media, Bill O'Reilly was still promoting them weeks later, teasing a segment by saying, "Al Gore is becoming extremely wealthy with all this global warming stuff." He added, "I believe that [Gore] is profiting by the green movement."[51]

This is the pattern Fox News follows on nearly every political issue: latch on to a conservative "fact" and broadcast it ad nauseam, even after it is proven false. Unlike with health care reform, conservatives were able to block President Obama's climate bill. Fox News played a vital role in the fight, turning the protection of big oil polluters into a populist cause.

Both battles demonstrated Fox's domination of the conservative movement. By pushing phony controversies such as death panels and Climategate into the mainstream, Fox News could shift the national conversation and influence conservatives all over the country, who trusted their favorite "news" network far more than any of their elected leaders.

The promotion of misleading ACORN tapes should have served as a warning to the media that Fox News could not be trusted. But fresh off the firing of Van Jones, traditional media outlets were not ready to accept this truth. Fox was still a "sister" news organization. This only encouraged the network to seek out more targets to attack.

At the end of September, Sean Hannity focused his energy on attacking an Obama appointee named Kevin Jennings, who served as assistant deputy secretary for the Office of Safe and Drug-Free Schools at the U.S. Department of Education. Jennings had been a leader for nearly two decades in the fight to ensure that LGBT students had a safe school environment. As a teacher at Concord

Academy in Massachusetts, Jennings founded the nation's first gay-straight alliance. He went on to cofound the Gay and Lesbian Independent School Teacher Network—later renamed the Gay, Lesbian and Straight Education Network (GLSEN)—in Boston in 1990 and grew it into a national organization. Following that success, Jennings was appointed by Republican governor William Weld to chair the Education Committee of the Governor's Commission on Gay and Lesbian Youth in 1992. He had also authored several books on his experience as a gay teacher, and most people considered him highly qualified for his new position in the administration.

On September 18, just days after ACORN's funding was stripped by Congress, Hannity quizzed his guests asking, "Who do you think is the most dangerous [czar]?" Republican strategist Noelle Nikpour responded, "Well, I think it's Kevin Jennings. Not only that, that he's a gay activist, but he was part of the GLSEN. He was the former director for GLSEN. They held a conference in which techniques for, I think it was, homosexuality, how to perform different techniques. That's insane." *The Wall Street Journal* editorial board member Stephen Moore then chimed in: "Remember, we—used to be that sex education was putting condoms on bananas. Lord knows what they're going to do now."[52]

A week later, Hannity took his case against Jennings further, claiming that "this is a guy that's advocated promoting homosexuality in schools. This is a guy we have talked about his past. He's had contempt for religion, et cetera, et cetera . . . Isn't the issue here that what they're teaching oftentimes, value-wise, contradicts what parents are teaching? And isn't that morally wrong?"[53]

Glenn Beck had received a huge boost in prominence following Van Jones's resignation. Sean Hannity now wanted a scalp of his own, and the rest of Fox News was happy to assist. During a segment on *Fox & Friends,* Brian Kilmeade claimed that Jennings wrote "a report on how he did not report an incident with an underage student who had sex with an older man, and also has expressed contempt for religion."[54]

FoxNews.com also got in on the act, describing Jennings as a "former schoolteacher who has advocated promoting homosexuality in schools, written about his past drug abuse, expressed his contempt for religion and detailed an incident in which he did not report an underage student who told him he was having sex with older men."[55]

This charge, like the "truther" allegation against Jones, escalated the anti-Jennings campaign into a full-fledged controversy. Led by Fox News, right-wing pundits and media outlets pushed the claim that two decades earlier, when Jennings was a twenty-four-year-old teacher at Concord Academy, he "cover[ed] up statutory rape" by not reporting a conversation he had with a student who told him about a relationship he had with an "older man."[56]

But the accusation was a lie; at the time of the conversation, the student in question was old enough to give his legal consent, making the statutory rape charge impossible. Additionally, the former student credited Jennings with helping him through a difficult period.

"Since I was of legal consent at the time, the fifteen-minute conversation I had with Mr. Jennings twenty-one years ago is of nobody's concern but his and mine," the former student said. "However, since the Republican noise machine is so concerned about my 'well-being' and that of America's students, they'll be relieved to know that I was not 'inducted' into homosexuality, assaulted, raped, or sold into sexual slavery."

He continued, "In 1988, I had taken a bus home for the weekend, and on the return trip met someone who was also gay. The next day, I had a conversation with Mr. Jennings about it. I had no sexual contact with anybody at the time, though I was entirely legally free to do so. I was a sixteen-year-old going through something most of us have experienced: adolescence. I find it regrettable that the people who have the compassion and integrity to protect our nation's students are themselves in need of protection from homophobic smear attacks.

"Were it not for Mr. Jennings' courage and concern for my well-being at that time in my life, I doubt I'd be the proud gay man that I am today,"[57] he concluded.

While the attacks on Jennings continued, they had lost their punch. *The Atlantic* reported,

> A few weeks ago, Kevin Jennings was in trouble. After social conservatives at the Family Research Council had opposed his nomination as director of the Education Department's Office of Safe and Drug-Free Schools earlier in the year, he came under a firestorm of criticism from conservative bloggers and Fox News pundits for counseling an underage student—a 15-year-old boy, it was reported—on a sexual relationship with an older man . . . While the fire hasn't completely died down—53 House Republicans sent a letter calling for his job last week—it has certainly lost steam. Jennings is no longer a topic du jour, mostly due to one simple fact: the boy wasn't actually underage.[58]

Before the Jennings episode, Fox News was more powerful than ever and the media felt obligated to pay attention to the network's attacks. When Fox's overreach was exposed, reporters and producers at other news organizations began to realize that stories on the network deserved extra scrutiny before they committed resources to covering them. Unfortunately, this belief was not universal. While some would heed the warning of the Jennings fiasco, others still gave Fox News the elevated platform of a non-partisan media organization.

Chapter 8

Willie Horton . . . Times a Thousand

There was a breakdown in the system, and it is being addressed. But it must say something about the power of Fox, that a week after she resigned, we're still talking about this.

—Fox News vice president Michael Clemente

After investigations cleared ACORN of any wrongdoing, at that moment, Andrew Breitbart's credibility in the press should have evaporated. If that wasn't the case, James O'Keefe's arrest in January 2010, after entering Democratic senator Mary Landrieu's office on false pretenses, should have made the rest of the media seriously doubt the journalistic integrity of Breitbart's operation.

Breitbart owned the "life rights" to O'Keefe's work. As such, he shared some responsibility—if not legal, then at least ethical—for the actions of his protégé. But even O'Keefe's criminal stunt in Louisiana wasn't enough for the media to write off Breitbart, whose talent for finding, or inventing, potentially explosive stories was too ratings-worthy to pass up.

Breitbart was finally exposed in July after he launched a racially tinged attack on Shirley Sherrod, an employee at the Department of Agriculture. In a posting on his Big Government website, Breitbart wrote:

> We are in possession of a video from [*sic*] in which Shirley Sherrod, USDA Georgia Director of Rural Development, speaks at the NAACP Freedom Fund dinner in Georgia. In her meandering speech to what appears to be an all-black audience, this federally appointed executive bureaucrat lays out in stark detail, that her federal duties are managed through the prism of race and class distinctions.
>
> In the first video, Sherrod describes how she racially discriminates against a white farmer. She describes how she is torn over how much she will choose to help him. And, she admits that she doesn't do everything she can for him, because he is white. Eventually, her basic humanity informs that this white man is poor and needs help. But she decides that he should get help from "one of his own kind." She refers him to a white lawyer.[1]

While that was the story that the video appeared to tell, it was not the full truth. Unfortunately, the White House had not learned its lesson about Breitbart and forced Sherrod to resign on the same day the video was posted. Fox News had pounced on the story already, failing to obtain the full video and jumping to conclusions about its significance.

Fox News framed the story around the NAACP's contention that elements of the Tea Party movement were racist. FoxNews .com reported, "Days after the NAACP clashed with Tea Party members over allegations of racism, a video has surfaced showing an Agriculture Department official regaling an NAACP audience with a story about how she withheld help to a white farmer facing bankruptcy."[2]

A little more than two and a half hours after Breitbart first posted his video, FoxNation.com's top headline read, "Caught on Tape: Obama Official Discriminates Against White Farmer." When Sherrod resigned, the headline was changed to read, "Obama Official Resigns After Discrimination Caught on Tape."[3] Both stories linked to Breitbart's original story and video.

At the tail end of his show that night, Bill O'Reilly said, "Sherrod was caught on tape saying something very disturbing. Seems a white farmer in Georgia had requested government assistance form Ms. Sherrod." O'Reilly then commented, "That is simply unacceptable. And Ms. Sherrod must resign immediately."[4]

Fifteen minutes later, Sean Hannity reported that Sherrod "resigned just a short time ago after she was caught on tape appearing to tell an audience that she had used her position to racially discriminate against white farmers."

During the "Great American Panel" later in the show, Republican strategist Kate Obenshain said, "It's just a shame that it takes an expose, it takes Breitbart having to put it on his website, for her resignation to be forced." Obenshain was followed by *Wall Street Journal* columnist John Fund, who exclaimed, "Obviously no one complained at the Georgia NAACP. No one complained. It would have passed unless they had this video which came out now."[5] Under pressure, the NAACP issued a statement condemning Sherrod a little after nine in the evening.

On *Fox & Friends* the next morning, Steve Doocy claimed Sherrod was caught "making a speech to the NAACP that sure sounded racist." Alisyn Camerota added that Breitbart's video showed Sherrod "touting this in this anecdote as though this is, you know, a feather in her cap, somehow, for her to be congratulated." The hosts also decided the Sherrod tape was "Exhibit A" of "what racism looks like." During their discussion, the on-screen text read, "RACISM CAUGHT ON CAMERA" and "USDA OFFICIAL ADMITS RACISM ON TAPE; FORCED TO RESIGN AFTER DICEY VIDEO LEAKS."[6]

That morning, CNN hosted Sherrod to respond to the charges against her. After she told her side of the story, host John Roberts said, "Miss Sherrod, let's make it clear, though, that this happened twenty-four years ago. You eventually worked with this white farmer. You eventually became friends, you say, with the farmer and his wife . . . So, the question I have is, when the U.S. Department of Agriculture came to you and said you have to step down, why didn't you just say, wait a minute, you don't know the full story. Here's the full story, why should I step down?"

Sherrod's answer was telling: "I did say that, but they, for some reason, the stuff that Fox and the Tea Party does is scaring the administration."[7]

By nine in the morning, Fox News had started walking back the story, reporting, "Sherrod says that that story is about something that happened twenty-four years ago . . . and that she uses the story when speaking to groups to point out how racism can and needs to be overcome."[8]

As the day progressed, Breitbart and Fox's story continued to unravel. In an appearance on CNN, the white farmer whom Sherrod spoke of in the video said that people who were calling her a racist "don't know what they are talking about."[9]

Glenn Beck devoted the first twenty minutes of his show to the story, airing a clip of Sherrod's CNN interview and asking if this "was a political assassination from the White House or from the NAACP." Beck added, "Context matters, but we don't have the full video. Andrew Breitbart is trying to get the full video."[10]

The network was in full retreat by 7 p.m., with host Bret Baier abruptly telling viewers, "Fox News didn't even do the story. We didn't do it on *Special Report*. We posted it online."[11]

At 7:45 p.m., the full video was released. Sherrod's was a story of redemption, not racism. Instead of denying the white couple service, she had worked to save their farm and befriended them in the process. According to Sherrod, Fox News never contacted her for comment before running with the story.

Sherrod didn't hesitate to criticize Breitbart and Fox for playing the race game. "When you look at their reporting, this is just another way of seeing that they are [racist]," she said. "But I have seen that before now. I saw their reporting as biased during the Bush administration and the Clinton administration."[12]

In reality, there were several parties who wronged Sherrod: Breitbart and Fox News, the White House, and even the NAACP. Yet Sherrod's hasty punishment had been instigated by the deceitful conservatives promoting the story.

The network, clearly embarrassed, tried to rewrite the history of the Sherrod saga. "Fox News Channel did not touch this story until she had actually quit,"[13] Steve Doocy insisted. Likewise, correspondent James Rosen stated that "the idea that Fox News was somehow a catalyzing agent in this" was a "myth."[14]

One Fox News personality, Shepard Smith, was honest about the incident and implicitly criticized the rest of the network. "We here at *Studio B* did not run the video and did not reference the story in any way for many reasons, among them: We didn't know who shot it, we didn't know when it was shot, we didn't know the context of the statement, and because of the history of the videos on the site where it was posted," Smith stated. "In short, we do not and did not trust the source."[15]

Eventually, Fox News admitted that running with Breitbart's

story was a mistake. In an interview with *Politico,* Fox News vice president Michael Clemente said, "There was a breakdown in the system, and it is being addressed. But it must say something about the power of Fox, that a week after she resigned, we're still talking about this."[16] It did say something about the power of Fox to slander a woman and nearly destroy her life.

Roger Ailes's work on the Nixon and George H. W. Bush campaigns, Bill Sammon's search for racial subtext in Barack Obama's writings, and Glenn Beck's statement that the president was "a racist" all demonstrate a willingness among the network's employees to engage in race baiting. The Shirley Sherrod story simply followed in line with these despicable incidents. However, she was not alone.

With Roger Ailes's history of using race as a political weapon, it's no surprise the network would employ the same tactics. During the 2008 campaign, statements of President Obama's pastor, Jeremiah Wright, were played ad nauseam on the network, delivering the message to viewers that while Obama positioned himself as a post-racial candidate, he had a murky past.

In March 2008, Dick Morris pointed out to Bill O'Reilly the significance of Fox News in spreading the story. O'Reilly began his show by informing his audience, "This man, Chicago preacher Jeremiah Wright, is Barack Obama's pastor. He even married the senator and his wife. Well, Fox News has obtained portions of Reverend Wright's sermons that are anti-American, to say the least. Viewer warning, some offensive material coming up."

He then played some of Reverend Wright's controversial statements and concluded, "Now, there's no question that Reverend Wright is a problem for Senator Obama." O'Reilly continued,

"How big a problem remains to be seen. Most Americans love their country and believe it is noble. That kind of extreme rhetoric, the kind that Wright traffics in, is only acceptable to the far left. So Senator Obama will have to deal with this."[17]

Later in the episode, discussing the political implications of Reverend Wright, O'Reilly asked Morris, "This is Willie Horton—who was used to destroy Michael Dukakis's campaign, a criminal in Massachusetts—times a thousand. If you were McCain, do you use this against Obama?"

Morris replied, "He doesn't have to. You just did."[18]

Morris realized how much had changed since 1988 in politics and the way it was covered by the media. Then, with fewer major news sources, each of which held itself to a higher standard in terms of what constituted real news, the Willie Horton story had to be floated as a paid advertisement. Had Fox News existed in 1988, the Willie Horton commercial would never have needed to be aired—the network would have carried the story for the GOP.

A little more than a month after his colloquy with O'Reilly, Morris again spelled out Roger Ailes's strategy behind the Reverend Wright story and the other racially tinged coverage on Fox: "The determinant in the election will be whether we believe that Barack Obama is what he appears to be, or is he somebody who's sort of a sleeper agent who really doesn't believe in our system and is more in line with Wright's views?"[19]

In the summer of 2010, another story with racial overtones would dominate Fox's airwaves. On the night of Obama's election in 2008, Fox News anchors had mentioned in passing that members of the New Black Panther Party were intimidating voters at a polling station in Philadelphia. During the summer, a former

Justice Department employee, J. Christian Adams, came forward to claim that the Obama administration's Department of Justice had declined to pursue charges against the New Black Panthers.

In the June 25, 2010, edition of *The Washington Times,* Adams wrote, "The New Black Panther case was the simplest and most obvious violation of federal law I saw in my Justice Department career. Because of the corrupt nature of the dismissal, statements falsely characterizing the case and, most of all, indefensible orders for the career attorneys not to comply with lawful subpoenas investigating the dismissal, this month I resigned my position as a Department of Justice (DOJ) attorney."[20]

Adams continued, "Based on my firsthand experiences, I believe the dismissal of the Black Panther case was motivated by a lawless hostility toward equal enforcement of the law."[21] According to Adams, the New Black Panthers were never charged because of reverse racism at the Justice Department.

The story fit perfectly into the Ailes-Sammon-Beck racial framework. It didn't matter that not a single voter came forward to claim he or she had been intimidated, or that the facts didn't line up with Adams's story. It was not the Obama Justice Department that chose not to pursue a criminal complaint against the New Black Panthers. Appearing before the U.S. Commission on Civil Rights, Assistant Attorney General Thomas Perez testified that the *Bush* Justice Department had "determined that the facts did not constitute a prosecutable violation of the criminal statutes." And, in fact, "the Department did, however, file a civil action on January 7, 2009."[22]

The Obama administration took additional action in the case in May 2009. "Based on the careful review of the evidence, the Department concluded that the evidence collected supported the allegations in the complaint against Minister King Samir Shabazz,"

Perez said. "The Department, therefore, obtained an injunction against defendant King Samir Shabazz, prohibiting him from displaying a weapon within 100 feet of an open polling place on any Election Day in the City of Philadelphia."[23]

Furthermore, the New Black Panther Party case was not the only incident of alleged voter intimidation in which the Justice Department had recently declined to pursue criminal charges. After Election Day in 2006, the *Austin American-Statesman* reported, "In Arizona, Roy Warden, an anti-immigration activist with the Minutemen, and a handful of supporters staked out a Tucson precinct and questioned Hispanic voters at the polls to determine whether they spoke English . . . Armed with a 9mm Glock automatic strapped to his side, Warden said he planned to photograph Hispanic voters entering polls in an effort to identify illegal immigrants and felons."[24] In his testimony to the civil rights commission, Perez pointed out that the Bush Justice Department "declined to bring any action for alleged voter intimidation, notwithstanding the requests of the complaining parties."[25]

J. Christian Adams, whose charges were fueling the controversy, was a longtime Republican activist. In 2001, Adams filed an ethics complaint against Hillary Clinton's brother, Hugh Rodham, which was dismissed. In 2004, he served as a Bush poll watcher in Florida. Additionally, the legal news website Main Justice reported that Adams had "volunteered with the National Republican Lawyers Association, an offshoot of the Republican National Committee that trains lawyers to fight on the front lines of often racially tinged battles over voting rights."[26]

Although he was supposedly a "career" employee in the Justice Department and not a political appointee, Adams's position in the agency was based on his partisan affiliation. According to Joseph Rich, the former head of the Bush Justice Department's

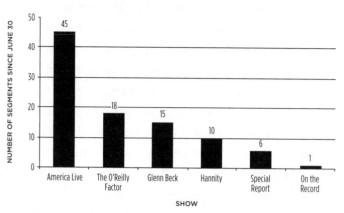

NUMBER OF FOX SEGMENTS DISCUSSING
NEW BLACK PANTHER CASE

Civil Rights Division Voting Section, Adams was "Exhibit A of the type of people who had been hired" under a process the DOJ Inspector General determined was improperly influenced by politics.[27]

Fox News wasn't concerned with the facts or their source. In July alone, the network ran a whopping ninety-five segments on the fake controversy. Forty-five of them occurred on Megyn Kelly's show, which purportedly was part of Fox's "news" programming.

Despite the coverage on Fox, the New Black Panther Party was a fringe organization that the Southern Poverty Law Center labeled a hate group. There was really no reason to pay much attention to them—unless the objective was to scare a mostly white audience about the president's ties to radical black activists.

Only one network saw fit to give the New Black Panthers wide-ranging coverage. Dating back to 1998, the group's leadership had appeared fifty-one times on Fox News, with the majority of those appearances coming on Sean Hannity's program. There was no news value in hosting the New Black Panthers; the appearances were orchestrated to create the same tension as Ailes's notorious furlough ad. Therefore, Fox was unconcerned with the fact that Adams couldn't give detailed accounts of why the Justice Department made certain decisions in the New Black Panther Party case because, in his words, "I don't know. I wasn't there."[28] His accusations were perfect for the story that Fox wanted to tell.

Conservative blogger and CNN contributor Erick Erickson linked the New Black Panthers controversy directly to Roger Ailes, writing a blog post titled "King Samir Shabazz Should Be 2010's Willie Horton" (Shabazz was the New Black Panther who had been sanctioned at the request of the Justice Department). In the post, Erickson wrote, "Republican candidates nationwide should seize on this issue. The Democrats are giving a pass to radicals who advocate killing white kids in the name of racial justice and who try to block voters from the polls . . . The Democrats will scream racism. Let them. Republicans are not going to pick up significant black support anyway."[29]

On his radio program, Glenn Beck declared that the New Black Panther Party was part of Obama's "army of thugs."[30] A few days later, he adopted an even more hysterical tone. "They want a race war. We must be peaceful people. They are going to poke and poke and poke, and our government is going to stand by and let them do it," he said. "We must take the role of Martin Luther King, because I do not believe that Martin Luther King believed in, 'Kill all white babies.' "[31]

Finally, Abigail Thernstrom, a conservative scholar and Bush-appointed vice chair of the Commission on Civil Rights, told the truth about Adams's charade. In an interview with *Politico,* Thernstrom said, "This doesn't have to do with the Black Panthers, this has to do with their fantasies about how they could use this issue to topple the [Obama] administration." She added, "My fellow conservatives on the commission had this wild notion they could bring Eric Holder down and really damage the president."[32]

Neither Shirley Sherrod nor the New Black Panthers were national figures, and neither had a platform or constituency that warranted major news coverage. Yet, in both cases, Fox News seized on unfounded allegations, without checking the facts, to create a national controversy. Roger Ailes had used race as a wedge throughout his entire political career. Fox's coverage of Sherrod and the New Black Panthers were just additional evidence that he would use the same strategy to turn Americans against President Obama.

Part III

The Campaign

Chapter 9

A Vote for Liberty

WHAT CAN BROWN DO FOR YOU?
      —Fox News chyron

With sixty Democratic votes, a filibuster-proof majority, in the Senate, it was likely the president's health care reform legislation would become law. But in August 2009, Ted Kennedy passed away after a sixteen-month battle with brain cancer. Holding on to his seat in the Senate was critical to passing the legislation, which the Massachusetts senator had fought for his entire career. As the special election heated up, Obama's top priority hung in the balance.

Martha Coakley, the state's popular attorney general, was the first candidate to officially enter the race, on September 1. Having already won a statewide election, Coakley was a formidable contender. She cruised to victory in the Democratic primary, beating Congressman Michael Capuano by more than twenty points and finishing even further ahead of City Year cofounder Alan Khazei and Boston Celtics co-owner Stephen Pagliuca.

Coakley's general-election opponent was Republican state senator Scott Brown, and most observers expected the Democrats to retain their sixtieth vote in the Senate. However, as 2010 began, the race suddenly began to tighten. Following her primary victory, Coakley made only limited efforts to raise funds and left the campaign trail to take a vacation. Scott Brown took full advantage of her absence, and Fox News was ready to help his campaign cross the finish line.

In the weeks leading up to the election, the network hosted Brown for numerous interviews, serving, in effect, as a glorified telethon for his campaign. On January 8, he appeared on *Hannity,* telling viewers, "If people are kind of fed up with the way things are going, they can go to BrownForUSSenate.com, and they can make a difference and they can stop the business as usual—not only in Massachusetts, but more importantly nationally."[1]

Three days later, Brown told the audience of *On the Record,* "And if people want to learn more, they can certainly go to BrownForUSSenate.com. But we have a money bomb right now that's hitting, and you can go to RedInvadesBlue.com, and you can help me fight back against the machine, because the negative ads—the second I walked off the stage, the negative ads have started."[2]

And, appearing two days later on *Fox & Friends,* Brown said, "And if people want to help, they can go to BrownForUSSenate .com, and they can donate so I can fight against the machine. Because I can win this race if the people in Massachusetts look at the issues."[3]

While other networks discouraged candidates from explicitly

promoting their websites or fund-raising on the air, no such rules existed at Fox News.

Enabling candidates to raise money on its airwaves was not a new practice at Fox. In the two weeks leading up to the 2009 off-year election, New York Conservative Party congressional candidate Doug Hoffman, New Jersey Republican gubernatorial candidate Chris Christie, and Virginia Republican gubernatorial candidate Bob McDonnell appeared on the network and its personalities' radio shows for a total of sixteen interviews, consuming more than 114 minutes of airtime. During these appearances, the candidates repeatedly beseeched Fox's conservative audience to support their campaigns.[4]

Fox hosts also used the network to raise funds for their own political committees. In October 2009, Mike Huckabee directed viewers on multiple occasions to "go to BalanceCutSave.com" and sign a petition urging Congress to "balance the budget," "cut their spending," and "save American families."[5] But the website was merely a front for Huckabee's PAC, whose primary mission was to support Republican candidates. After signing the "Balance, Cut, Save" petition, visitors were redirected to a page asking for donations and received e-mails asking them to "take a moment now to make phone calls to voters"[6] on behalf of McDonnell, Hoffman, and California Republican David Harmer.

Other Fox News contributors took advantage of the Massachusetts race to raise funds for their own organizations. For example, in a January 11 appearance on *Hannity,* Dick Morris urged viewers to "go to DickMorris.com . . . to help elect Brown" because "if we win this fight, then there will never be another victory for Obama."[7] At Morris's website, visitors were asked "to help us raise $300,000 for a last minute media buy to push Brown and the Republicans to victory."[8]

From: Governor Mike Huckabee <mikehuckabee@huckpac.com>
Date: Sun, Nov 1, 2009 at 9:06 PM
Subject: Final Push for Votes Begins Now
To: ████████████████████

NEWSLETTER

This Tuesday voters will head to the polls and cast votes for three very important candidates: Bob
McDonnell (candidate for Virginia Governor) and David Harmer and Doug Hoffman candidates for
Congress in California and New York. We need to help get each of these fine men elected.

We are past the point where a donation to their campaign will matter that much, what we need now is to
reach as many voters as possible within the next 36 hours and let them know Americans are focused on
helping elect elect Bob McDonnell, David Harmer and Doug Hoffman.

Today I am emailing to ask if you will take a moment now to make phone calls to voters. We have set up
phone banks for Bob McDonnell and David Harmer and you can begin calling voters immediately.
Tomorrow we will launch a phone bank for Doug Hoffman. Even if you can only make a call or two, you
will help make a positive difference in the final hours before votes are cast on Tuesday.

Also, if you know friends or family who will have a chance to vote on Tuesday for one of these
candidates please make sure they do. Huck PAC volunteers have already made over 20,000 calls in
Virginia and helped Bob immensely. I know if we make these final calls we can do more of the same.

Fighting for Bob, David and Doug,

Mike Huckabee

Mike Huckabee

You may login to begin making phone calls here:

http://my.huckpac.com/?Fuseaction=PhoneBank.Home

Donor acquisition is an expensive process, but Fox News, by
granting access to its audience, helped to ease the burden. The network provided selected candidates easy access to a large pool of
potential contributors who were ready to fill their campaign cof-
fers with small-dollar contributions. This practice distinguished

Fox from any other cable news network. MSNBC, for example, suspended Keith Olbermann and Joe Scarborough, two of the network's most prominent personalities, for their off-air political activities. In issuing Olbermann's suspension, NBC News president Phil Griffin was clear: "I became aware of Keith's political contributions late last night. Mindful of NBC News policy and standards, I have suspended him indefinitely without pay."[9]

Along with helping to fill Scott Brown's bank account, Fox hosts made a concerted effort to build the narrative that Martha Coakley could not be trusted. Although some of Coakley's mistakes—like describing Red Sox World Series hero Curt Schilling (who was supporting Brown) as a "Yankees fan"—were her own doing, Fox also cropped, edited, and misrepresented the Democratic candidate's words at every turn.

During the final debate of the campaign, moderator David Gergen asked, "How do you think we succeed in Afghanistan?" Coakley replied, "I'm not sure there is a way to succeed. If the goal was—and the mission in Afghanistan was to go in because we believed that the Taliban was giving harbor to terrorists. We supported that. I supported that goal. They're gone. They're not there anymore. They're in, apparently, Yemen, they're in Pakistan. Let's focus our efforts on where Al-Qaeda is." She added, "The focus should be getting the appropriate information on individuals who are trained, who represent a threat to us, and use the force necessary to go after those individuals."[10]

Coakley's answer was noncontroversial. Many members of the foreign policy and military establishment had been making similar statements for months. For instance, National Security Adviser Jim Jones told CNN in October, "The good news is, that Americans should feel at least good about in Afghanistan, is that the Al-Qaeda presence is very diminished. The maximum estimate is less than one hundred operating in the country. No bases. No ability to launch attacks on either us or our allies."[11]

In May, when CNN's John King asked whether it was "an exaggeration" to say there was "no Al-Qaeda at all in Afghanistan," General David Petraeus responded, "No, I would agree with that assessment."[12]

Nonetheless, Fox News went on the attack. The hosts of *Fox & Friends,* in particular, wrongly accused Coakley of claiming there were no terrorists at all in Afghanistan and saying the Taliban was "no longer a threat."[13] In context, there was nothing extraordinary about Coakley's remarks, but Fox repeated the charges over and over again to portray her as naïve.

A few days before the election, Fox News attempted to drum up a new controversy. "She says Catholics shouldn't be working in emergency rooms," Sean Hannity declared. "This is Massachusetts. I lived in Rhode Island five years. A lot of Catholics in Massachusetts. So what's happening?"[14]

Likewise, Glenn Beck stated, "Now, the next one is religious bigotry. Do we have that with Coakley? Oh, sure. Catholics—pay attention to this one." After playing a truncated audio clip of Coakley saying, "You can have religious freedom, but you probably shouldn't work in the emergency room," Beck said: "Oh, well, thank you very much. I appreciate that. Hey, Catholics, as soon as we get all of the—you know, all of the universal health care, if you got to provide abortions or something, you're a nurse and you don't want to do that, well, go find another job. And practice that religious freedom elsewhere."[15] FoxNation.com linked to a blog post by right-wing blogger Jim Hoft under the headline: "Coakley: Catholics Shouldn't Work in the ER."[16]

But Fox News distorted what Coakley, a Roman Catholic, actually said. In a local radio interview, host Ken Pittman asked if

Coakley would support "a health care bill that had conscientious objector toward certain procedures, including abortion." Coakley responded that she didn't "believe that would be included in the health care bill," and that she would oppose legislation that would allow health care workers who "don't want to provide services that are required under the law" to "individually decide not to follow the law."

As Coakley then pointed out, "Scott Brown filed an amendment to a bill in Massachusetts that would say that hospital and emergency room personnel could deny emergency contraception to a woman who came in who had been raped." This led to the following exchange:

PITTMAN: Right, if you are a Catholic, and you believe what the Pope teaches, you know, that any form of birth control is a sin. And you don't want to do that, that—

COAKLEY: No, but we have a separation of church and state here, Ken, let's be clear.

PITTMAN: Yeah, but in the emergency room, you still have your religious freedom.

COAKLEY: The law says that people are allowed to have that. And so, then, if you—you can have religious freedom, you probably shouldn't work in the emergency room.

PITTMAN: Wow. Okay, so if you have religious conviction, stay out of the emergency room.

COAKLEY: Well, no, I'm not—look, you're—you're the one who brought the question up. I don't believe that the law allows for that, and I know that we accommodate all kinds of differences all the time. I think Roe vs. Wade has made it clear that women have a right to choose, and in Massachusetts, particularly if someone has been the victim of a rape, an

assault, and she goes to an emergency room to get contraception, someone else should say, "Oh, no, I don't believe
in this, so I'm going to affect your constitutional rights"?[17]

The dishonest attacks on Coakley did not occur in a bubble.
Each distortion spread through blogs and talk radio, creating an
endless loop of misinformation. While Brown made unforced
errors, his gaffes were mostly overlooked or forgiven, while Coakley's were blown up, exaggerated, or just lied about to the point
that she was unable to recover.

Beyond its aggressive campaigning, Fox News overhyped the
significance of a possible Brown victory, even suggesting that
viewers would profit from a Republican triumph. On the January 19 edition of *Fox & Friends,* Fox Business host Stuart Varney
said that "investors would love" Brown's election and that "your
401(k) could do well" as a result.[18] In the same interview, Fox
aired the following on-screen graphic:

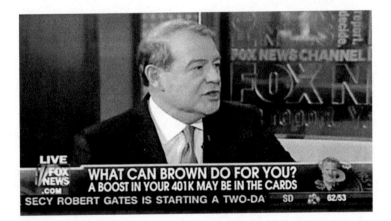

Moreover, FoxNation.com proclaimed in a headline: "Brown Win Could Cause Huge Stock Rally":[19]

January 18, 2010
05:57 PM EST

Brown Win Could Cause Huge Stock Rally

🗨 **51 Comments**

On the day before the election, Fox dropped the pretense of being fair or balanced. The top headline at FoxNation.com read "Massachusetts Miracle" and linked to a video proclaiming that "our liberty is threatened by another tyrannical government" and a "vote for Scott Brown is a vote for liberty."[20]

By Election Day, it was hard to tell the difference between Scott Brown and Fox News staffers. At a campaign rally on January 19, *ThinkProgress* blogger Lee Fang witnessed Fox News reporter Carl Cameron "relaxing after the speech with Brown campaign volunteers, hugging staffers, and autographing Brown for Senate campaign materials." Fang reported that "when *Think-*

Progress approached Cameron to question him about Fox News's journalism ethics, he ducked the question and ran away from the event, saying 'Dude, I'm on a deadline. I can't.' "[21]

It was no surprise that Cameron wouldn't address Fox News's unethical role in the campaign. His network had spent the previous three weeks airing Scott Brown infomercials, unapologetically soliciting donations, and unfairly attacking his opponent.

When all was said and done, Brown defeated Coakley by just under four percentage points, and the Democrats' supermajority was gone.

.   .   .

One week before Scott Brown's election, Fox News scored another victory when Sarah Palin signed on to the network as a contributor. The multiyear deal would reportedly pay the half-term governor more than one million dollars. Six months earlier, on July 3, 2009, Palin had resigned as governor of Alaska. In a rambling speech outside her home, Palin told the assembled media, "I love my job and I love Alaska, and it hurts to make this choice, but I'm doing what's best for them."[22]

Palin continued, "As I thought about this announcement that I would not seek reelection, I thought about how much fun other governors have as lame ducks. They maybe travel around their state, travel to other states, maybe take their overseas international trade missions . . . I'm not going to put Alaskans through that. I promised efficiencies and effectiveness. That's not how I'm wired. I'm not wired to operate under the same old politics as usual."[23]

While only Palin knew the truth, there was plenty of speculation about the real reasons she was stepping down. Palin's life changed forever when John McCain chose her as his running mate, instantly catapulting her from obscurity into the national spotlight. She went from being a relatively unknown governor with no national platform to one of the most recognizable faces in the country. And that came with perks: a bevy of staff, security, and tens of thousands of dollars of designer clothing for her and her family.

When the campaign ended in defeat, it all disappeared. In a Cinderella moment, Palin's carriage turned back into a pumpkin and life returned to normal, with no adoring crowds or throngs of press following her every move. She was even forced to return her expensive new wardrobe to the Republican National Committee. Trapped in Alaska, Palin lost most of the perks of stardom.

Palin was also in a position to earn significant fees for speaking engagements, playing pundit, and putting her name on books. But every day she spent in the world of Alaska politics was a lost opportunity to promote conservative issues, and herself, on a national stage. Plus, governing was boring; being a media star was exciting.

On the campaign trail, Palin had learned an important lesson: the press could be her greatest friend and her worst enemy—often at the same time. This was a major difference between Palin and McCain, who was so close with D.C. journalists that he at one time called the media his "base." The stories of McCain's "straight talk" on the back of the campaign bus were legendary. Unlike Palin, McCain was a creature of the world the press inhabited. He had spent thirty years in Washington, D.C., advancing his political career alongside many of the nation's top reporters.

Palin came from a different world and quickly cast the press as her enemy. Early on, the media were impressed by Palin's poise during her announcement speech, her gleeful hostility toward Obama at the Republican National Convention, and her ability to weather the media firestorm created by her seventeen-year-old daughter, who was pregnant out of wedlock. But soon the sheen wore off, and the campaign was unable to hide Palin's inexperience and ignorance. An interview with *CBS Evening News* anchor Katie Couric was particularly embarrassing, because of Palin's remarkable response to a softball question about what magazines and newspapers she read:

> COURIC: And when it comes to establishing your worldview, I was curious, what newspapers and magazines did you regularly read before you were tapped for this—to stay informed and to understand the world?
>
> PALIN: I've read most of them again with a great appreciation for the press, for the media—

COURIC: But, like, what ones specifically? I'm curious, that you—

PALIN: Um, all of them, any of them that have been in front of me over all these years.

COURIC: Can you name a few?

PALIN: I have a vast variety of sources where we get our news. Alaska isn't a foreign country, where, it's kind of suggested and it seems like, 'Wow, how could you keep in touch with what the rest of Washington, D.C., may be thinking and doing when you live up there in Alaska?' Believe me, Alaska is like a microcosm of America.[24]

Rich Lowry, writing in the conservative *National Review,* called Palin's performance "dreadful."[25] However, many conservatives disagreed. To them, Couric's ordinary question was another example of the media's "liberal bias." A few weeks later, Palin lashed out at Couric in an interview with Fox News's Carl Cameron:

It's like, man, no matter what you say, you're going to get clobbered. If you choose to answer a question, you're going to get clobbered on the answer. If you choose to try to pivot and go on to another subject that you believe that Americans want to hear about, you get clobbered for that, too . . . But, in those Katie Couric interviews, I did feel that there were a lot of things that she was missing, in terms of an opportunity to ask what a V.P. candidate stands for. What the values are represented in our ticket . . . So, I guess I have to apologize for being a bit annoyed. But, that's also an indication of being outside of that Washington elite, outside of the media elite, also. And just wanting to talk to Americans without the filter and let them know what we stand for.

Most conservatives agreed with Palin: it wasn't her fault; the media were just out to get her. Now that she was back in Alaska, it was more of the same—reporters out to get her and political operatives launching "frivolous" investigations—but there was a whole nation of conservatives eagerly waiting to hear her voice.

Stepping down as governor allowed Palin to share her message with the nation. After a summer of Twitter and Facebook posts, Palin released her memoir, *Going Rogue,* in November 2009. The book was filled with enough falsehoods and distortions to make a Fox News fact-checker blush.

Going Rogue strayed so far from the truth that the Associated Press took the step of fact-checking it, writing:

> Sarah Palin's new book reprises familiar claims from the 2008 presidential campaign that haven't become any truer over time. Ignoring substantial parts of her record if not the facts, she depicts herself as a frugal traveler on the taxpayer's dime, a reformer without ties to powerful interests and a politician roguishly indifferent to high ambition. Palin goes adrift, at times, on more contemporary issues, too. She criticizes President Barack Obama for pushing through a bailout package that actually was achieved by his Republican predecessor George W. Bush— a package she seemed to support at the time.[26]

After receiving the dubious honor of creating PolitiFact's "Lie of the Year," Palin was ready for the logical next step: signing a contract with Fox News. There had always been a certain synergy between Palin and Fox. During the campaign, the network had been a safe place for Palin to voice her opinions without the threat of difficult questions that could trip her up. And in January 2009 she was the first guest to appear on Glenn Beck's Fox show. After another interview in January 2010, Beck commented on his radio program, "The one thing I learned about Sarah Palin is we're very similar in our experiences."[27]

Beck wasn't the only Fox News host with a Palin connection. Greta Van Susteren's husband, John Coale, had, in his own words, "started the PAC" (SarahPAC) and "helped start a legal defense fund for her."[28] While most news organizations would prohibit reporters from covering subjects that represented such conflicts of interest, Fox News executive Bill Shine had a different philosophy. "There are always some sort of, let's just say, unique relationships that happen when you live in Washington," he said. "It's the culture of that town."[29] Now Sarah Palin herself became a Fox employee.

The factually challenged governor and the factually challenged network were a perfect match. Palin could use her perch at Fox News to address the issues of the day and speak to the conservative voters who would be crucial to any future political ambitions. Additionally, Palin could take advantage of the power of Fox's platform. Eric Deggans, the *St. Petersburg Times* media critic, states, "[Fox] gave a platform to the Tea Party it might not have had otherwise, it gave a platform to extremely conservative voices. Sarah Palin is considered credible in part because she has a voice on all of these platforms, and Fox is the biggest one."[30]

In return, Fox got the premier voice of the conservative movement on its payroll and ready to attack—exclusively on Fox—at any moment.

Fox's relationship with Palin and other potential presidential candidates without a doubt would affect its coverage of the upcoming presidential election. George Washington University's Michael Shanahan points out, "Having people who are going to run for president, or who are seriously likely to run for president, as commentators on your television network certainly skews politics and political outcomes."[31]

The Washington press corps still hung on Palin's every word, but for Roger Ailes, the acquisition meant something more. With Newt Gingrich, Karl Rove, and Mike Huckabee already on the payroll, Ailes had locked up almost every prominent political figure on the right (not serving in government), except Mitt Romney. With Palin on the roster, the Republican faithful would be forced to turn to his network if they wanted to hear from their heroes.

In her first appearance as a Fox News contributor, Palin told Bill O'Reilly that Americans were "tuning in to Fox News" because they were tired of "biased journalism."[32]

Palin's first interview with O'Reilly attracted a huge audience, but the ratings success did not last. Her show, *Real American Stories,* generated controversy because it recycled an old interview Fox News had conducted with rapper/actor LL Cool J and promoted it as Palin's work. The controversy didn't compel viewers to tune in. In its debut, 2.073 million people watched the show, 10 percent fewer than the number who watched Van Susteren's show in the same time slot one week earlier.[33]

Palin's ratings were irrelevant. With few exceptions, Palin wouldn't talk to other outlets. Therefore, reporters who wanted to cover Palin were often forced to promote Fox—another victory for Roger Ailes.

Chapter 10

One Million Dollars

News Corporation believes in the power of free markets, and the RGA's pro-business agenda supports our priorities at this most critical time for our economy.

—News Corp. spokesperson Jack Horner

Although Fox's transition was readily apparent to anyone who was paying attention, other media outlets still treated the network like a journalistic enterprise. Since January 2009, Fox News had not only supported the Tea Party movement and relentlessly attacked President Obama and his agenda, but it campaigned for Republicans every chance it got. Over the course of the 2010 election cycle, more than thirty Fox News employees endorsed, raised funds, or campaigned for over three hundred Republican candidates and organizations.

West Virginia congressional candidate David McKinley explained the importance of a Fox News endorsement after Dick Morris visited his district and announced support for his candidacy. "I think people that have followed Fox News and get a lot of their news that way, maybe this is something that they can relate to," McKinley said. "But this man has a national voice that understands this economy."[1]

Other networks prohibited the use of their brand for partisan activities, but Fox News had no such rules. Around the country, Republicans touted their support from Fox personalities. In a promotional video, the Republican Party of Pinellas County in Florida highlighted Morris's network affiliation. Similarly, an invitation to a fund-raising dinner for the Republican Party of Allen County in Indiana described Mike Huckabee as the "Host of 'Huckabee' on FOX News" above a line noting that he was the "Former Governor of Arkansas and Republican Presidential Candidate."[2]

In a press release, Tennessee congressional candidate Chuck Fleischmann boasted that "conservative leader, and Fox News host, Mike Huckabee will be coming to the 3rd District to campaign for Chuck."[3]

Republican Congressman Ron Paul of Texas hyped a barbecue to kick off his reelection, writing on his campaign website: "I am pleased to announce that we will be joined by a good friend of mine, and someone that you will recognize from his regular appearances on Fox News Channel—Judge Andrew Napolitano!"[4]

Florida attorney general candidate Pam Bondi made no secret of the fact that she was flaunting the Fox News brand to win over conservative voters. The *Palm Beach Post* wrote, "Bondi's not shy about dropping the names of her FOX friends. She touts her connections with Hannity and Palin's endorsement at each of her stump speeches and in Ocala delighted the audience with her praise of the network."[5]

The power of these endorsements to help candidates raise funds and establish themselves as serious contenders would not have been missed by Ailes. Decades earlier, candidates sought to use his name to demonstrate the seriousness of their campaigns. "Among my team is Roger Ailes, who, in addition to working on President Reagan's media, successfully handled Westchester County Executive Andrew O'Rourke's media in 1983,"[6] wrote Congressional candidate Joe DioGuardi to potential supporters in the summer of 1984.

That same year, the Bill Hendon for Congress Committee wrote to its supporters, "Our excellent TV and radio ads, done by Ailes Communications, Inc., started airing last week."[7]

Fox News employees worked tirelessly to elect Republicans and sometimes even offered to help them on the air. In October 2009, Glenn Beck was eager to assist Representative Michele Bachmann, asking, "How can I help you raise money?" After Bachmann plugged her campaign website, Beck said, "We should have a fund-raiser for you, Michele."[8]

Newt Gingrich aided the National Republican Congressional Committee and the National Republican Senatorial Committee, raising $14.5 million for the party apparatuses during a joint fund-raiser. Gingrich's own political organization, American Solutions for Winning the Future, raised approximately $25 million to fund its attacks on Democratic candidates.

Mike Huckabee's PAC, which he promoted aggressively on Fox News, raised more than $1.6 million in 2009–10. Sarah Palin's PAC raised more than $4 million, and nobody's endorsement was in higher demand in Republican primaries than the former Alaska governor's. Rick Santorum, who was using his gig as a Fox contributor to revive his political career, raised close to $2.5 million for Republican candidates through his America's Foundation PAC.

Perhaps nobody on the Fox News payroll was more brazen

about his political activities than Dick Morris, who regularly promoted the efforts of his Super PAC for America and other campaign committees on Fox shows.

Karl Rove topped them all, raising more than $50 million through his new groups American Crossroads and Crossroads GPS, and running more than 27,000 ads targeting Democrats around the country. Other than the U.S. Chamber of Commerce and AFSCME, few outside groups could claim that kind of footprint in the 2010 election.

This widespread behavior drew a clear contrast between Fox News and MSNBC, which suspended those who violated the network's rules against partisan activities. The disparity betrayed not only Fox's lack of journalistic standards but also its ideological bias: virtually all of the political work done by the network's contributors benefited the Republican Party.

A result of Fox's hiring its "contributors" was to enable their partisan activities. Political work is often more intensive and less lucrative than the private sector. But Fox contributors are paid handsomely. Their cushy network gigs afforded the Republican heavyweights more time to spend on their political projects, which in turn made them more relevant as on-air contributors.

Tellingly, none of the left-leaning contributors on Fox News were as politically active or influential as their Republican counterparts.

With all of the political work of its employees, it was hardly surprising when Fox's parent corporation itself decided to directly invest in Republican organizations. In mid-August 2010, *Bloomberg News* broke the story that News Corp. had donated $1 million to the Republican Governors Association (RGA), making it the group's largest corporate donor. The RGA's only other seven-figure donation came from libertarian billionaire and notorious right-wing funder David Koch.

While political contributions from large corporations are not unusual, a gift of that size from a publicly traded company was extraordinary. Moreover, such contributions are typically balanced, as corporations attempt to win influence with politicians on both sides of the aisle.

For instance, in 2010 General Electric's PAC, at the time the parent company of MSNBC, gave $30,000 apiece to the Democratic Congressional Campaign Committee, the National Republican Congressional Committee, the Democratic Senatorial Campaign Committee, and the National Republican Senatorial Committee. News Corp. did write checks for several thousand dollars to Democrats, including Senators Harry Reid and Chuck Schumer, but none of the contributions rivaled its gift to the RGA.

Fox's parent company had crossed an ethical boundary. According to Kelly McBride, an expert on media ethics at the Poynter Institute, "[Political contribution by news companies] reinforces the notion that the media organization itself has a political bias. For the consumer who wants non-partisan news, they are less likely to seek out that source." She added, "To be perfectly ethical, they should not make the donation—you are compromising the appearance of fairness."[9]

News Corp. saw no problem with its actions. As spokesman Jack Horner wrote in an e-mail to *Politico* reporter Ben Smith, "News Corporation believes in the power of free markets, and the RGA's pro-business agenda supports our priorities at this most critical time for our economy."[10] News Corp. was no longer afraid to acknowledge its political agenda.

Rupert Murdoch offered a different explanation for the contribution, saying, "It had nothing to do with Fox News. The RGA [gift] was actually [a result of] my friendship with John Kasich."[11] Kasich was the former Fox News host who would go on to be elected governor of Ohio.

In September, *Politico* reported that News Corp. had also donated $1 million to the U.S. Chamber of Commerce. Despite the role of local chapters nationwide, this was not simply a gift to a business-friendly trade association. The Chamber was in the midst of a $72 million negative ad campaign targeting Democrats. The commercials, which were funded in part by Fox News's parent company, included some of the most dishonest ads of the cycle.

For example, an ad running in Arizona attacked Democratic representative Gabrielle Giffords, stating: "But Gabrielle, your change has meant massive job loss. Unemployment has doubled since you took office. You voted with President Obama ninety percent of the time; for government-run health care and an energy bill that would raise taxes and kill more than forty thousand Arizona jobs."[12] These misleading claims distorted Giffords's record and the impact of the policies she supported.

Another ad targeting several endangered Democrats included various falsehoods about health care reform: "Unemployment. Spending. Debt. Washington's broken and [insert name's] policies are making it worse. [Insert name] voted for Nancy Pelosi's trillion-dollar big-government health care. And [insert name] voted to gut Medicare by five hundred billion dollars. More than [insert population/state] seniors face reduced benefits because of [insert name]. Government-run health care, Medicare cuts."[13]

Finally, some of the ads were simply derisive, such as this attack on Florida representative Alan Grayson: "Tired of big-mouth politicians ignoring our big problems? Alan Grayson is the most extreme. [GRAYSON:] 'Die quickly. The Republicans want you to die quickly. Die quickly.' But when it comes to Nancy Pelosi, big barker Grayson turns into a lapdog. Obamacare, job-killing energy taxes, union giveaways. Good boy, Alan."[14]

Between August 1 and Election Day, the Chamber paid to broadcast more than twenty-five thousand political attacks.[15] The magnitude of the Chamber's campaign push was likely part of the reason News Corp. wasn't eager to disclose its gift. When asked if he expected the company's political contributions to become public, Murdoch said, "The RGA we did," but "we didn't expect the other one."[16] Why would a news organization feel the need to keep its giving a secret? At the company's annual meeting in October, Murdoch finally admitted the company's motivation, saying it was "in the interest of the country and of all the shareholders . . . that there be a fair amount of change in Washington."[17]

With the company's blessing, Fox News hosts didn't feel the need to conceal their support for the Chamber, either. In response to accusations that the Chamber was using foreign money to fund its electoral activities, Glenn Beck announced, "I would like to make this the biggest fund-raising day in the Chamber's history." After pledging to contribute ten thousand dollars on his own, Beck said, "So put your money where your mouth is. If you have a dollar, please go to GlennBeck.com or to the U.S. Chamber of Commerce and donate today. Let's break all records. Let's show these people that we—we actually believe in something different than what Barack Obama and Joe Biden are saying."[18]

Beck's efforts paid off. That day, the Chamber received more than $312,000 in online donations, the organization's largest single-day haul ever. The Chamber was appreciative of Beck's support, with spokesman Tom Collamore writing, "We just wanted to say thank you to Mr. Beck and his many loyal listeners who believe in our mission of protecting and advocating for the principles of free enterprise. And for those of you who didn't have a chance to contribute yesterday—or who want to contribute again—just click here."[19]

Glenn Beck's advocacy for the Chamber wasn't his biggest contribution to the Republican campaign effort. His "Restoring Honor" rally on August 28 brought the conservative movement to Washington, D.C., for a pre-election conclave.

He had announced the rally the previous November at a retirement community in Florida. In front of a crowd of approximately twenty thousand, Beck proclaimed:

> Next year, we're holding—I've divided the country up into seven separate regions, and I'm having conventions around the country. They're education conventions. You're going to get up early on a Saturday morning and you're going to go to bed late. And you are going to learn about history, you're going to learn about finance, you're going to learn about community organizing. You're going to learn everything we need to know. If you want to be a politician, we're going to teach you how to be a politician . . . We're going to do seven of these, is the initial thought. And then, come August 28—I would like you to make your plans now—to join me at the feet of Abraham Lincoln in Washington, D.C."[20]

The event was supposed to be part of Beck's "100-year plan" to stop the "ticking time bomb" that progressives had set in motion a century earlier to create a "socialist utopia."[21] From there, it morphed into a fund-raiser for the Special Operations Warrior Foundation. The charity's tax status required the rally to be non-political, so it became about "Restoring Honor."

Throughout the summer, Beck promoted the rally nightly on

his show, proclaiming that it would be a "historic" day, signifying a "turning point in America" that your "children will remember." Beck claimed that in planning the event, he did not recognize that August 28, 2010, was already historic: it was the fortieth anniversary of Dr. Martin Luther King's "I Have a Dream" speech, which was delivered in the same area where Beck intended to hold his event. When he became aware of his oversight, Beck decided to hijack the civil rights hero's message, claiming the scheduling error was "divine providence."[22] Beck went on to assert that his rally would "pick up Martin Luther King's dream that has been distorted and lost and we say, we bought it when he first said it, it is time to restore it and to finish it."[23]

In addition to Beck's flacking, others on Fox News promoted the event as well. In a segment devoted to the Reverend Al Sharpton's criticism of Beck, *Fox & Friends* directed viewers to Beck's website for more information about the rally. Bill O'Reilly also hosted Beck to defend the event's timing and message. It was during this interview that Beck claimed, "I don't think black people own the legacy of Dr. Martin Luther King."[24]

When August 28 finally arrived, it was obvious that Beck's rally was far from nonpartisan. The Tea Party Patriots provided four hundred volunteers to satisfy the National Park Service's requirement for a permit. Additionally, the National Rifle Association, FreedomWorks, Americans for Prosperity, and other conservative groups participated by promoting the rally, holding corresponding events, and even bussing members to Washington, D.C.

Beck also relied on Republican politicians to help pay for the event. Senator Orrin Hatch and Representative Jason Chaffetz, both of Utah, joined Beck at a Salt Lake City fund-raiser in July. Beck also auctioned off a personal tour of the Capitol with Michelle Bachmann, which raised $27,500 toward "Restoring Honor."

Furthermore, Beck was unambiguous about his political motivations. "On August 28, I'm going to Washington, D.C., and I'm going to be at the feet of Abraham Lincoln and facing the Washington Monument," he said. "Everybody tries to fix the capital. I'm telling you, the capital will fix itself if we just stand between Washington and Lincoln and try to be those people. Restore honor in the country, and we'll be fixed."[25]

The actual event was an odd mix of a religious revival, a political protest, and a celebrity parade. On the night before the gathering, Beck announced the creation of the "Black Robe Regiment." He explained the next day, "The Black Robe Regiment is back again today. These 240 men and women of all faiths are standing here today . . . These 240 men and women from all faiths represent thousands of clergy that we couldn't fit into this area that are amongst you now—thousands that have come here to the Mall to stand with America and God. And those thousands that are here represent 180 million people."[26] Beck's regiment primarily consisted of anti-gay members of the clergy, one of whom later publicly fantasized about the president begging for forgiveness for destroying America.

Breaking Beck's pledge to keep politics out of it, featured speaker Sarah Palin took a not-so-thinly veiled shot at the president. Referencing Obama's statement that his election would "fundamentally transform" the country, Palin said, "I must assume that you too, knowing that, no, we must not fundamentally transform America as some would want, we must restore America and restore her honor."

Beck capped the day with an odd prediction. "Somewhere in this crowd—I know it. I have been looking for the next George Washington. I can't find him. I know he is in this crowd. He may be eight years old, but this is the moment. This is the moment that he dedicates his life, that he sees giants around him. And twenty-five years from now, he will come not to this stair, but to those stairs. And he can proclaim, 'I have a new dream.' That must be our goal: to raise the next great monument."[27]

While the blend of religion, politics, and theater was somewhat confusing, the real impact of the event had been bringing tens of thousands of right-wing voters to Washington, D.C., giving conservative advocacy groups such as FreedomWorks a golden opportunity to organize and train activists for the election fight ahead. These would be the activists on the ground that would help the GOP win on Election Day.

After Tea Party darling Christine O'Donnell shocked the political world in September with her primary victory in the Delaware Senate race, Sarah Palin imparted some sage wisdom to the newly minted Republican nominee. Appearing on *The O'Reilly Factor,* Palin advised O'Donnell to "go with her gut, get out there and speak to the American people, speak through Fox News and let the independents who are tuning in to you, let them know what it is that she stands for, the principles behind her positions."[28]

That weekend, O'Donnell canceled interviews on CBS's *Face the Nation* and *Fox News Sunday* at the last minute. Apparently, even Fox host Chris Wallace represented too tough a challenge for the candidate, who opted instead for an interview with Sean Hannity a few days later.

Here are just a handful of the softball questions Hannity posed during the sixteen-minute interview:

- "There seems to be, if you look at Lisa Murkowski, and a lot of other races, Charlie Crist, as an example, I'm almost calling it the sore loser syndrome. Is [Mike Castle], what is your take on him?"

- "You made an appearance [on Bill Maher's *Politically Incorrect*] talking I guess about a boyfriend when you were a teenager . . . saying that you had dabbled into witchcraft. Why don't you explain to people, what was that about?"

- "[Maher is] promising to keep bringing out old tapes, and other people promising to dredge up old comments that you've made, what is your reaction to that?"

- "One of the things I've noticed is that there is, in this campaign, I don't hear any Democrats running on health care, running on the stimulus, their support for Obama, Reid, and Pelosi. So, what are we to make of the attacks against you?"[29]

At one point, Hannity brought up another bit of guidance from Palin, saying, "Governor Sarah Palin tweeted and I thought she gave you some interesting advice and I want to get your take on it. 'Christine O'Donnell's strategy, time's limited, use it to connect with local voters who you'll be serving versus appeasing national media seeking your destruction.' "[30]

"She's absolutely right," O'Donnell replied, explaining that her campaign was taking national media appearances "off the table"[31] to focus on local events. Hannity was the exception. Indeed, even on Fox News, his show was a uniquely welcoming place for Republicans.

O'Donnell's cancelation and subsequent appearance on Hannity raised questions among many in the media. "I would like to see us in a position where candidates don't get to pick and choose which shows they go to," said Kevin Smith, president of the Society of Professional Journalists. "Tough questions have to get asked. I think the voters in Delaware would like to see that."[32]

Christine O'Donnell should never have been the Republican nominee. The Party had a clear shot at capturing the seat previously held by Vice President Joe Biden. Congressman Mike Castle, the former governor who had represented Delaware's at-large district in the House for seventeen years, was the frontrunner in the race. He was a moderate who was popular among independents. Meanwhile, the Democratic Party had failed to recruit a top-tier candidate, such as Joe Biden's son Beau, and nominated a little-known county executive named Chris Coons.

In any other year, Castle probably would have sailed into the Senate, but he was the victim of bad timing. While Delaware was a moderate state, the Republican Party was dominated by Tea Party supporters who didn't care about O'Donnell's lack of experience or her thirty-point loss to Biden two years earlier. They were also willing to ignore her sketchy personal history, which included an IRS lien against her for more than $11,000 in back taxes and allegations that she had used campaign funds for personal benefit.

O'Donnell's victory revealed a fissure in the Fox News family. Karl Rove bemoaned O'Donnell's nomination, saying that "this is not a race we're going to be able to win." This provoked a response from Palin, who retorted on *The O'Reilly Factor*, "Some of these good old boys—and I have nothing against Karl Rove personally, you know he's the expert—but Bill [O'Reilly], some of these folks, they are saying that people like Christine O'Donnell and others, Tea Party Americans, can't win because they don't want them to win, because they know that . . . these folks are gonna shake it up. And they are going to do what's right for America, not necessarily what is right for a political party machine."[33]

In a trend that also played out in Alaska, Palin was able to best Rove in the primary, but the general election would be a different story. Within days, it became obvious that Rove was right.

As the official organs of party support realized her campaign was a lost cause, O'Donnell began using their lack of enthusiasm and financial support to raise money on her own. There was evidence that at least some of the division among Republicans was kabuki theater. Indeed, *The Huffington Post*'s Howard Fineman reported on a strategy meeting at which O'Donnell told Republican officials, "I've got Sean Hannity in my back pocket, and I can go on his show and raise money by attacking you guys."[34] Hannity's program was a platform to raise money from the Tea Party crowd—and to pressure the Republican establishment to fall in line.

Hannity continued helping O'Donnell through Election Day. In a remarkable display of hypocrisy, Hannity attacked the media for paying attention to O'Donnell's "witchcraft" comments because they occurred in the past, despite repeatedly attacking Coons as a "bearded Marxist," which was a reference to the tongue-in-cheek headline of an article Coons wrote in college. Recognizing the value of Hannity's support, O'Donnell praised him as "a leader of the band in saying we have got to stand on our principles."[35]

O'Donnell wasn't the only Republican candidate who understood the benefits of Sean Hannity's support. California Senate candidate Carly Fiorina, Ohio gubernatorial hopeful John Kasich, and a myriad of other Republican candidates went on his show to solicit campaign funds.

Sharron Angle, who was running against Senate Majority Leader Harry Reid, was particularly shameless about using Fox News and Hannity to raise money. On September 10, Angle appeared on Hannity's show to tout her push to raise $1 million by the end of the month. Angle called Hannity—who had previously said that Nevada voters "have a duty"[36] to defeat Reid—a "great American." After Hannity accused Reid of running negative ads and asked how Angle would respond, she said, "Harry Reid has $25 million, and I need a million people with $25 to go to SharronAngle.com."[37]

Angle went so far as to actually attach a monetary value to her appearances on his show. At a Nevada house party she was recorded saying,

> I've been criticized for saying that I like to be friends with the [press]—but here's the deal: when I get a friendly press outlet—not so much the guy that's interviewing me—it's their audience that I'm trying to reach. So, if I can get on Rush Limbaugh, and I can say, "Harry Reid needs twenty-five million dollars. I need a million people to send twenty-five dollars to SharronAngle.com" . . . When I said it on Sean Hannity's television show we made forty thousand dollars before we even got out of the studio in New York. It was just [great]. So that's what I'm really reaching out to is that audience that's had it with Harry, and you can watch that happen when I go on those shows. Go on my website, it starts coming in.[38]

No wonder Republicans loved appearing on Fox News at 9 p.m. Less than fifteen minutes of time could bring in forty thousand dollars, far more efficient than almost any other form of grassroots fundraising.

In an interview with the Christian Broadcasting Network's David Brody, Angle expounded on her strategy, noting that Fox News was the only major network that would let her raise funds on the air:

DAVID BRODY: Not to harp on the point, but when you're on Fox News or talking to more conservative outlets but maybe not going on *Meet the Press* or a *This Week*, those type of news shows, then the perception and the narrative starts to be like you are avoiding those mainstream media outlets.

SHARRON ANGLE: Well, in that audience will they let me say I need 25 dollars from a million people go to Sharron Angle.com send money? Will they let me say that? Will I get a bump on my website and you can watch whenever I go on to a show like that we get an immediate bump. You can see the little spinners. People say, "Oh, I heard that. I am going and I'm going to help Sharron out" because they realize this is a national effort and that I need people from all around the nation. They may not be able to vote for me but they can certainly help.[39]

Hannity not only assisted Angle's fund-raising efforts, but he also helped spread lies about her opponent. In October, he praised one especially dishonest attack ad that claimed Reid "voted to use taxpayer dollars to pay for Viagra for convicted child molesters and sex offenders" as "the template that I think every candidate could use against Democrats."[40] Contrary to Hannity's insistence that it was "in the [health care] bill," the law included no such provision.

And whenever Republican candidates committed a gaffe, Hannity could be counted on to come to the rescue. For instance, after Rand Paul attracted widespread criticism for suggesting that elements of the Civil Rights Act were unconstitutional, Hannity was eager to help him recover. In an interview with the Kentucky Tea Party candidate, Hannity said, "When I first saw the news coverage of it, I said, 'What? He doesn't support the Civil Rights Act?' That's how it was portrayed. And you clearly laid out just the opposite, and it was very clear."[41] It was the media, Hannity claimed, that were at fault and had "tried to purposely distort" Paul's words.

Fox News was not the only venue for Hannity's political efforts. In March, Hannity was the keynote speaker at a fund-raiser for the National Republican Congressional Committee that raised $7 million for the party. According to *Roll Call,* "The dinner is traditionally one of the committee's biggest single sources of fundraising for the year."[42]

Hannity's political activism extended back several years. In 2008, he helped raise money for Rudy Giuliani's presidential campaign. As the *Daily News* reported, "It's no secret that Sean Hannity, the conservative Fox News commentator, has helped to raise Rudy Giuliani's profile—but now he's helped the former mayor raise money, too. In a little noticed event this month, Hannity— co-host of Fox News' *Hannity & Colmes* and host of a popular WABC radio show—introduced the Republican front-runner at a closed-door, $250-per-head fund-raiser Aug. 9 in Cincinnati, campaign officials acknowledge."[43]

Two years earlier, Hannity pledged on his radio show to contribute "the maximum that I can give" to Republican Jeanine Pirro's campaign to unseat Hillary Clinton in New York. He also told his radio audience, "Listen, I'm gonna have to run, but I want people to donate to your campaign."[44]

According to Bill Shine, all of this was okay because "Sean is not a journalist—Sean is a conservative commentator." He added, "Sean doesn't hide, and never has hidden, his beliefs from anyone."[45]

In the final days of the campaign, Sean Hannity continued his all-out efforts to elect Republicans to office. Raising funds, attacking their opponents, and Hannitizing their campaign for Fox News's activist audience. More than any host on Fox, Sean Hannity could be counted on to help Republican candidates in need.

In 2010 there was no Democrat whom Republicans wanted to defeat more than Senate Majority Leader Harry Reid. Even though the party had to nominate their strongest candidate, according to public polling, Tea Party darling Sharron Angle was running ahead. With the economy reeling and anticipation of a Republican wave in November, Reid appeared likely to lose. Fox News was dedicated to making that happen.

A little more than a week before Election Day, the network unveiled an October surprise for Reid. Blared across the home page of FoxNews.com was the headline "Harry Reid Aide Lied to Fed over Sham Marriage." According to the article, "An aide to Senate Majority Leader Harry Reid repeatedly lied to federal immigration and FBI agents and submitted false federal documents to the Department of Homeland Security to cover up her illegal seven-year marriage to a Lebanese national who was the subject of an Oklahoma City Joint Terror Task Force investigation, FoxNews.com has learned."[46]

The story had all the elements of a Fox News scandal: race, terrorism, and a leading Democratic member of Congress. The report, though, was much ado about nothing, at least as it pertained to Reid. The aide was never charged with a crime, and the incident had occurred years before she joined the senator's staff.

Reid's office was quick to respond. In a statement, Reid spokesman Jim Manley said, "Our office was not previously aware of these allegations and, following an internal investigation, the staffer at issue is no longer with our office. The conduct alleged, which took place several years before the staffer worked for Senator Reid, was clearly wrong. But the bottom line remains that this story was a desperation measure by partisan Republicans, who have stooped to slinging mud about junior staffers to score points in the waning days of her campaign."[47]

The banner headline was hypocritical, considering the network had essentially ignored reports that an aide to Louisiana Republican Senator David Vitter had been arrested for attacking his ex-girlfriend with a knife. Not only did Vitter not fire the staffer following his arrest, but he allowed him to continue working on women's issues. The aide resigned only after ABC News reported on the investigation several months later. Fox mentioned the story only once in passing.

The next day, Bret Baier introduced the Reid story, claiming, "The last thing Senate Majority Leader Harry Reid needed was a political scandal as he fights to hold on to his seat from Nevada. But he has one tonight."[48] To keep the "scandal" alive, Fox deceptively cropped Manley's quote to eliminate the sentence making it clear that the incident took place before the staffer in question worked for Reid, as well as the fact that the senator's office had not been aware of her actions. Fox's version of the quote read, "The staffer at issue is no longer with our office . . . the bottom line remains that this story was a desperation measure by partisan Republicans, who have stooped to slinging mud about junior staffers to score points in the waning days of [Sharron Angle's] campaign."[49] Due to the specious nature of the charges, the story died and did not have an impact on the election.

After kicking off election week with a dubious attack on Reid, Fox News began a nonstop promotional campaign for Republican candidates on its airwaves. This final push began on October 26, when *Fox & Friends* interviewed Republican National

Committee chairman Michael Steele from inside the "Fire Pelosi" bus, on which he had been touring the country. "You want a job, then you're going to have to fire Pelosi," Steele proclaimed, "because she's the one who's blocking your ability to get that job."[50]

In the next hour, Fox hosted Kentucky Senate candidate Rand Paul to respond to charges that one of his campaign volunteers had assaulted a female member of the progressive organization MoveOn.org outside of a debate.

Later, Neil Cavuto hosted Florida gubernatorial candidate Rick Scott to attack his Democratic opponent for her debate performance. Glenn Beck hosted Tea Party superstars Jim DeMint, Michele Bachmann, and Jason Chaffetz, complimenting the trio as "good representatives in Washington that are—that are standing there in a lion's den every day" and "good guys that need your help." Doing everything he could for his friends, Beck asked, "What kind of help do you need?"[51]

In prime time, Sean Hannity hosted Michael Steele for his second Fox News appearance of the day. During the interview, Steele insulted President Obama as "not very presidential"[52] and presented Hannity with a "Fire Pelosi" baseball cap and miniature football.

After chatting with Steele, Hannity interviewed Sean Bielat, who was running against Massachusetts congressman Barney Frank. Hannity introduced the segment by playing a clip of Frank saying, "The right-wing media, talk-show hosts decided to target me. I've had Hannity, Limbaugh, Beck, basically saying things about me that weren't true." Hannity responded, "Nice try, Congressman, but I think the reason you are in the toughest race of your career has nothing to do with me or any other talk show host and everything to do with our next guest."[53] Bielat proceeded to ask for contributions and plug his website.

Hannity also included California congressional candidate Nick Popaditch on that night's "Great American Panel." Popaditch used the platform to level attacks on the president, who he claimed was "out there only representing some of the people, and a pretty extreme some."[54]

The only Democratic official who appeared on Fox News that day was Democratic National Committee Chairman Tim Kaine, whose interview on *Fox & Friends* took on a far different tone. Rather than friendly banter, Kaine had to respond to combative statements, such as Gretchen Carlson's claim that "one of the things the voters are upset about with many of the Blue Dogs and Democrats in general was that they voted for health care."[55]

"You could go state to state, any of those closely contested races where the candidate aligned with the Fox ideology got easy access to the airwaves,"[56] said Tom Fiedler, dean of the Boston University College of Communications.

Although some hosts claimed that candidates had turned down requests for interviews, the fact was that Democrats had nothing to gain by appearing on Fox so close to the election. With the network in campaign mode, they wouldn't get a fair shake.

Meanwhile, Fox's attacks became even more outlandish. For instance, President Obama had been using variations of the following metaphor on the campaign trail since August:

> Finally we got this car up on level ground. And, yes, it's a little beat up. It needs to go to the body shop. It's got some dents; it needs a tune-up. But it's pointing in the right direction. And now we've got the Republicans tapping us on the shoulder, saying, "We want the keys back." You can't have the keys back. You don't know how to drive. You can ride with us if you want, but you got to sit in the backseat. We're going to put

middle-class America in the front seat. We're looking out for them.[57]

Suddenly, a week before the election, Fox News heard racial overtones in the president's stump speech. On Fox News, the bad driver in the backseat of the car was a reference to segregation. "Talk about sit in the back of the bus," Sean Hannity commented, wondering aloud what would happen if "a talk show host and a conservative commentator made such a reference."[58] Echoing Hannity, Stuart Varney said, "When I looked at that, being foreign born, I know the association that that was bringing to the public mind . . . It's unpresidential."[59]

On Fox & Friends, Peter Johnson, Jr., described Obama's metaphor as "a peculiar and strange and haunting and really backward reference that we're seeing by the president and what we're really seeing is a reference to the notion of being in the back of the bus, and that's a matter of sad American history, embarrassing American history."[60]

In the afternoon, Monica Crowley stated, "I think after the civil rights movement of the 1950s, riding in the back certainly does have some civil rights and racial overtones to it and you can't tell me that the president of the United States was not aware of that when he said it."[61]

Obama had spoken about Republicans driving the country into a ditch for months without controversy. The quote obviously had nothing to do with the institutional racism of the South. Fox News simply couldn't pass up the chance to stir up racial divisions one last time before the 2010 elections.

On the second day of election week, Fox's lineup skewed even more toward Republicans, as the network didn't host a single Democratic candidate or party official. On America's Newsroom,

Martha MacCallum bent over backward to help California gubernatorial candidate Meg Whitman improve on her performance in
the previous night's debate. "Did you think that was a fair question from Matt Lauer last night?" MacCallum asked, referencing
Lauer's attempt to get the candidates to renounce negative ads.
"Was it fair that he put you both on the spot in that way?" Later in
the interview, MacCallum told Whitman, "I'm going to give you a
do-over right now."[62]

Megyn Kelly talked with a lawyer representing Sharron Angle,
who claimed that Harry Reid would attempt to steal the election.
"We follow the law—try to follow the law scrupulously, and we're
always held to a higher standard," the lawyer claimed. "We get
punished when we get even close to the line; the Democrats skate
very close to the line."[63]

Sean Hannity hosted West Virginia senatorial candidate John
Raese, whom he referred to as a "real Republican," and accused
Democrat Joe Manchin of "running as far away from being a
Democrat and Barack Obama and Harry Reid [as] anybody else
out there."[64]

Greta Van Susteren concluded the evening by giving Meg
Whitman an opportunity to respond to allegations from her former housekeeper, saying that the woman's lawyer, Gloria Allred,
was "ambushing" the gubernatorial candidate.

The next day offered more of the same, as *Fox & Friends* started
by interviewing conservative Senate hopefuls Marco Rubio and Pat
Toomey. On *America's Newsroom,* Bill Hemmer interviewed New
York gubernatorial candidate Carl Paladino. Opening the interview, Hemmer said, "You started your campaign as a guy—you
were mad as hell, and that's what all your yard signs said. And
people are like, 'Yeah, I'm mad as hell, too, Carl.' "[65] Later, Hannity hosted one of his favorite candidates, Christine O'Donnell, as

well as New York congressional candidate Michael Grimm. Van Susteren ended the night with Arizona governor Jan Brewer.

Tim Kaine, Democratic Senate candidate Kendrick Meek, and Republican-turned-Independent Charlie Crist were the only non-Republicans to show up.

In the final twenty-four hours before the election, Fox News hosted thirteen Republican candidates or officials and just three Democrats (along with one candidate from the right-wing Constitution Party). From Carly Fiorina in California to Joe Miller in Alaska to Tom Coburn in Oklahoma, Republican candidates flocked to Fox News, where they were given free rein to promote their campaigns and urge the party faithful to get out the vote. Several of the hosts seemed to cheer on their favorite candidates. During an interview with former Republican congressman Tom Tancredo, who was running for Colorado governor as a member of the conservative Constitution Party, Neil Cavuto gushed, "Tom Tancredo, who was written off, now has the momentum maybe to be the next governor . . . If the polls are right, you're on fire."[66]

Later that evening, Sean Hannity closed his interview with Sharron Angle by expressing excitement about her potential victory. "I think there are a lot of conservatives like myself looking forward to the announcement tomorrow,"[67] he said.

The Democrats who appeared on the network received no such treatment. Maryland Congressman Chris Van Hollen was asked by Bill Hemmer how Democrats would "work with Tea Party candidates that—who will no doubt be swept into office tomorrow" if "you lose the House and you come razor thin to even hanging on in the Senate."[68]

There was no balance. The line between news and opinion did not matter. Fox News had chosen its team and was rooting them on. Hope was high as the voting began. Now all that was left was the counting. For two years, Fox had worked toward this moment. It had served as the communications hub of the Republican Party, contributed more than two million dollars and raised tens of millions more, and used the Tea Parties to build a movement that supplied bodies for the Republican field operation. Now it was time to see the fruits of that labor materialize.

Part IV

The Aftermath

Chapter 11

The Puppet Master

Without exception, Fox has become a political player. It is not a news source, it is a political player.

—Tim McGuire, Arizona State University School of Journalism

Republicans won sixty-three seats in the House of Representatives, the largest gain by any party since 1948, capturing the chamber and elevating John Boehner to Speaker. In the Senate, Republicans gained six seats, allowing Democrats to maintain a slim majority. Fox's role in this victory did not go unnoticed. The night after the election, *Fox News Sunday* host Chris Wallace strode onto the set of *The Daily Show* and was greeted by Jon Stewart: "Congratulations to your team at Fox. Great job. You guys did it, you worked hard and you pulled it off. Terrific."

"You mean the fact that we had the highest ratings," Wallace answered. "More ratings than CNN and MSNBC combined."

Stewart interrupted, "No, no, no, no, no, retaking control of the House of Representatives. You did it. It was not an easy job, you know. This was a two-year plan."[1]

In the two days following the election, Fox News hosted a televised victory party featuring more than twenty-nine interviews with Republican candidates and other party officials celebrating their success. However, under this veneer of jubilation, a new battle had begun: the 2012 Fox primary.

In 2010, all the elements of the Republican Party united under a single roof, advocating for the defeat of Democrats. With that battle won, Republicans would now fight for the soul of their own party. This squabbling pitted the establishment, led by Karl Rove, against the loud voices of the Tea Party movement, best personified by Sarah Palin.

Establishment Republicans, while elated about Republican gains in the House, were insistent that Palin and her wing of the party had cost Republicans control of the Senate and the single biggest electoral prize—unseating Senate Majority Leader Harry Reid, who not only won reelection but maintained control of his chamber.

Rove had a point. Sue Lowden, the establishment candidate, had lost the Republican primary thanks to a combination of her own missteps—such as suggesting Nevadans could barter chickens in exchange for health care—and the rising popularity of Tea Party favorite Sharron Angle.

The state was the recession's ground zero. Unemployment remained in the double digits, and a few miles from the Las Vegas strip whole developments stood empty, either never occupied or foreclosed on by lenders. Some strip malls in Clark County were offering free rent to anyone willing to open up a business. As a result, Harry Reid's approval rating was mired in the low forties or worse.

However, Sharron Angle seemed determined to lose the election, committing gaffe after gaffe. Despite her popularity among conservative diehards, Angle clearly was not ready for prime time.

Ultimately, though he trailed in nearly every public poll, Harry Reid ended up winning the election by five percentage points.

In Delaware, what would have been almost a sure victory for Republican Mike Castle ended with Chris Coons defeating Christine O'Donnell by more than sixteen points. Sarah Palin's support and Sean Hannity's barrage of promotion could not persuade voters in the moderate state to send O'Donnell to the Senate.

In Colorado, Tea Party favorite Ken Buck lost to appointed Senator Michael Bennet by just under 1 percent of the vote. Buck had defeated Lieutenant Governor Jane Norton in the Republican primary. Norton, having already won a statewide election, would have been a favorite to win the seat.

Some argued that these seats—and the extra resources the national party and allied groups were forced to divert from other competitive races to contest them—cost Republicans control of the Senate. In the final weeks before the election, this feud spilled out into the open.

Just days before voters headed to the polls, Karl Rove attacked fellow Fox News contributor Sarah Palin in *The Daily Telegraph,* implying the reality show she had filmed was unpresidential.[2] Palin fired back, asking on Greta Van Susteren's show why Rove felt "so threatened and so paranoid?"[3]

The fighting among Fox News contributors foreshadowed what was to come. The network had positioned itself at the center of the battle for the future of the Republican Party. As *Politico* noted in September 2010, "With the exception of Mitt Romney, Fox now has deals with every major potential Republican presidential candidate not currently in elected office."[4]

There was no medium better equipped to reach Republican primary voters than Fox News. Its audience was comprised of the most active members of the conservative base, who not only would provide votes but were also a proven source of grassroots contributions and boots on the ground. Winning over viewers in the Fox primary was perhaps as important as reaching out to voters in Iowa, New Hampshire, and South Carolina.

Potential candidates employed by the network received more than eighty-five hours of airtime in 2010, often fielding softball questions from their colleagues. An aide to one of those who wanted to take on the president in 2012, but did not work for the network, told a Fox employee, "I wish we could get that much airtime, but, oh yeah, we don't get a paycheck."[5]

Mike Huckabee, who hosted his own show, led the pack with forty-eight hours on the air, followed by Sarah Palin, who spent fourteen hours on the network in 2010. Newt Gingrich was on for nearly twelve hours, followed by Rick Santorum, who spent six hours talking directly to Republican primary voters on the network. The value of being a "Fox News Contributor" was far greater for Newt Gingrich and Rick Santorum than others. Sarah Palin and Mike Huckabee, as the Republican Party's vice presidential nominee and the winner of the 2008 Iowa caucus respectively, were already assumed to be major figures in the party. Newt Gingrich and Rick Santorum had been outside of electoral politics for years. Instead of being forgotten, they had access to the Republican base with regular appearances on Fox.

Even John Bolton, the ambassador to the United Nations under George W. Bush, suggested he might run. "I am thinking about it," Bolton told Fox Business Network's Stuart Varney, "because I think legitimate issues of national security should be more at the center of the national debate than they have been for the last two years."[6] Bolton spent just under six hours on Fox promoting himself, while receiving a healthy paycheck for his services.

The value of airtime can be tabulated using data from the Cam-

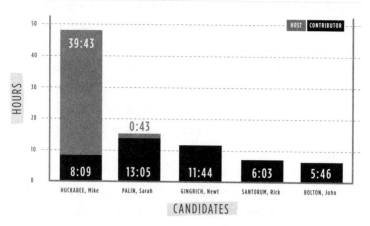

TOTAL AIR TIME ON FOX NEWS FOR POTENTIAL REPUBLICAN CANDIDATES WHO ARE ALSO FOX NEWS CONTRIBUTORS, 1/1/2010 - 12/31/2010

paign Media Advertising Group (CMAG). The time on the network these prospective candidates received from Fox was valued at more than $54 million. As Media Matters noted in a report, "Advertisers would have spent about $31 million for Huckabee's time for the entire year. Gingrich's and Palin's time each would

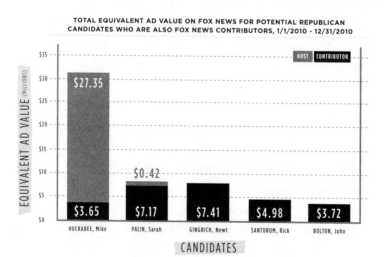

TOTAL EQUIVALENT AD VALUE ON FOX NEWS FOR POTENTIAL REPUBLICAN CANDIDATES WHO ARE ALSO FOX NEWS CONTRIBUTORS, 1/1/2010 - 12/31/2010

have cost advertisers about $7.5 million each for the entire year. Santorum's estimated ad-value equivalency for the year comes to almost $5 million, while Bolton's is approximately $3.7 million."[7]

Fox News intended to take full advantage of its privileged position as the primary employer of the potential Republican field. Partnering with the South Carolina Republican Party, the network announced it would host the first debate of the 2012 primary season in May 2011. Now all it needed was for candidates to enter the race.

In the 2008 election, candidates from both parties had formed exploratory committees by late winter of the previous year. However, even with Barack Obama at a weak point in his presidency, Republicans hesitated to jump in. As the winter turned to spring, not a single major candidate had announced his or her intention to run.

Following the midterm election, there were countless questions to be answered: Would Obama be able to govern with Republicans in control of the House? Would health care reform be repealed? What investigations would Republican committee chairmen with newly granted subpoena power undertake? What was the impact on the president's reelection chances?

To Glenn Beck, though, there were much more important issues to cover. On election night, he was busy promoting his special about George Soros, which would air one week later. He referred to the billionaire philanthropist as a "puppet master" and questioned his Jewish identity.

Beck's rhetoric, while not overtly bigoted, was rooted in deeply anti-Semitic tracts such as the *Protocols of the Elders of Zion,* an

early-twentieth-century text proposing conspiracy theories that center on Jewish plots to control the world. Additionally he had established a pattern of using the words of anti-Semites to attack Soros and other progressives.

For example, a month earlier, he told his audience, "Many, including the Malaysian prime minister, believe it was billionaire speculator George Soros who helped trigger the [Southeast Asian] economic meltdown."[8]

The statement Beck was referring to was actually an anti-Semitic diatribe by the prime minister, who said, "We do not want to say that this is a plot by the Jews, but in reality it is a Jew who triggered the currency plunge, and coincidentally Soros is a Jew. It is also a coincidence that the Malaysians are mostly Muslim."[9]

Beck's "special" included the recitation of a decades-old lie that Soros had collaborated with the Nazis during World War II. According to Beck, Soros "had to help the government confiscate the lands of his fellow Jewish friends and neighbors."[10]

As a fourteen-year-old boy in occupied Hungary, Soros was hidden from the Nazis by a Christian family. The man hiding Soros was assigned to go inventory the estate of a wealthy Jewish family and brought Soros along to protect him. Soros himself was never part of any property confiscation.

Jewish leaders roundly criticized these attacks. Abe Foxman, director of the Anti-Defamation League, which had recently honored Rupert Murdoch at a banquet in New York, told *Jewish Week,* "Look, I spit on Jews when I was six years old . . . Does that make me an anti-Semite?" The Holocaust, Foxman explained, "is so sensitive that I'm not even sure Holocaust survivors themselves are willing to make such judgments." He continued, "For a political commentator or entertainer to have the audacity to say, there's a Jewish boy sending Jews to death camps, that's horrific. It's totally off limits and over the top."[11]

In January 2011, the attempted assassination of Representative Gabrielle Giffords and the murder of six others outside a strip mall in Arizona sent shock waves through the political world. People on all sides of the political spectrum called for the violent rhetoric that had emerged the previous summer to be toned down. Even Roger Ailes had had enough. In an interview two days after the shooting, Ailes told hip-hop mogul Russell Simmons that his message to Fox employees was, "Shut up, tone it down, make your argument intellectually."[12] Apparently, the memo was not received.

Three days after the tragedy, Glenn Beck used his Fox News show to scare the network's audience about the political implications of the Arizona shooting. He falsely claimed politicians were "pushing a ban on certain symbols and words, a ban on guns, a ban on talk radio."[13] This baseless fear of the Obama administration's taking away people's guns had already inspired Richard Poplawski, who allegedly killed three police officers in Pittsburgh, but Beck defied his boss's wishes and went on the attack.

Within hours of the shooting, online journalists dug up an image Sarah Palin had promoted before the election on her political action committee website—a map of the United States with what looked like gun sights on targeted congressional districts. One of them was aimed squarely at the district represented by Gabrielle Giffords.

Palin aide Rebecca Mansour insisted the crosshairs were actually surveyor's marks, but Palin herself had contradicted Man-

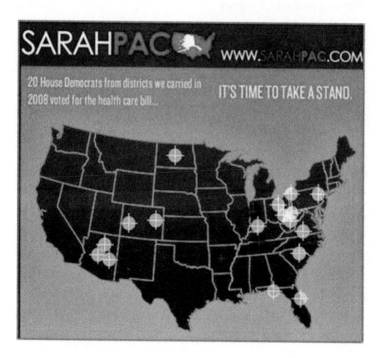

@SarahPalinUSA
Sarah Palin

Remember months ago "bullseye" icon
used 2 target the 20 Obamacare-lovin'
incumbent seats? We won 18 out of 20
(90% success rate;T'aint bad)

4 Nov via Twitter for BlackBerry®   ☆ Favorite ⇄ Retweet ↰ Reply

Retweeted by scopedbylarry and 100+ others

sour's claim two days after the midterm election, writing on
Twitter: "Remember months ago 'bullseye' icon used 2 target
the 20 Obamacare-lovin' incumbent seats? We won 18 out of 20
(90% success rate;T'aint bad)."[14]

Palin wanted to respond to her critics aggressively, but Roger
Ailes had other ideas. "Lie low," the network chief advised her.
"If you want to respond later, fine, but do not interfere with the
memorial service."[15]

Palin ignored Ailes's advice, and her response only made matters worse. In a video message posted on her Facebook page, Palin
said, "Especially within hours of a tragedy unfolding, journalists
and pundits should not manufacture a blood libel that serves only
to incite the very hatred and violence they purport to condemn.
That is reprehensible."[16]

The term "blood libel" referred to the anti-Semitic myth from
the Middle Ages that European Jews ritualistically murdered
Christian children in order to use their blood in religious ceremo-
nies. Comparing criticism of her actions, regardless of its fairness,
to historic religious persecution was outrageous and put Palin at
the center of another controversy. Ailes was livid. According to

one Republican close to him, he now believes "Palin is an idiot. He thinks she's stupid. He helped boost her up. People like Sarah Palin haven't elevated the conservative movement."[17]

As the spring began, protests erupted in Tunisia and Egypt. After the fall of Egyptian president Hosni Mubarak, they continued to spread throughout the Middle East. While many Americans across the political spectrum cheered the democracy movements in the Arab world, Glenn Beck had a different take. He warned his audience of "a Muslim caliphate that [would control] the Mideast and parts of Europe."[18]

Many experts and pundits in conservative foreign policy circles had been waiting their entire careers for the dictatorships of the Middle East to be overthrown and, they hoped, be replaced with pro-Western democracies. Beck's conspiracy theory was the proverbial straw that broke the camel's back. Conservatives who had been fearful of criticizing Beck suddenly came out in full force against the host.

Fox News contributor Bill Kristol led the charge, writing in *The Weekly Standard,* "[Beck] brings to mind no one so much as Robert Welch and the John Birch Society. He's marginalizing himself, just as his predecessors did back in the early 1960s."[19]

But it wasn't only conservative commentators who recognized the problem with Beck. "I've heard, from more than a couple of conservative sources," wrote Joe Klein on *Time* magazine's *Swampland* blog, "that prominent Republicans have approached Rupert Murdoch and Roger Ailes about the potential embarrassment that the paranoid-messianic rodeo clown may bring upon their brand."[20]

Beck's time at Fox News was coming to an end. Down almost one million viewers since his peak, and faced with a successful advertiser boycott that culminated in more than three hundred sponsors pulling their ads, Beck's show had lost its value to the network. In late March, Joel Cheatwood, the executive who brought Beck to Fox, foreshadowed what was coming when it was leaked that he was leaving the network to join Beck's company, Mercury Radio Arts. By the first week in April, Fox and Beck announced that his daily show would end. Roger Ailes told the press, "Glenn Beck is a powerful communicator, a creative entrepreneur and a true success by anybody's standards. I look forward to continuing to work with him."[21]

Ailes later told reporters, "Half of the headlines say he's been canceled, the other half say he quit. We're pretty happy with both of them."[22]

In March, mainstream Republican candidates still seemed loath to enter the race against President Obama. To the party's detriment, this allowed possible fringe candidates to grab the spotlight. Donald Trump, who had flirted with running for president before, made another go at it. As part of his efforts to curry favor with the conservative base, the *Celebrity Apprentice* host repeatedly questioned the authenticity of Barack Obama's birth certificate.

The birther issue had been virtually absent from Fox News's airwaves in 2009 and 2010. When the issue was covered, Fox hosts mocked the fringe political actors espousing conspiracy theories. Bill O'Reilly said "those demanding [Obama's birth certificate] look unhinged,"[23] and Glenn Beck called them "idiots."[24] Mike Huckabee was forced to backpedal after suggesting that Obama grew up in Kenya during an appearance on a New York radio show.

Trump, however, embraced birtherism, and Fox enthusiastically followed. Broadcasting the real estate mogul's pronouncements, the network devoted fifty-two segments to the subject of the president's birthplace in March and April. While other networks also covered Trump's statements, Fox News made barely any effort to report the truth. In forty-four of the fifty-two segments, the false charges went completely unchallenged.[25]

Sarah Palin applauded Trump, saying, "more power to him."[26] Sean Hannity cheered Trump on in segment after segment, making statements such as, "Do I think he was [born in America]? Yes. Do I think this is odd that they won't produce the birth certificate? It's beginning to get odd to me."[27] As *The New York Times* incredulously reported, "The so-called birther controversy stubbornly refuses to go away" and "now appears to have staying power as the political season lurches toward 2012."[28]

As Alex S. Jones, director of the Shorenstein Center at Harvard University, noted, "Fox is more unrelentingly, especially in its prime time, hyper politics. It is stridently anti-Obama, it kept the birther story alive."[29]

At the end of April, Barack Obama decided to end the "silliness" by asking the state of Hawaii to release his long-form birth certificate, which it did.

A few weeks later, NBC announced its fall lineup, which included *Celebrity Apprentice*. As a result, Trump was forced to announce he would not run for president. The reality host had snookered the media into covering his every word for weeks while he promoted his television show. Fox merely took advantage of the situation to air segment after segment questioning Barack Obama's birth certificate.

.   .   .

As the Fox debate in South Carolina neared, a robust Republican field had yet to emerge. For several potential competitors, one factor weighed heavily on their minds. As Mike Huckabee told *Fox News Sunday* host Chris Wallace in November 2009, "The reason I wouldn't [run] is because this Fox gig I've got right now, Chris, is really, really wonderful." Huckabee added, "A lot of it depends on how the elections turn out next year and whether Roger Ailes continues to like my show on the weekends."[30] Huckabee was reportedly earning $500,000 per year to appear on the network. Potential candidates such as Newt Gingrich and Rick Santorum were also receiving significant amounts. Jumping into the presidential race meant giving up these lucrative contracts.

Toward the end of February, Fox began taking action. Bill Shine and other executives made calls to potential candidates to inquire if they were running. In some cases, they scheduled individual meetings to have the conversation. While Sarah Palin was on the outs in Roger Ailes's eyes, she had not taken any affirmative steps toward a run.

This was not the case for Newt Gingrich, whose contract was suspended by the network in early March. "We can't have Speaker Gingrich on our payroll while he is in the midst of an exploratory committee to see if he's going to run for office," said Fox vice president of legal and business affairs Dianne Brandi. "It's a clear conflict."[31] Rick Santorum had committed to participating in the first Fox News debate, a clear sign he was running, and the network suspended his contract as well. Huckabee was given leeway and permitted to continue broadcasting his show while he made up his mind.

By the end of April, it was evident that Fox's first debate would turn out to be a dud. Other than former Minnesota Governor Tim Pawlenty, whose campaign never caught fire and folded in

August, none of the GOP's top-tier talent would participate. Pawlenty was joined onstage by Santorum, Texas representative Ron Paul, former New Mexico governor Gary Johnson, and former Godfather's Pizza CEO Herman Cain, who at the time was at the bottom of the GOP pack. On the day of the debate, Fox formally terminated its agreements with Gingrich and Santorum.

Huckabee ultimately chose his network deal over the chance to compete for the presidency, announcing his decision on the May 14 episode of his show on Fox News. Even some of Huckabee's closest advisers were surprised by the decision.

Feeling burned by Palin, Ailes had no candidate to get behind. Published reports indicated that every mainstream Republican candidate had spoken with Ailes, but he could not find a single one to support. Each had potential political or ideological weaknesses that prevented Ailes from backing his or her campaign.

Ever the strategist, he even tried to recruit a favorite candidate into the race. Gabriel Sherman reported in *New York* magazine, "A few months ago, Ailes called Chris Christie and encouraged him to jump into the race. Last summer, he'd invited Christie to dinner at his upstate compound along with Rush Limbaugh, and like much of the GOP Establishment, he fell hard for Christie."[32] But Christie rejected Ailes's advances, preferring to stay in New Jersey and out of the 2012 election.

Nevertheless, Fox News would play a defining role in the Republican primary. "They have taken a shot at manipulating the 2012 election by supporting certain candidates, having party regulars like Karl Rove as regulars, commentators," says Tim McGuire, Frank Russell Chair for the business of journalism at Arizona State University's Walter Cronkite School of Journalism and Mass Communication. "Without exception, Fox has become a political player. It is not a news source, it is a political player."[33]

There was no venue on any medium that provided more direct access to conservative voters. If a trip on Sean Hannity's show was worth $40,000 to a Senate candidate in 2010, access to the network could be worth millions in a Republican primary. No matter who ran for the GOP nomination in 2012, they would have to go through Roger Ailes.

Epilogue

These revelations show a culture run amuck within News Corp. and a board that provides no effective review or oversight.

—from News Corp. shareholder lawsuit

On June 2, Fox announced that Glenn Beck's show would conclude at the end of that month. In May, his audience had declined 30 percent among viewers ages twenty-five to fifty-four, a critical advertiser demographic, and 15 percent overall.[1] A roundtable discussion show called *The Five,* featuring a rotating cast of four conservatives and a token liberal, would now occupy the 5 p.m. time slot.

As Glenn Beck's last week on the network began, Fox launched an aggressive campaign against Media Matters. It was not the first time Fox's hosts had singled us out for attack. As early as December 2004, just months after our founding, Bill O'Reilly called us "character assassins,"[2] and, more recently, Glenn Beck had made us the focus of multiple episodes of his program. However, this latest attack took the shape of a coordinated campaign across numerous shows, each pushing its audience to file complaints against Media Matters with the Internal Revenue Service in the hope that we would be stripped of our nonprofit tax status.

The campaign began with a June 22 column in *The Washington Times* by former White House counsel to George H. W. Bush C. Boyden Gray, a former Fox contributor and board member of the Tea Party group FreedomWorks.

In his column, Gray argued that Media Matters should have its tax-exempt status stripped for two reasons. "First," he wrote, "IRS rulings make clear that attacks on individuals, statements of positions that are unsupported by facts, and use of inflammatory language and other distortions will cost an organization its tax-free status. Second," he continued, "in declaring 'guerrilla warfare' on Fox as the 'leader' and 'mouthpiece' of the Republican Party and in developing a sophisticated Democratic-leaning media training boot camp, [Media Matters] has transformed itself into an aggressive advocate for Democratic and progressive causes and thus produced a second deviation from exempt educational activities."[3] Gray's charges were wholly without merit. Media Matters has always ensured that our behavior remains well within the legal confines set by the IRS, and we have never received the slightest hint the agency was concerned with our efforts.

After witnessing and documenting coordinated attacks by Fox on ACORN, Planned Parenthood, Van Jones, and numerous other progressives, we knew this was the beginning of a campaign against Media Matters. Sure enough, the next night Bill O'Reilly interviewed Gray during the "Impact" segment of his show. By July 10, two and a half weeks later, Fox News had run thirty-five segments on Media Matters's tax status and actively encouraged its viewers to file complaints with the IRS. Prominent links topping the Fox Nation website directed users to a pre-filled complaint form, and *Fox & Friends* dedicated several segments to interviewing viewers who filed complaints with the IRS. Additional segments were run on the Fox Business network, and links to the stories remained atop Fox Nation for nearly a month. As a point of comparison, Fox ran just six segments and thirteen news briefs on New York State's historic decision that week to allow same-sex marriage.[4]

As the campaign against Media Matters continued, the segments Fox ran became increasingly personal in nature. On July 5, Steve Doocy asked on *Fox & Friends,* "What goes on in [David Brock's] head?" He then brought on psychiatrist and Glenn Beck coauthor Dr. Keith Ablow to speculate. Brock, he diagnosed, is "full of self-hatred, which he then projects on the world around him in order to get love. So he's got to have somebody to hate because he thinks that's the way—the best way to galvanize the love in his direction . . . There's very sexual connotations here, too," Ablow continued. "Taking the father figure down. This is a guy who was adopted. I don't know whether he has deep-seated feelings about whether he wasn't loved. He was given up for adoption."[5] The segment concluded with Ablow stating that David was a "very dangerous man."[6]

That same day on *Fox & Friends,* Brian Kilmeade and Juan Williams went on the attack in a segment in which they discussed, "Who's this guy Ari?"

Williams informed the audience, "He has a political background. He has no background in journalism . . . This is a guy who comes from the world of politics working for the likes of Al Gore and other top Democratic operatives and the whole idea of negative research, negative commercials. Apparently, that's where his mind-set is centered. For example, he brags about trying to disrupt Fox's business interests."[7] While they spoke, the chyron read, "ARI RABIN-HAVT USES YOUR $ TO TARGET FOX NEWS."

As the attack took shape, it began to look like another run through the Fox Cycle:

Step 1: Make an inaccurate charge designed to make progressives look bad:

Former Fox News consultant and current FreedomWorks Foundation board cochairman C. Boyden Gray publishes a column in The Washington Times *suggesting Media Matters should lose its tax status.*

Step 2: Devote disproportionate coverage to the story.

In three weeks, Fox News runs more than thirty-five segments on the story.

Step 3: Attack mainstream journalistic outlets for ignoring the "story."

In the third week of coverage, Fox repeatedly asked on air why only a single mainstream outlet reported on the story.

Because we could identify the Fox Cycle, we were able to put the brakes on it, ensuring it would not reach Steps 4 and 5, where the real damage is done. We were aided by the fact that Fox could not gain any traction for its story, because the law is clearly on our side. In IRS filings we inform the agency that Media Matters is "dedicated to comprehensively monitoring, analyzing, and correcting conservative misinformation in the U.S. Media."[8] Similarly, Brent Bozell's Media Research Center, which has been operating since 1987, maintains its 501c3 status. As Marcus Owens, a partner at the law firm Caplin & Drysdale and former director of the Exempt Organizations Division of the IRS, succinctly put it to *Politico* in its article on Fox's non-story: "I'm afraid Fox loses this round."[9]

Undeterred by the facts, Fox continued its campaign well into August. The network invested resources into running a several-thousand-word, three-part series on the Fox Business website.

As we write this final chapter, no government entity has contacted us about any investigation into our tax status, nor have we been officially informed by the IRS of any complaints filed against us. In fact, the only complaints we've seen are a cover page faxed to us by Fox News's chief Washington correspondent, James Rosen, who was seeking comment, and C. Boyden Gray's complaint, which was posted by *Washington Post* media blogger Eric Wemple in early August.

Far from muzzling our efforts, Fox's campaign was a clear signal that our work struck a nerve at the organization. If anything, we would press even harder to advocate for better journalistic practices by the network.

As Fox launched its attacks on Media Matters, its parent company, News Corporation, began to face perhaps the largest and most damning media scandal in history. Editors and reporters at *News of the World,* a 160-year-old British tabloid owned by News Corp., had been caught hacking into the voice mails of possibly thousands of individuals to further coverage on their gossip pages. As the sordid and shocking story unfolded, Fox News's incurious and at times scant coverage of this major news story raised further questions about its objectivity and trustworthiness as a news organization.

The scandal began in 2005, when *News of the World* reported that ITV political editor Tom Bradby had lent Prince William some video-editing equipment. The seemingly innocuous report read, "If ITN do a stocktake on their portable editing suites this week, they might notice they're one down. That's because their pin-up political editor Tom Bradby has lent it to close pal Prince William so he can edit together all his gap year videos and DVDs into one very posh home movie."[10]

Since few people knew of the arrangement between the Prince and Bradby, it immediately aroused William's suspicion. Bradby told William, "When I was royal correspondent, [phone hacking] was kind of an open secret and I remember having chats with tabloid hacks about how phone hacking is, you know, kind of rife."[11] An earlier story about a knee injury suffered by the prince also raised suspicions.

Shocked by the news, William's office complained to Scotland Yard, which launched an investigation into the incident. In January 2007, *News of the World*'s royal editor and Glenn Mulcaire, a private investigator hired by the paper, both pleaded guilty to hacking the voice mails of members of the royal family. Each was sentenced to several months in prison. That month, *News of the World* editor Andy Coulson also resigned. Less than six months later, he was named communications director for the Conservative Party.

In court, Mulcaire also confessed that the hacking went well beyond members of the British royal family and included model Elle Macpherson and Member of Parliament Simon Hughes.

While the story faded from the headlines, a flurry of civil lawsuits kept the scandal alive. *Guardian* reporter Nick Davies spent nearly three years working on the case. The results of his dogged reporting were a series of investigative pieces that blew the case back into the mainstream. Davies explained his interest in the story, telling Media Matters, "Not only were there a lot of journalists doing a lot of illegal things within the Murdoch organization, the former editor [of the paper in question] happened to have gone to work for the man about to become the prime minister. Instantly, the significance of the story is raised a level." Davies continued, "And then you have the fact that the largest police force in the country clearly failed to investigate, or inform all of the victims. And I found out early on that one of the hacking victims was the deputy prime minister—a man who knew about economic and military secrets."

In April 2011, News Corp. began to settle cases involving phone hacking, most prominently with actress Sienna Miller. However, that did not stop the story from expanding further.

The story finally began to reach a tipping point after Davies reported in *The Guardian* that *News of the World* "illegally targeted the missing schoolgirl Milly Dowler and her family in March 2002, interfering with police inquiries into her disappearance."[12] Most shockingly, Davies discovered that voice mails on the victim's phone "were deleted by journalists in the first few days after Milly's disappearance in order to free up space for more messages. As a result friends and relatives of Milly concluded wrongly that she might still be alive. Police feared evidence may have been destroyed."[13]

Prior to the publication of the Milly Dowler story, the known victims of these invasions of privacy were limited to members of the British elite, the royal family, Members of Parliament, and sports and movie stars. In the Dowlers' case, not only had the phone of a non-public figure been hacked, but *News of the World* had committed a grievous injustice against the murder victim's family. Because messages were being deleted by *News of the World* employees, the murdered girl's parents held out hope their daughter was still alive.

After Davies's story on the Dowlers, reports about other potential victims of phone hacking began to emerge, including the relatives of British troops killed in Iraq and Afghanistan, individuals murdered in the bombings of the London Underground in 2005, and, perhaps most shockingly, the mother of a girl who had been murdered by a pedophile. The grieving parent, Sara Payne, was embraced by *News of the World* editor Rebekah Brooks, who advocated for "Sarah's Law," named after Payne's daughter, which allowed parent-controlled access to the U.K.'s registry of sex offenders.

Evidence mounted that the tabloid potentially targeted almost "3,870 names, 5,000 landline numbers and 4,000 mobile numbers."[14] This was an invasion of privacy on a massive level, and as more and more details of this widespread illegal activity came out, it became clear that the misbehavior was not isolated to a few bad apples—the core of *News of the World* was rotten. And it came from a culture that was created by News Corp.'s CEO himself, one that pushed for shock headlines and ever-more-sensational stories that would lead to higher sales, unbound by journalistic ethics or common decency. As *The New York Times* reported, "Mr. Murdoch expects his tabloids to beat the competition with aggressive, intrusive reporting that results in splashy exclusives that expose sexual misbehavior or debunk the establishment line." The *Times* continued, "It is this expectation, former editors and reporters say, that has pushed his tabloids' editors into ever more adventurous news gathering practices."[15]

By early July, the pressure reached a boiling point for News Corp. For the first time, the phone-hacking scandal was being covered in both the U.K. and U.S. media. This accelerated the pace of the story. News Corp. announced on July 7 that the following Sunday would be the last edition of *News of the World,* ending the paper's storied 160-year history.

Andy Coulson, who resigned as British prime minister David Cameron's spokesman in January because of his ties to the scandal, was arrested on July 8. Clive Goodman, who had already spent time in prison, was arrested again, this time for payments made to the police in connection with the phone hacking stories.

When the scandal broke, Rupert Murdoch had been in the process of trying to acquire full ownership of the British satellite television service BSkyB. After nearly a year fighting to gain regulatory approval, News Corp. was on the verge of closing the deal.

A potential parliamentary investigation forced News Corp. to formally withdraw its bid for the company on July 13. Phone hacking would have serious implications for the rest of the Murdoch empire. In August, the New York Department of Education canceled a $27 million contract with News Corp. State controller Thomas DiNapoli wrote, "In light of the significant ongoing investigations and continuing revelations with respect to News Corp., we are returning the contract with Wireless Generation unapproved."[16]

As the walls crumbled around him, Rupert Murdoch did not seem to take the scandal seriously. In an interview with *The Wall Street Journal*, the CEO claimed that News Corp. "handled the crisis 'extremely well in every way possible,' making just 'minor mistakes.' "[17]

The next day, *Wall Street Journal* publisher Les Hinton resigned from the paper and as CEO of Dow Jones over his role in covering up the scandal. Hinton previously was chairman of News International and, according to *The Guardian,* had "been accused of giving misleading information to parliament on two occasions, in 2007 and 2009, by saying there was no evidence of widespread malpractice within the company."[18]

That same day, Rebekah Brooks, who some had said Murdoch closed down *News of the World* to save, resigned as chief executive of News International.

That weekend, News Corp. ran an advertisement in every

major newspaper in the U.K. with the headline "We are sorry." A day later, Brooks was arrested for her role in the scandal. Despite this fact, the *Telegraph* reported that "she remains on the company payroll."[19]

On July 19, Rupert Murdoch and his son James, who ran the subsidiary of News Corp. that owned *News of the World* and approved settlement claims related to the hacking, were called to testify before Parliament. Rupert Murdoch called it "the most humble day of my life."[20] The father-son testimony did little to stem the scandal, as criminal probes widened and more were arrested in the U.K. The FBI opened an investigation to determine if any U.S. laws were broken and if any 9/11 victims' phones had been hacked, as was alleged by one media organization. Many speculate that *News of the World*'s payments to members of the Metropolitan Police violated the Foreign Corrupt Practices Act, which makes it illegal to bribe foreign officials.

Fox News covered the testimony in full. This was a marked difference from its coverage the previous weeks. As the scandal emerged in the United States, Fox had barely mentioned the story in comparison to its competitors. From July 4 to July 13, CNN ran 108 segments on the phone hacking scandal, MSNBC ran 71 segments, and Fox News ran 30 segments on this fast-breaking story.[21]

Even Fox's own weekend media criticism program, *Fox News Watch*, did not mention the scandal during its July 9 broadcast. Behind-the-scenes video revealed this was an act of intentional self-censorship, as opposed to an editorial oversight. FoxNews .com often posted "Behind the Breaks" videos of panelists conversing during commercial breaks. The following conversation occurred that day off-air:

CAL THOMAS (Fox News contributor): Anybody want to bring up the subject we're not talking about today for the—for the [online] streamers?

JAMES PINKERTON (Fox News contributor): Sure. Go ahead, Cal!

THOMAS: No, go ahead, Jim.

(*Laughter*)

THOMAS: *I'm not going to touch it.*

JUDY MILLER (Fox News contributor): With a ten-foot [inaudible].[22]

CNN reporter Brian Todd later confirmed that the panelists were discussing the *News of the World* scandal during this segment.

Media Matters released a study highlighting Fox's lack of coverage of the scandal that garnered significant attention, leading to a dramatic increase in reporting by the network. While Fox ran only 30 segments on the scandal in the ten-day period from July 4 through July 13, in the six days between July 14 and 19, it ran 72 segments. The 102 total segments the network ran still trailed MSNBC and CNN, which ran 138 and 199 segments, respectively.

Of course, several of these segments were simply defenses of News Corp.'s behavior. Bill O'Reilly led the charge on behalf of his employer, claiming on July 20, "You have *The New York Times* absolutely running wild with the story," he said. "Front page, front page, front page. Column, column, column. Vicious stuff, vicious stuff. And it's all ideological, is it not?"[23]

Regardless of coverage, the impact of the phone hacking scandal continues to spread. As of our writing, at least eleven News Corp. employees, among them several senior executives, have been arrested in connection with the scandal. Paul Stephenson, the commissioner of the Metropolitan Police of London, and

John Yates, the assistant commissioner, were both forced to resign over the mishandling of the case and accusations that *News of the World* staff members paid police officers for information published in the paper.

In the United States, a shareholder suit filed earlier in the year challenging Murdoch's acquisition of his daughter's production company, Shine, for $675 million was amended to include the phone hacking scandal. The filings allege that the phone hacking "revelations show a culture run amuck within News Corp. and a Board that provides no effective review or oversight."[24]

Some suggest that the phone hacking will mean the end of Rupert Murdoch's reign over the company; he has been criticized for running it more like a family business than a publicly traded institution. Certainly, it has paused speculation that Murdoch's son James would succeed him as CEO.

However, its effect on Fox News and its political actions remains unknown. Running an incredibly profitable division of the company, Roger Ailes would likely be untouched in any transition. The question is whether a new CEO would give him free rein to run Fox News as his own political fiefdom, as Murdoch has permitted.

The end of Glenn Beck's tenure at Fox would also mark his departure from broadcast television and a renewed focus on developing a new platform. For years he had been more than just a television and radio host—Beck's reach spanned nearly every media platform, each venue serving as a promotional vehicle for the others. Even while hosting his show at Fox, his largest audience and paycheck came from his syndicated radio show. Beck also was a prolific writer. In two and a half years at Fox, while broadcasting three hours of radio and an hour of television every weekday, he wrote seven books in multiple genres, including a novel, titled *The Overton Window,* and a self-help book called *The 7: Seven Wonders That Will Change Your Life.*

Post-Fox, Beck also took his act on the road, performing at venues around the country, with crowds and ticket prices that matched bands on the Billboard Top 100.

But Beck's largest area of growth was his online presence. In the fall of 2010, he launched TheBlaze.com, his version of *The Huffington Post.* He also began to provide his audience with original paid content such as "Insider Extreme," which allowed subscribers to watch a live video feed of his radio show and an extra hour of content from his cohosts and producers, Pat and Stu.

In 2010, Beck had launched an online "university" offering courses focused on faith, hope, and charity that used guests from his show as teachers. One of them was David Barton, who had previously been condemned by the Anti-Defamation League. The organization wrote in its 1994 book *The Religious Right* that his "ostensible scholarship functions in fact as an assault on scholarship: in the manner of other recent phony revisionisms, the history it supports is little more than a compendium of anecdotes divorced from their original context, linked harum-scarum and laced with factual errors and distorted innuendo."[25] Most damningly, the ADL wrote that "Barton's 'scholarship,' like that of Holocaust denial and Atlantic slave trade conspiracy-mongering, is rigged to arrive at predetermined conclusions, not history." At Glenn Beck University, Barton taught a series of courses titled Faith 101, 102, and 103.

Though Beck's salary from Fox was near the bottom of his list of revenue sources, the network did provide him with his most influential platform. Because of the network's position as the go-to place for conservative news, it opened up Beck to an entirely new audience. With frequent guest appearances with Bill O'Reilly and on *Fox & Friends,* Beck took full advantage of his television home.

When Fox executive Joel Cheatwood left the network to join Beck's production company, Mercury Radio Arts, there were rumors that Beck would attempt to form his own television network. *The New York Times* went so far as to speculate that Beck "could follow a road paved by Oprah Winfrey when she started OWN: The Oprah Winfrey Network in January."[26]

At the time, we asked a senior executive at a major cable company if he believed Beck was launching his own network. The executive responded that this was extremely unlikely. While Beck had proven himself a ratings star, he had not shown the ability to create the additional stream of attractive programing required to operate a cable network. It was suggested Beck might try to create an On-Demand channel or go the more lucrative route of an Internet subscription model.

Sure enough, on June 6, just after Fox announced his departure date, Mercury Radio Arts announced the creation of an online network called GBTV. In spite of his professed disdain for the "liberal" *New York Times,* Beck gave it the exclusive story on the formation of his channel. Media reporter Brian Stelter wrote, "On Tuesday, Mr. Beck will announce a first-of-its-kind effort to take a popular—but also fiercely polarizing—television show and turn it into its own subscription enterprise." Stelter, who interviewed Beck for the story, concluded, "It is an adaptation of the business models of both HBO and Netflix for one man's personal brand—and a huge risk, as he and his staff members acknowledged in interviews in recent days."[27]

Beck's press release described the network's content by stating that it "will feature an exclusive behind-the-scenes reality show about the making of GBTV. GBTV subscribers will also get access to a video simulcast of Glenn's daily three-hour radio program, original documentaries, and in-depth coverage of live events, such as Glenn's 'Restoring Courage' event in Israel on August 24th."[28]

By the day of GBTV's launch on September 12, 2011, Beck had already signed up more than 230,000 customers. While comprising 10 percent of his television audience, at a cost to subscribers of $9.95 per month, Mercury Radio would earn more than $25 million in revenue, nearly ten times his reported salary at Fox News. If he managed to enlist one million subscribers, the company would earn more than $100 million a year, making Beck one of the highest-paid broadcasters in history. The question was whether Glenn Beck's brand was strong enough to bring in such astronomical numbers. It's one thing to attract a primarily passive radio and television audience; it is completely another to attract an audience willing to shell out a monthly fee to watch your programming. Furthermore, no regularly scheduled online program has ever achieved such a large audience.

Glenn Beck, however, was ready to test the strength of his brand. Following up on his Restoring Honor rally a year earlier, Beck would now host another mega-event—this time, outside the United States. He would journey to Israel at the end of August to host a rally he titled "Restoring Courage."

Ever the showman, Beck announced the event in mid-May using the same self-aggrandizing language he had a year earlier for the Restoring Honor event and two years earlier in the announcement of the 9/12 Project. He called the Restoring Courage rally "a life-changing, life-altering event" and said, "This will be a— I think, a pinnacle moment in your life. It will define you. In the end, this event will define you."[29] He even borrowed from the Gettysburg Address, saying that "possibly for the first time in man's history, God will remember and make note of what we do there."[30]

In the run-up to the event, Beck began linking himself to members of the far right of Israel's conservative Likud Party. In July, he was even invited to testify before a committee of the Knesset. Danny Danon, a member of the body, became one of Beck's principal advocates in Israel. He was warmly received, save for an awkward conversation in which Beck expressed his concern about not wearing a tie before the legislative body.

Beck's hyperbole continued throughout the promotion of the event, turning more and more messianic as the date drew closer. On August 12, he told his radio audience, "Somebody sent this to me last night—a religious figure that I respect. He said it was sent in by somebody else and he said, 'I've looked into this, and I think this might be right.' " Beck continued, "He said, 'The Restoring Courage event,' he said, 'I believe may be, may be, a fulfillment of Zechariah prophecy.' Listen to this from Zechariah. He's talking about, and in the days when all hell breaks loose this is what the Lord Almighty says."[31]

This followed Beck's August 10 broadcast, on which he proclaimed, "I wouldn't be surprised if this did alter the world. I wouldn't be surprised if a pillar of fire showed up. Sky is the limit. I have seen miracles on this."[32]

The pillar of fire never appeared. In fact, Beck's presence in the country became somewhat unwelcome. His record of statements about the Holocaust and references to anti-Semitic literature were too much for many Israelis.

In early August, Knesset members Nachman Shai and Danny Danon debated about Glenn Beck on the popular Israel Defense

Forces Radio program *Ma Boer*. Danon tried to defend Beck, claiming, "Yes, he has made problematic comments and let me tell you a secret. He is going to make problematic comments in the future also." The show's host asked Nachman Shai, "Does this man do more harm to Israel than good?" To which Shai responded, "Of course! Of course!"[33]

Prominent Israeli blogger Noam Sheizaf published an op-ed in *The Jewish Daily Forward* summing up the Israeli case against Beck, writing, "This is not the kind of help Israel needs. Beck's religious rhetoric, his radical conservative positions and his fondness for the idea of Armageddon present a real danger to the well-being of Israelis and Palestinians alike."[34]

Not only did the Israeli left object to Glenn Beck's rally, but many on the right in Israel were not welcoming either. Several rabbis and religious figures called for a boycott of the rally, led by Mina Fenton, "a former Jerusalem council woman for the National Religious Party."[35]

In the lead-up to the event, Beck and his allies in Israel promoted the idea that U.S. politicians, led by Joe Lieberman, would attend. As the day drew closer, this became less and less likely. The only presidential candidate publicly committed to appear was Herman Cain, who at the time was trailing far behind in the Republican field.

AIPAC and other pro-Israel organizations sponsored trips to the nation for more than eighty lawmakers in August. Many assumed that these leaders would participate in Beck's rally. However, the House ethics committee told lawmakers they couldn't attend a political event while on official travel. Beck was informed of this on air by Representative Joe Walsh, who told him, "Lo and behold, ethics yesterday said—did not approve the trip . . . They said your portion of the fact-finding mission had the appearance of a political event."[36]

Beck lashed out at Speaker of the House John Boehner, saying, "Speaker Boehner, you should be ashamed of yourself. The Republican Party should be ashamed of themselves. They don't have to attend my event. Let them come to our biggest ally and our only friend in the Middle East in their hour of need. They don't have to attend my event! In fact, I'll ban them. Does that make you happy?"[37]

After several back-and-forth reports, Lieberman confirmed he would not attend Restoring Courage, and early supporters such as Eric Cantor, the Republican House Majority Leader and highest-ranking Jewish officeholder in the United States, also declined Beck's invitation.

Ultimately, Beck's series of Israel events would each be attended by only several thousand people. Most telling, however, was the fact that the event was mentioned only once on Fox, not by a network employee, but by Herman Cain, during an interview. It did not receive the banner coverage or promotion that Beck's previous efforts had been granted on Fox and other news channels. Without the broadcast platform of Fox, Beck had been relegated to a crank in the swamps of talk radio and the Internet. Observer David Weigel wrote in a post at *Slate,* "Post–Fox News, I meet conservative activists in primary states who say they miss Beck. Without Fox, his imprint on the culture is barely noticeable."[38]

It had been a wild two-and-a-half-year ride to prominence, but the consequence to Beck after losing his platform on Fox was evident. Even though he still hosted one of the top radio programs in the country, within two months of leaving the network he was no longer culturally significant.

. . .

As the summer of 2011 began, the Republican presidential primary was finally in full swing, with a multitude of candidates competing to challenge the president. All eyes turned to the first test of the election, the Iowa Straw Poll, held every four years in the city of Ames. Though the event awards no convention delegates, the media has inflated its importance over the years, seeing it as a critical first test of how well candidates can organize a successful campaign for the upcoming caucuses. Consequently, candidates spend tens of thousands of dollars on staff and tents, complete with food and entertainment, hoping to make a good first impression. In 2007, Mitt Romney trounced the competition, receiving more than 31 percent of the vote. Mike Huckabee, who would ultimately win the caucuses, received just over 18 percent. Four years later, Mitt Romney, now the overwhelming front-runner, would choose not to compete in the straw poll.

It did not matter. With voters casting ballots, even meaningless ones, the political media had a story to report. Fox News positioned itself at the center of the event, hosting a debate with *The Washington Examiner* in Iowa on August 11, just two days before the straw poll. Ignoring the first debate, which was full of second-tier candidates, Fox vice president Michael Clemente announced the event by stating, "FOX News is proud to partner with *The Washington Examiner* and the Iowa GOP to kick off the 2012 election season and provide viewers the most thorough coverage of this important debate."[39]

The debate was moderated by Fox hosts Bret Baier and Chris Wallace, who were joined by *The Washington Examiner*'s Byron York and Susan Ferrechio. When it was done, several observers seemed more focused on Fox's performance than the candidates', declaring the news network the winner of the debate based on the performance of its staff. *The Baltimore Sun*'s David Zurawik praised Baier, writing, "I cannot remember seeing a moderator this side of CNN's Wolf Blitzer who opened a debate with a more focused, well-researched barrage of questions . . . He set the bar high for every moderator who follows this presidential season."[40]

Time magazine media critic James Poniewozik wrote, "Fox assumed, rightly, that its audience tuned in to watch a 2012 Presidential debate in August 2011, and thus was interested enough not to need things jazzed up for them."[41]

What little criticism there was of the debate moderators came from the right. During the debate, Newt Gingrich went on the attack against Baier after he used quotes from several of the candidates' appearances on Fox with regard to Libya. At first, Gingrich had called for a no-fly zone over the country, but then criticized President Obama for taking that very action. In response, Gingrich said, "This is an example of a gotcha question. The fact that I was commenting on Fox about a president who changes his opinion every other day ought to be covered by a Fox News commentator using all the things I said and not picking and choosing the ones that fit your premise."[42]

Keach Hagey of *Politico* summed up the feelings of many who covered the event, writing, "Instead of providing a platform from which candidates could complain about the bias of the mainstream media—a role the channel often played during the 2010 election cycle—Fox News came across as a robust part of that mainstream media."[43]

Was this the sign of a new, more objective Fox News, one that would hold Republican candidates up to the same level of scrutiny it traditionally reserved for Democrats? It seems unlikely. In the case of the debate, the network simply did not have to choose sides. Asking robust questions of all candidates in a Republican primary was to its advantage. Fox would gain nothing by outwardly taking sides in a primary when its real goal was to challenge the president. The network was the go-to place for Republican voters to hear from their candidates.

In fact, while garnering positive coverage for its handling of the debate, Fox continued its outlandish attacks on progressives, the president, and his policies, with the clear goal of victory in 2012. When news in late July turned to the frantic negotiations between Democrats and Republicans over raising the nation's debt ceiling, Fox inflamed the issue with a series of false claims. Additionally some Fox figures cheered for no deal and some even welcomed a default by the United States on its debt obligations. After the deal was struck, Fox turned overwhelmingly to Republican figures for analysis of what happened. Of its guests following the compromise, twenty-five were Republicans and only eight were Democrats. This imbalance persisted across its straight news and opinion programing.[44]

Additionally, while receiving praise for its debate performance, Fox's donation of airtime to Republican candidates continued at a record pace. In the ten and a half weeks from June 1 to August 14, the week of the Ames Straw Poll, Fox hosted Republican candidates and potential candidates for president 239 times, totaling more than twenty-eight hours of exposure.[45]

Michele Bachmann alone appeared on the network twenty-one times during that period, averaging two appearances a week. Ron Paul appeared on the network twenty-six times; Herman Cain twenty-three times; Newt Gingrich and Rick Santorum each appeared sixteen times. Trailing all these candidates was Mitt Romney, who appeared only five times on the network. As the front-runner and the leader of the pack in terms of fund-raising, Romney could stay above the fray for the moment. Rick Perry appeared four times, but he was not yet a candidate for president.

Sarah Palin, while not a candidate, appeared ten times as a paid contributor. She used this platform to continue to feed anticipation about a potential campaign, telling Sean Hannity on August 8, "I am still considering a run, Sean." Palin was interrupted with cheers from the live audience before continuing, "You know, I think the good folks here in Iowa—you can do a man-on-the-street here, you can ask anybody here and I think that they would tell you: it's time that this country is put back on the right track, that the economy is strengthened, that jobs are created via the private sector. And they are ready for some positive change to allow that from Washington, D.C."[46]

And this is perhaps one of the most powerful things Fox can give the conservative politicians it favors: a platform from which to run for president. Without the support of the establishment, which Mitt Romney had, or an elected office to run from, Fox gives political exiles and marginal political figures the opportunity to compete without the party machinery.

Michele Bachmann is a third-term representative, with no record of legislative accomplishment and a history of outlandish and radical statements. And yet there she was: a much-discussed voice in Republican politics. Fox gave her the ability to gain supporters and a platform that afforded her the option of running for the nation's highest office.

Rick Santorum was a two-term senator who had been defeated in a landslide in 2006. Now, five years later, he was running for president. Without Fox and his contributor contract, he would never have remained in the spotlight and have been long forgotten by the Republican Party's base. Additionally, the network provided the former senator with nearly $239,000[47] in income in 2010 and 2011 as he planned his run—a hefty sum for what amounted to a few hours a week of work.

Former Speaker of the House Newt Gingrich, while a more prominent figure than Santorum, had resigned his position more than a decade before this presidential election cycle. He also would not have maintained a platform to run for president without his contributor contract.

The Republican Party was still not pleased with the field. The day of the straw poll, sensing an opportunity, Texas governor Rick Perry entered the race and immediately became a front-runner. After a series of poor debate performances, and a surge by Herman Cain, Perry fell from his elevated status.

Yet Sarah Palin remained mum on whether she would run. Most assumed that if she were to enter the race, she would have launched her campaign by August to participate in the straw poll.

Karl Rove attacked Palin for her indecisiveness. After he suggested she would need to enter the race at a September 3 rally in Iowa, her PAC issued a release criticizing the Republican strategist. Rove shot back on Greta Van Susteren's show, telling the host and friend of Palin, "I would just recommend she might get a slightly thicker skin because if she's got this thin a skin now, when people are saying, Well, I think she might be a candidate, what kind of—how's she going to react if she does get into the campaign and gets the scrutiny that every presidential candidate does get?" Rove continued, "I mean, that's not going to be a pretty sight if she's as thin-skinned in the fray as she is on the edges of it."[48]

Sarah Palin's status in the Republican party began to diminish after she reportedly disobeyed Ailes's directive to "lie low"[49] following the attempted assassination of Gabrielle Giffords. Ultimately, Palin recognized that giving up a lucrative Fox News contract and paid speeches was not worth it for a quixotic campaign. If she were to lose, it would ultimately diminish her power within the Republican Party and her ability to continue her position as a political celebrity.

Palin's announcement demonstrated the fracture in her relationship with Roger Ailes. On the morning of October 5, the Associated Press released a profile of the Fox News boss in which he claimed, "I hired Sarah Palin because she was hot and got ratings."[50] The comment clearly could be interpreted as a sexist insult directed at the network contributor.

Sarah Palin got her revenge late that afternoon, when conservative radio host Mark Levin read an exclusive statement from the former Alaska governor announcing that she would not be running for president. Levin was then granted the first interview with Palin. She would appear on Fox News only several hours later, in the friendly confines of Greta Van Susteren's show in the 10 p.m. hour.

Gabriel Sherman reported Roger Ailes was "livid" with Palin and considered "pulling her off the air entirely." He reportedly told Fox vice president Bill Shine, "I paid her for two years to make this announcement on my network." Palin, according to Sherman, decided to broadcast her decision on Levin's show because she was "upset that Fox News has given a platform to Karl Rove, one of her principal critics."[51]

When Fox host Mike Huckabee elected not to run for president, he used the moment to promote his show. The executive producer of his program released a statement the day before his announcement stating, "Governor Huckabee will announce tomorrow night on his program whether or not he intends to explore a presidential bid."[52] Palin's decision could have been an even larger affair, driving ratings and influence. By making her announcement to Mark Levin, who was syndicated by Citadel, she denied Fox that opportunity.

Palin, however, was not critical to Ailes's place at the center of the GOP primary. For months Republican candidates sought out the Fox News boss for advice as they launched their campaigns. "Perry stopped by [Ailes's] midtown Manhattan office a few months back," Howard Kurtz reported. Perry "was still weighing whether to make a run, and confided that he was worried about being able to raise the big bucks. 'Money will find you if people believe in your message,' Ailes assured him."[53]

Perry was not the only Republican candidate who was given guidance by Ailes. Kurtz reported that Mitt Romney also met with the network boss. After a pasta dinner, "the Fox chief was struck by a sense of humor rarely displayed in public. 'You ought to be looser on the air,' he said while dropping off the former Massachusetts governor at his hotel."[54]

No other network head was so actively sought out by candidates for advice on their campaigns. Still, many in the press expressed surprise that Fox hadn't actively taken sides in the Republican primary, crediting the network for its newfound neutrality. They quickly forgot that Ailes failed to recruit his preferred candidate, New Jersey governor Chris Christie, into the race.

However, his previous denials of any plan to run for president did not stop Fox, or in fact the entire political media establishment, from continually musing about a Christie run. The speculation reached fever pitch by the start of October. In response, the New Jersey governor held a press conference in Trenton on October 4, making it clear he would not be running for president in 2012.

By early October Herman Cain shot to the head of the Republican pack in several national polls. It's no surprise during that period he also took the lead in terms of appearances and airtime on Fox News. Between June 1 and October 16, Cain was a guest on the network fifty-four times. In comparison, Ron Paul, who followed Cain in appearances, had been a guest forty-four times. Herman Cain's more than seven hours of airtime eclipsed all other candidates. His closest rival, Newt Gingrich, had been granted little more than four and a half hours on air.[55]

A few weeks later Cain's polling began to fade and Newt Gingrich climbed to the top of the primary field. During the week of November 14–20, the same week Gingrich took the lead in national polls, the former House speaker also led other candidates in terms of airtime on Fox, appearing for 34 minutes on the network, 9 and 10 minutes longer than Rick Perry and Mitt Romney respectively.[56]

Without Christie in the race, Ailes knows his power is based on Fox's perceived neutrality between Republican candidates, ensuring the network remains the venue of choice for the GOP hopefuls.

Each of the top Republican contenders made a pilgrimage to kiss their Svengali's ring. The Fox boss now sits in the middle, with each member of the primary field knowing that Fox's audience will ultimately pick the Republican who will face off against President Obama.

Roger Ailes, granted unprecedented freedom by Rupert Murdoch and utilizing his unique production talent, has built Fox News into cable news's Goliath, dominating the ratings with an audience that is both large and dedicated to the network's brand. Fox is loved by the conservative base and feared by politicians of both parties.

Ailes could have used his production genius to build a constructive force. Instead, he has built one that has fundamentally damaged our political and media landscape, leaving a legacy of cynicism and destruction. Joe McGinniss, the author of several books, including the classic *The Selling of the President* and *The Rogue,* a 2011 book on Sarah Palin, has been a friend of Ailes's for forty-four years, yet still believes that "from Richard Nixon to Rupert Murdoch, I think everyone he's ever worked for has harmed this country in some way. I also think Fox News is an excrescence."[57]

At Fox, Ailes has ushered in the era of post-truth politics. The facts no longer matter, only what is politically expedient, sensationalistic, and designed to confirm the preexisting opinions of a large audience. It's a world where a *news* organization encourages people to believe that Barack Obama attended a madrassa, even though he did not; and encourages its viewers to believe the Earth is not warming, in spite of the fact that virtually every scientific authority says it is. It is an organization that consciously reports that the Democrats' health care bill contains death panels, despite the fact that it does not.

In each of these cases, Fox broadcasted and laundered these lies and others like them until they became gospel for a segment of the population. Once, this role was reserved for talk radio or small-circulation ideological publications. Now the highest-rated cable news network in America broadcasts them. Most problematic, once these lies take hold, no amount of fact-checking by Media Matters or websites such as PolitiFact or Factcheck.org will ever convince the segment of the population that is predisposed to believe them.

There is simply nothing comparable on the left. No mainstream left-of-center media organization—however broadly you define that category—departs so willingly and extensively from journalism's fundamental mission to report facts as fairly and objectively as possible. No outright lie is accepted as widely on the left as distortions like the "death panels" have been on the right.

Beyond the lies, Roger Ailes has been at the forefront of a political culture that seeks to divide our country. On the Nixon and Bush campaigns, he worked to fragment America along racial lines. Now at Fox, he has continued that effort, in addition to dividing us by party and ideology. Balkanizing our nation makes it practically impossible for our leaders to work together. There could be no compromise on the health care bill because Republicans feared an attack from Fox. There can be no working together to solve the climate crisis because Fox has convinced its audience that global warming does not exist. Republicans felt compelled to push our nation to the edge of default because they feared the reaction of their Fox News–watching base.

Ironically, Ailes's quest to divide has also damaged the Republican Party. Mike Castle would likely be the senator from Delaware had Fox not whipped the Tea Party into a frenzy. This pattern holds true for the Republican Party in Colorado as well. Twenty years ago, Orrin Hatch was considered one of the most conservative Republicans in the Senate. Today, it is speculated he might face a primary challenge because he is not ideologically pure enough for the Tea Party. These are the results of Roger Ailes and Fox News pushing the Republican Party far to the right and, in many cases, well outside the mainstream of American politics.

Nevertheless, there are encouraging signs that the narrative is changing. Consider the fact that in the fall of 2009, White House communications director Anita Dunn caused a stir by simply observing, "It's opinion journalism masquerading as news . . . They are boosting their audience. But that doesn't mean we are going to sit back."[58] Her comments caused an uproar, not only on Fox, but

among members of the White House press corps and media critics. Fox had been on the offensive against her boss for nearly three
years, yet a light slap back was enough to cause a case of vapors
among the chattering class. Less than a year later, *Politico* reporter
Ben Smith observed on his blog, "That's a campaign [the 2012 Republican Primary] in which Fox News is just undoubtedly the single
most important player—it pays the candidates, and reaches the
electorate." Smith continued, "Its executives' and hosts' specific decisions will be crucial to deciding the nominee. Coverage that treats
Fox as an observer, not a player, will miss much of the point."[59]

Now, two years later, Dunn's comments would be uncontroversial among many of those who were up in arms. It is a widely
accepted fact that Fox's product is far from fair and balanced.

By mid-2009 it became clear from our daily monitoring that
Fox was changing. No longer was it simply a conservative news
network. It had morphed into a political campaign. We witnessed
the promotion of the Tea Party in April that year and the heated
rhetoric at town halls over the summer. In the spring of 2010, as
the idea behind *The Fox Effect* germinated, we witnessed the network take an unprecedented role in fund-raising for Republican
candidates.

In a confessional interview with Howard Kurtz, Ailes himself
acknowledges the network overstepped its boundaries during the
2010 election cycle. According to Kurtz, "[Ailes] calls it a 'course
correction,' quietly adopted at Fox over the last year. Glenn Beck's
inflammatory rhetoric—his ranting about Obama being a racist—
'became a bit of a branding issue for us' before the hot-button host
left in July, Ailes says. So too did Sarah Palin's being widely promoted as the GOP's potential savior—in large measure through her
lucrative platform at Fox."[60]

Vindicating Anita Dunn, Ailes even went so far as to acknowledge Fox's strategy, telling Kurtz, "Every other network has given all their shows to liberals. We are the balance."[61]

The metamorphosis from "Fair and Balanced" to "we are the balance" is a significant admission. Fox's version of "balance"—according to its president—isn't to provide its viewers with an equal hearing of all sides. Rather, its purpose is to supply right-wing bias to correct what it wrongly perceives to be an error in the media cosmos.

Now, as the 2012 election draws near, it is clear Fox will attempt to repeat its performance from 2010. Karl Rove, still a network employee, has promised to raise hundreds of millions of dollars to defeat Barack Obama. Its prime-time lineup is as committed to the Republican Party as ever, and its "news" hosts continue to echo GOP talking points. We can anticipate lies about the president's policies and smears of his advisers.

However, Fox News will no longer be able to conduct its campaign under the false pretense that the network is a journalistic institution. There is heightened awareness in the progressive community and the general public of the damage Fox causes. In early 2011, protests erupted at the Wisconsin State Capitol Building over Governor Scott Walker's attempt to strip public employee unions of their right to collective bargaining. Media outlets rushed to cover the protests. On multiple occasions, as Fox reporters began their live feeds, the crowd around them shifted its focus to the network, chanting, "Fox lies," "Fox News lies," and "Tell the truth."[62] Ultimately, while the network's audience believes Fox's lies, the vast majority of Americans want their media to tell the truth. And that, in the end, is why Roger Ailes will fail.

Notes

Introduction: Not Necessarily the News

1. Eric Hananoki, "Cruise Ship Confession: Top Fox News Executive Admits Lying On-Air About Obama," MediaMatters.org, March 29, 2011, mediamatters.org/blog/201103290006.

2. Eric Hananoki, "FoxLeaks: Bill Sammon's October Surprise," MediaMatters .org, February 1, 2011, mediamatters.org/blog/201102010022.

3. Ibid.

4. Ibid.

5. *Fox & Friends,* Fox News, October 28, 2008; Hananoki, "Bill Sammon's October Surprise."

6. Bill Sammon, "Obama Affinity to Marxists Dates Back to College Days," FoxNews.com, October 28, 2008; Hananoki, "Bill Sammon's October Surprise."

7. Joe Strupp, "Veteran D.C. Bureau Chiefs Rip Sammon: 'This Isn't Journalism,' " MediaMatters.org, March 31, 2011, mediamatters.org/blog/201103310026.

8. Howard Kurtz, "Obama a Socialist? Fox News Exec Said So, but Didn't Believe It," *Daily Beast,* March 29, 2011, www.thedailybeast.com/blogs -and-stories/2011–03–29/obama-a-socialist-fox-news-exec-said-so-but -didnt-believe-it.html.

9. Natalie Gewargis, " 'Spread the Wealth'?" *Political Punch* (blog), ABC News, October 14, 2008, blogs.abcnews.com/politicalpunch/2008/10/spread -the-weal.html.

10. *The Live Desk,* Fox News, October 14, 2008; Hananoki, "Bill Sammon's October Surprise."

11. Strupp, "Veteran D.C. Bureau Chiefs Rip Sammon."

12. Chuck Todd, Mark Murray, Domenico Montanaro, and Ali Weinberg,

"First Thoughts: Obama's Good, Bad News," *First Read* (blog), NBC News, August 19, 2009, firstread.msnbc.msn.com/_news/2009/08/19/4431138 -first-thoughts-obamas-good-bad-news.

13. Mark Howard, "Study Confirms Watching Fox News Makes You Stupid," Alternet, October 15, 2010, www.alternet.org/media/149193/study _confirms_that_fox_news_makes_you_stupid.

14. David J. Lynch, "Economists Agree: Stimulus Created Nearly 3 Million Jobs," *USA Today,* August 30, 2010, www.usatoday.com/money/ economy/2010–08–30-stimulus30_CV_N.htm.

15. Brian Stelter, "Study: Some Viewers Were Misinformed by TV News," Media Decoder (blog), *New York Times,* December 17, 2010, mediadecoder .blogs.nytimes.com/2010/12/17/study-some-viewers-were-misinformed -by-tv-news/.

16. James O. Goldsborough, "The Media and Public Misconceptions," *San Diego Union-Tribune,* October 13, 2003.

17. Interview with Media Matters for America. Conducted by Joe Strupp. May 17, 2011.

18. Michael Wolff, *The Man Who Owns the News: Inside the Secret World of Rupert Murdoch* (New York: Broadway Books, 2008), 346.

19. Stefano DellaVigna and Ethan Kaplan, "The Fox News Effect: Media Bias and Voting," *The Quarterly Journal of Economics* 122 (August 2007): 1187–234.

20. *Nightline,* ABC News, March 22, 2010, can be viewed at mediamatters.org/ mmtv/201003230020.

21. David Frum, "Waterloo," *Frum Forum* (blog), March 21, 2010, www .frumforum.com/waterloo.

22. Ibid.

Chapter 1: Roger's Rise

1. David Carr and Tim Arango, "A Fox Chief at the Pinnacle of Media and Politics," *New York Times,* January 9, 2010, www.nytimes.com/2010/01/10/ business/media/10ailes.html.

2. Ibid.

3. Tom Junod, "Why Does Roger Ailes Hate America?" *Esquire,* January 18, 2011, www.esquire.com/features/roger-ailes-0211.

4. "Nixon's Roger Ailes," *Washington Post,* February 13, 1972, www.scribd .com/doc/53543922/Roger-Ailes-I-Dont-Try-to-Fool-Voters.

5. Ibid.

6. Joe McGinniss, *The Selling of the President* (1969; repr. New York: Penguin, 1988), 100.

7. Ibid., 101.

8. Rick Perlstein, *Nixonland: The Rise of a President and the Fracturing of America* (New York: Scribner, 2008), 331.

9. McGinniss, *The Selling of the President,* 102.

10. Tom Junod, "Roger Ailes on Roger Ailes: The Interview Transcripts, Part 2," *Esquire.com,* January 27, 2011, www.esquire.com/blogs/politics/ roger-ailes-quotes-5072437.

11. Ibid.

12. "A Conversation with Roger Ailes," *The Kalb Report,* C-SPAN, April 5, 2007, www.c-spanvideo.org/program/Aile.

13. Junod, "Roger Ailes on Roger Ailes."

14. "Television: Mommy's Boy," *Time,* October 6, 1967.

15. Letter from Roger Ailes to H. R. Haldeman, February 9, 1971, Nixon Presidential Library and Museum.

16. Ron Ziegler, Memorandum for H. R. Haldeman, re: Roger Ailes appearance on CBS morning news show, March 14, 1970, Nixon Presidential Library and Museum.

17. Letter from Jim Allison, Jr., deputy chairman of the Republican National Committee, to Roger Ailes, May 25, 1970, Nixon Presidential Library and Museum.

18. Letter from Jon M. Huntsman to Roger Ailes, May 21, 1971, Nixon Presidential Library and Museum.

19. Letter from H. R. Haldeman to Roger Ailes, June 2, 1971, Nixon Presidential Library and Museum.

20. Talking Paper, Roger Ailes Meeting, Nixon Presidential Library and Museum.

21. Ibid.

22. Roger Ailes, Confidential Report–Television, November 1968, Nixon Presidential Library and Museum.

23. Roger Ailes, Confidential Report to Bob Haldeman re: White House Television, December 1969, Nixon Presidential Library and Museum.

24. Roger Ailes, Confidential Report to Bob Haldeman re: White House Television, 1971, Nixon Presidential Library and Museum.

25. "A Plan for Putting the GOP on TV News," unsigned, undated memo, Nixon Presidential Library and Museum.

26. Ibid.

27. Ibid.

28. Stanhope Gould, "Coors Brews the News," *Columbia Journalism Review,* March/April 1975, 17–29.

29. Ibid.

30. Ibid.

31. Ibid.

32. Ibid.

33. Ibid.

34. Ibid.

35. Ibid.

36. Ibid.

37. Ibid.

38. Ibid.

39. Kerwin Swint, *Dark Genius: The Influential Career of Legendary Political Operative and Fox News Founder Roger Ailes* (New York: Union Square Press, 2008), 60.

40. Gould, "Coors Brews the News."

41. Swint, *Dark Genius,* 72.

42. David Beckwith and Richard Stengel, "The Republicans: The Man Behind the Message," *Time,* August 22, 1988, www.time.com/time/magazine/article/0,9171,968180,00.html.

43. David Brock, "Roger Ailes Is Mad as Hell," *New York*, December 8, 1997.

44. Swint, *Dark Genius,* 47.

45. Beckwith and Stengel, "The Republicans."

46. Ibid.

47. Ibid.

48. Bernard Weinraub, "Campaign Trail; A Beloved Mug Shot for the Bush Forces," *New York Times,* October 3, 1988.

49. Deposition of Roger E. Ailes, Transcript of Proceedings of Federal Election Commission, August 29, 1991.

50. Ibid.

51. Ibid.

52. Joe Klein, "A Rudy Awakening," *New York,* October 16, 1989.

53. Howard Kurtz, "Giuliani Ad in N.Y. Yiddish Paper Links Dinkins and Jackson," *Washington Post,* September 29, 1989.

54. Ina Jaffe, "Giuliani Struggled with Issue in First Campaign," *Morning Edition,* National Public Radio, September 12, 2007, www.npr.org/templates/story/story.php?storyId=14304913.

55. Swint, *Dark Genius,* 40.

56. Ibid.

57. Ibid., 41.

58. Sam Roberts, "Giuliani Ads Remain Harsh in Last Days," *New York Times*, November 4, 1989, www.nytimes.com/1989/11/04/nyregion/giuliani-ads-remain-harsh-in-last-days.html.

59. Howard Kurtz, "With Ailes's Aid, Convict Becomes 'Willie Horton' of N.Y. Campaign," *Washington Post,* October 20, 1989.

60. Ibid.

61. Swint, *Dark Genius,* 118.

62. Ibid.

63. David R. Runkel, ed., *Campaign for President: The Managers Look at '88* (Dover, Mass.: Auburn House, 1989), 136.

64. Michael Wolff, *The Man Who Owns the News: Inside the Secret World of Rupert Murdoch* (New York: Broadway Books, 2008), 282–83.

65. Rush Limbaugh, "Rush and Roger Ailes Speak at Boy Scouts Awards Dinner," RushLimbaugh.com, November 11, 2009, www.rushlimbaugh

.com/daily/2009/11/11/rush-and-roger-ailes-speak-at-boy-scouts-awards -dinner.

66. "Nixon's Roger Ailes."

67. Roger Ailes, "Candidate + Money + Media = Votes," Town Hall of California, June 8, 1971, Nixon Presidential Library and Museum.

68. *The Rush Limbaugh Show,* EIB Network, January 20, 2009, www.rush limbaugh.com/daily/2009/01/16/limbaugh-i-hope-obama-fails.

69. Mark Silva, "Palin: Obama's Terrorist . . . Pallin' Around," The Swamp (blog), *Chicago Tribune,* October 4, 2009, www.swamppolitics.com/news/ politics/blog/2008/10/palin_obamas_terrorist_pallin.html.

70. Steven Beardsley, "Fox News Founder Roger Ailes Jabs Mainstream Media, Health Care Reform During Ave Maria Speech," *Naples Daily News,* April 26, 2010, www.naplesnews.com/news/2010/apr/26/fox-news -founder-roger-ailes-jabs-mainstream-media/.

71. Bob Woodward, *Bush at War* (New York: Simon & Schuster, 2002), 207.

72. Timothy Noah, "Roger Ailes Strikes Back," *Slate,* November 18, 2002, www.slate.com/id/2074145/.

73. Bill Carter and Jim Rutenberg, "Fox News Head Sent a Policy Note to Bush," *New York Times,* November 19, 2002, www.nytimes.com/2002/11/19/ politics/19ROGE.html.

74. Alex Koppelman and Erin Renzas, "Rudy Giuliani's Ties to Fox News," *Salon,* November 16, 2007, news.salon.com/2007/11/16/regan.

75. Russ Buettner, "Fox News Chief, Roger Ailes, Urged Employee to Lie, Records Show," *New York Times,* February 24, 2011, www.nytimes .com/2011/02/25/nyregion/25roger-ailes.html.

76. *Morning Joe,* MSNBC, June 21, 2010, can be viewed at mediamatters.org/ mmtv/201006210002.

77. Eric Boehlert, "Fox News Insider: 'Stuff Is Just Made Up' " Media Matters.org, February 10, 2011. Interview with Media Matters, mediamatters .org/blog/201102100007.

78. Wolff, *The Man Who Owns the News,* 345.

79. Tim Dickinson, "How Roger Ailes Built the Fox News Fear Factory." *Rolling Stone,* May 25, 2011, www.rollingstone.com/politics/news/how-roger -ailes-built-the-fox-news-fear-factory-20110525#ixzz1gGiXGg5o.

80. John Cook, "Fox News Chief Roger Ailes Can't Stop Calling the Cops," *Gawker,* April 29, 2011, gawker.com/5797078/fox-news-chief-roger-ailes -cant-stop-calling-the-cops.

81. John Cook and Hamilton Nolan, "Roger Ailes Caught Spying on the Reporters at His Small-Town Newspaper," *Gawker,* April 18, 2011, gawker.com/5793012/roger-ailes-caught-spying-on-the-reporters-at-his -small+town-newspaper.

82. Ibid.

83. Ibid.

84. John Cook, "Roger Ailes Continues to Ruin His Adopted Home," *Gawker,* May 10, 2011, gawker.com/5800439/roger-ailes-continues-to-ruin-his -adopted-home.

85. Ibid.

86. Wolff, *The Man Who Owns the News,* 346.

Chapter 2: The Path to the Top

1. Transcript of news conference as shown in *Outfoxed: Rupert Murdoch's War on Journalism,* Carolina Productions, 2004, www.outfoxed.org/docs/ outfoxed_transcript.pdf.

2. Al Franken, *Lies and the Lying Liars Who Tell Them: A Fair and Balanced Look at the Right* (New York: Dutton, 2003), 62.

3. Kerwin Swint, *Dark Genius: The Influential Career of Legendary Operative and Fox News Founder Roger Ailes* (New York: Union Square Press, 2008), 172.

4. Mark Lander, "Giuliani Pressures Time Warner to Transmit a Fox Channel," *New York Times,* October 4, 1996, www.nytimes.com/1996/10/04/ nyregion/giuliani-pressures-time-warner-to-transmit-a-fox-channel .html?pagewanted=all&src=pm.

5. Scott Collins, *Crazy Like a Fox: The Inside Story of How Fox News Beat CNN* (New York: Penguin, 2004), 101.

6. Clifford J. Levy, "Lobbying at Murdoch Gala Ignited New York Cable Clash," *New York Times,* October 13, 1996, quoted in ibid.

7. Collins, *Crazy Like a Fox,* 104–105.

8. Ibid., 70.

9. Ibid., 119.

10. Ibid., 143.

11. Ibid., 155.

12. Seth Ackerman, "The Most Biased Name in News: Fox News Channel's Extraordinary Right-Wing Tilt," *Extra!* (published by FAIR: Fairness & Accuracy in Reporting), July/August 2001, www.fair.org/index .php?page=1067.

13. Collins, *Crazy Like a Fox,* 158.

14. Martha T. Moore, "Bush Cousin Helped Fox Make Call," *USA Today,* November 14, 2000, quoted in Collins, *Crazy Like a Fox,* 159.

15. "Election Night 2000 Coverage by the Networks," hearing before the Committee on Energy and Commerce, House of Representatives, February 14, 2001, energycommerce.house.gov/107/hearings/02142001Hearing216/ print.htm.

16. Ibid.

17. Jane Mayer, The Talk of the Town, "Dept. of Close Calls George W.'s Cousin," *The New Yorker,* November 20, 2000, 36.

18. Ibid.

19. Collins, *Crazy Like a Fox,* 170.

20. Ibid.,170.

21. "CNN on Its Use of the Word 'Terrorist,' " CNN.com, September 30, 2001, archives.cnn.com/2001/US/09/30/terrorist/.

22. David Bauder, "Fox News Overtakes CNN in Ratings," Associated Press, January 29, 2002, www.mediapost.com/publications/index.cfm/?fa=Articles.showArticle&art_aid=3889, quoted in Collins, *Crazy Like a Fox,* 188–189.

23. Ibid.

24. Interview with Media Matters for America conducted by Joe Strupp, May 16, 2011.

Chapter 3: A "Terrorist Fist Jab"?

1. Sarah Lacy, "Barack Obama's Unlikely Supporter: Rupert 'Fox News' Murdoch," *Yahoo Finance Tech Ticker,* May 29, 2008, finance.yahoo.com/tech-ticker/article/20951/Barack-Obama's-Unlikely-Supporter-Rupert-'Fox-News'-Murdoch?tickers-ws,msft,yhoo,nyt.

2. David Carr and Tim Arango, "A Fox Chief at the Pinnacle of Media and Politics," *New York Times,* January 9, 2010, www.nytimes.com/2010/01/10/business/media/10ailes.html.

3. Chris Matthews, Democratic National Convention coverage, MSNBC, July 28, 2004.

4. Special Report with Brit Hume, Fox News Channel, November 3, 2004, quoted in "Conservatives Complained That Swift Boat Vets Were Ignored; Now They Tout Impact," MediaMatters.org, mediamatters.org/research/200411050002.

5. InsightMag.com, January 17, 2007; "Timeline of a Smear," MediaMatters.org, January 30, 2007, mediamatters.org/research/200701300007.

6. Eric Zorn, "Be Careful, Be Very Careful . . ." *Change of Subject* (blog), *Chicago Tribune,* January 9, 2007, blogs.chicagotribune.com/news_columnists_ezorn/2007/01/be_careful_be_v.html.

7. *Fox News Watch*, Fox News Channel, January 20, 2007; "Timeline of a Smear."

8. *Reliable Sources*, CNN, January 21, 2009; "Timeline of a Smear."

9. *Fox & Friends,* Fox News Channel, January 22, 2009; "Timeline of a Smear."

10. Howard Kurtz, "Hillary, Obama and Anonymous Sources," *Washington Post,* January 22, 2007, www.washingtonpost.com/wp-dyn/content/blog/2007/01/22/BL2007012200260_pf.html.

11. *The Situation Room,* CNN, January 22, 2009; "Timeline of a Smear."

12. Ibid.

13. Nedra Pickler, "Obama Debunks Claim About Islamic School," Associated Press, January 25, 2009, www.washingtonpost.com/wp-dyn/content/article/2007/01/24/AR2007012400371_pf.html.

14. "Atari 2600," *Political Punch* (blog), ABC News, January 26, 2009, blogs
.abcnews.com/politicalpunch/2007/01/atari_2600.html.

15. *Hannity & Colmes,* Fox News Channel, January 29, 2007; "Morris Still
Pushing Allegation That Clinton Camp Planted Obama Smear with
Insight," MediaMatters.org, January 30, 2007, mediamatters.org/
research/200701300009.

16. *Glenn Beck,* Fox News Channel, December 30, 2009; Jeremy Schulman,
"Coulter Brings Madrassa Lie Back to Fox News," MediaMatters.org,
December 31, 2009, mediamatters.org/blog/200912310001.

17. *The Big Story,* Fox News Channel, February 28, 2007; " 'Madrassa' Redux?
Gibson Cited Dubious Tabloid Article to Smear Obama, Clinton," Media
Matters.org, March 1, 2007, mediamatters.org/research/200703010011.

18. *Hannity & Colmes,* Fox News Channel, February 28, 2007; "Hannity Guest
on Obama's Church: Its 'Scary Doctrine' Is 'Something That You'd See in
More Like a Cult,' " MediaMatters.org, March 1, 2007, mediamatters.org/
research/200703010012.

19. "Ailes: 'Obama Is on the Move. I Don't Know if . . . Bush Called Musharraf
and Said: 'Why Can't We Catch This Guy?' " MediaMatters.org, March 9,
2007, mediamatters.org/research/200703100002.

20. *Hannity & Colmes,* Fox News Channel, August 24, 2007; "Hannity Refused
to Disallow Ted Nugent's Slurs Against Obama and Clinton," Media
Matters.org, August 27, 2007, mediamatters.org/research/200708270006.

21. *The O'Reilly Factor,* Fox News Channel, August 28, 2007; "Fox Graphics
Falsely Asserted Castro 'Wants' Clinton-Obama as 'Dream Team,' " Media
Matters.org, August 29, 2007, mediamatters.org/research/200708290012.

22. *Fox & Friends,* Fox News Channel, August 29, 2007; "Fox Graphics Falsely
Asserted."

23. Fidel Castro, *Granma Internacional,* August 28, 2007; "Fox Graphics Falsely
Asserted."

24. *Hannity & Colmes,* Fox News Channel, March 2, 2008; "After Asking, 'Do
the Obamas Have a Race Problem of Their Own?' Hannity Continued to
Smear Barack and Michelle Obama," MediaMatters.org, March 5, 2008,
mediamatters.org/research/200803050004.

25. Ibid.

26. Ibid.

27. "Ad Comparing Bush to Hitler Gets Heat," *FoxNews.com*, January 6, 2004,
www.foxnews.com/story/0,2933,107426,00.html.

28. *Tom Sullivan Show,* Fox News Radio, February 11, 2008; "Fox News Radio's
Tom Sullivan Aired 'Side-by-Side Comparison' of Speeches by Hitler
and Obama," MediaMatters.org, February 13, 2008, mediamatters.org/
research/200802130016.

29. *Hannity & Colmes,* Fox News Channel, April 3, 2008; "On *Hannity &
Colmes,* Coulter Again Made Obama-Hitler Comparison, Said Clinton

'Would Enjoy Torturing' Detainees," MediaMatters.org, April 4, 2008, media matters.org/research/200804040005.

30. *America's Pulse,* Fox News Channel, June 6, 2008; "Fox News' E. D. Hill teased discussion of Obama dap: 'A fist bump? A pound? A terrorist fist jab?' " MediaMatters.org, June 6, 2008, mediamatters.org/mmtv/200806060007.

31. *America's Pulse,* Fox News Channel, June 10, 2008; "Fox News' E. D. Hill Addresses Her 'Terrorist Fist Jab' Comment," MediaMatters.org, June 10, 2008, mediamatters.org/research/200806100009.

32. "Hume Falsely Claimed Obama's Half Brother Told *The Jerusalem Post* That Obama Had a 'Muslim Background,' " MediaMatters.org, June 18, 2008, mediamatters.org/research/200806180008.

33. Jake Tapper, "From the Fact Check Desk: What Did Obama's Half-Brother Say About Obama's Background?" *Political Punch* (blog), ABC News, June 18, 2008, blogs.abcnews.com/politicalpunch/2008/06/from-the-fact -c.html.

34. Michael Wolff, *The Man Who Owns the News: Inside the Secret World of Rupert Murdoch* (New York: Broadway Books, 2008), 398.

35. Ibid.

36. *Hannity & Colmes,* Fox News Channel, July 29, 2008; "Hannity Falsely Claimed Obama 'Abandon[ed] the Troop Visit' Because the Cameras Weren't Allowed," MediaMatters.org, July 30, 2008, mediamatters.org/research/200807300012.

37. *Morning Joe,* MSNBC, July 28, 2008; "*Morning Joe* Let McCain Campaign Manager Describe Attack Ad as 'the Truth,' Despite Colleague Mitchell's Reporting That It 'Literally Is Not True,' " MediaMatters.org, July 29, 2008, mediamatters.org/research/200807290006.

38. "On *Hannity & Colmes,* Another Corsi Falsehood About Obama," Media Matters.org, August 1, 2008, mediamatters.org/research/200808010003.

39. *Fox & Friends,* Fox News Channel, August 15, 2008; "Corsi's Claim That Obama Posted 'False, Fake Birth Certificate' Flatly Rejected by Hawaii Health Department," MediaMatters.org, August 15, 2008, mediamatters .org/research/200808150001.

40. *Hannity & Colmes,* Fox News Channel, August 18, 2008; "Fox News' Sammon Dismissed 'Nature of' Corsi Falsehoods as 'Relatively Innocuous,' " Media Matters.org, August 18, 2008, mediamatters.org/research/200808180009.

41. Jim Rutenberg and Julie Bosman, "Book Attacking Obama Hopes to Repeat '04 Anti-Kerry Feat," *New York Times,* August 12, 2008, www .nytimes.com/2008/08/13/us/politics/13book.html?pagewanted=all.

42. "Over Five-Day Period, Fox News Provided Far More Campaign Stump Time to Republicans Than to Democrats," MediaMatters.org, September 13, 2008, mediamatters.org/research/200809130005.

43. Colby Hamilton, "Jerrold Nadler, co-creator of the Permanent Cam-

paign?" The NYC Delegation. May 16, 2010, thenycdelegation.journalism
.cuny.edu/2010/05/16/jerrold-nadler-co-creator-of-the-permanent
-campaign/.

44. *Hannity & Colmes,* Fox News Channel, October 6, 2008; "Dick Morris'
Claim That Ayers 'Hired Obama' to 'Distribute the $50 Million That Ayers
Raised' Contradicted by *NY Times* Report," MediaMatters.org, October 7,
2008, mediamatters.org/research/200810070032.

45. Scott Shane, "Obama and '60s Bomber: A Look into Crossed Paths," *The
New York Times* October 3, 2008, www.nytimes.com/2008/10/04/us/
politics/04ayers.html.

46. *Hannity & Colmes,* Fox News Channel, October 13, 2008; "Dick Morris Falsely Claimed Obama Was 'General Counsel' for ACORN," Media
Matters.org, October 14, 2008, mediamatters.org/research/200810140011.

47. "Fox News Repeatedly Allowed Dick Morris to Solicit Funds on Air for
Anti-Obama Ad," MediaMatters.org, October 31, 2008, mediamatters.org/
research/200810310018.

48. Ibid.

49. *Fox & Friends,* Fox News Channel, October 30, 2008; "Fox News Repeatedly Allowed."

50. *Fox & Friends,* Fox News Channel, October 31, 2008; "Fox News Repeatedly Allowed."

51. Andrew O'Hehir, "I Watched Fox News for Five Hours Last Night," *Salon,*
November 6, 2008, www.salon.com/news/feature/2008/11/05/watching_fox.

52. Ibid.

53. Ibid.

Chapter 4: A Stalin-esque Mouthpiece

1. *Hannity & Colmes,* Fox News Channel, November 6, 2008; "Morris, Hannity, Limbaugh Implicate Obama in Stock-Market Decline—Analysts
Disagree," MediaMatters.org, November 7, 2008, mediamatters.org/
research/200811070011.

2. *Hannity & Colmes,* Fox News Channel, November 14, 2008; "Hannity,
Hewitt Revive 'Obama Recession' Claim," MediaMatters.org, November
17, 2008, mediamatters.org/research/200811170016.

3. Interview with Media Matters for America conducted by Joe Strupp,
May 17, 2011.

4. *Hannity & Colmes,* Fox News Channel, December 9, 2008; "Disregard-
ing Fitzgerald's Warning, Media Use Blagojevich Scandal to Engage in
Guilt-by-Association Against Obama," MediaMatters.org, December 10,
2008, mediamatters.org/research/200812100014.

5. Eric Boehlert, "Fox News Insider: 'Stuff Is Just Made Up,'" Media
Matters.org, February 10, 2011. Interview with Media Matters,
mediamatters.org/blog/201102100007.

6. "Koop Criticizes Evangelical Leaders on AIDS Stands," *Los Angeles Times,* June 10, 1989, articles.latimes.com/1989–06–10/local/me-1321_1_aids-epidemic-rev-d-james-kennedy-aids-stands.

7. John Dart, "Southern California File," *Los Angeles Times,* July 1, 1989.

8. Steve Rendall, "An Aggressive Conservative vs. a 'Liberal to Be Determined,' " *Extra!* (published by FAIR: Fairness & Accuracy in Reporting), November/December 2003, www.fair.org/index.php?page=1158.

9. Ibid.

10. Sean Hannity biography page, www.ksfo.com/showdj.asp?DJID=9876.

11. Ibid.

12. Matea Gold, "Fox News' Glenn Beck Strikes Ratings Gold by Challenging Barack Obama," *Los Angeles Times,* March 6, 2009, articles.latimes.com/2009/mar/06/entertainment/et-foxnews6.

13. *Unlikely Mormon: The Conversion Story of Glenn Beck* (DVD; Salt Lake City: Deseret Book, 2008), excerpt viewable at www.youtube.com/watch?v=rpVi6JwjjGU&feature=player_embedded.

14. Product Description on Amazon.com, www.amazon.com/Strategery-Terrorists-Outwitting-Confounding-Mainstream/dp/product-description/B001PTG3GU.

15. " Sammon and Boughton Officially Upped at Fox News," *FishbowlDC* (blog), Mediabistro, February 26, 2009, www.mediabistro.com/fishbowldc/sammon-and-boughton-officially-upped-at-fox-news_b15133.

16. Joe Strupp, "Sources: Fox Management Slanting D.C. Bureau's News Coverage," MediaMatters.org, October 29, 2010, mediamatters.org/blog/201010290023?lid=1147907&rid=56347393.

17. Ibid.

18. Howard Kurtz, "Journalist Major Garrett Leaves Fox News TV for National Journal Print," *Washington Post,* August 26, 2010, www.washingtonpost.com/wp-dyn/content/article/2010/08/25/AR2010082504484.html.

19. Interview with Media Matters for America conducted by Joe Strupp, May 17, 2011.

20. Bill Sammon e-mail, obtained by Media Matters for America, October 27, 2009.

21. *Hannity,* Fox News Channel, August 18, 2009; "Luntz Births Another GOP Talking Point: It's a 'Government Option' Not a 'Public Option,' " Media Matters.org, August 19, 2009, mediamatters.org/mmtv/200908190002.

22. *Special Report,* Fox News Channel, October 27, 2009; Ben Dimiero, "Leaked Email: Fox Boss Caught Slanting News Reporting," *County Fair* (blog), MediaMatters.org, mediamatters.org/blog/201012090003.

23. Ibid.

24. *Special Report,* Fox News Channel, October 26, 2009; Dimiero, "Leaked Email."

25. *Special Report,* Fox News Channel, January 14, 2010.

26. *Fox News Sunday,* Fox News Channel, January 17, 2010.

27. "33 Internal FOX Editorial Memos Reviewed by MMFA Reveal FOX News Channel's Inner Workings," MediaMatters.org, July 14, 2004, media matters.org/research/200407140002.

28. Howard Kurtz, "Tilting at the Right, Leaning to the Left," *Washington Post,* July 11, 2004, www.washingtonpost.com/wp-dyn/articles/A41604 –2004Jul10.html.

29. *The Rush Limbaugh Show,* EIB Network, January 20, 2009, rushlimbaugh .com/daily/2009/01/16/Limbaugh-i-hope-obama-fails.

30. *Glenn Beck,* Fox News Channel, January 20, 2009, www.youtube.com/ watch?v=35eRxxZ-Ar0.

31. *Hannity,* Fox News Channel, January 21, 2009, www.youtube.com/ watch?v=35eRxxZ-Ar0.

32. *The O'Reilly Factor,* Fox News Channel, January 22, 2009, www.youtube .com/watch?v=35eRxxZ-Ar0.

33. *Glenn Beck,* Fox News Channel, January 23, 2009, www.youtube.com/ watch?v=35eRxxZ-Ar0.

34. *Huckabee,* Fox News Channel, January 24, 2009, www.youtube.com/ watch?v=35eRxxZ-Ar0.

35. *Fox News Sunday,* Fox News Channel, January 25, 2009, www.youtube .com/watch?v=35eRxxZ-Ar0.

36. *Fox & Friends,* Fox News Channel, January 27, 2009, www.youtube.com/ watch?v=35eRxxZ-Ar0.

37. *Glenn Beck,* Fox News Channel, January 30, 2009, www.youtube.com/ watch?v=35eRxxZ-Ar0.

38. *Hannity,* Fox News Channel, February 2, 2009, www.youtube.com/ watch?v=35eRxxZ-Ar0.

39. *Special Report,* Fox News Channel, February 5, 2009, www.youtube.com/ watch?v=35eRxxZ-Ar0.

40. *Happening Now,* Fox News Channel, February 10, 2009; "Fox Passes Off GOP Press Release as Its Own Research—Typo and All," MediaMatters .org, February 10, 2009, mediamatters.org/research/200902100019.

41. *Happening Now,* Fox News Channel, April 1, 2009; "Cut and Paste: 'FOXfact[s]' About GOP Budget Nearly Identical to GOP Rep. Ryan's Op-Ed," MediaMatters.org, April 1, 2009, mediamatters.org/mobile/ research/200904010017.

42. *America's Newsroom,* Fox News Channel, April 23, 2009; "Fox News' Hemmer 'Keeping Track of the Stimulus Money' by Lifting Research from GOP Website," MediaMatters.org, April 23, 2009, mediamatters.org/ research/200904230018.

43. *The O'Reilly Factor,* Fox News Channel, January 28, 2009; "On *O'Reilly Fac-*

tor, Morris Falsely Claimed Aid to States in Recovery Plan 'Doesn't Stimulate Anything,' " MediaMatters.org, January 29, 2009, mediamatters.org/research/200901290001.

44. Mark Zandi, testimony before the Committee on Small Business, U.S. House of Representatives, July 24, 2008, www.economy.com/mark-zandi/documents/Small%20Business_7_24_08.pdf.

45. *Special Report,* Fox News Channel, January 29, 2009; "AP's Retracted Stimulus Bill Falsehood Finds a New Home at Fox," MediaMatters.org, January 30, 2009, mediamatters.org/research/200901300002.

46. *Fox & Friends,* Fox News Channel. January 29, 2009; *"Fox & Friends'* Doocy Repeated False Claim that Stimulus Package Includes $4 Billion for ACORN," MediaMatters.org, January 29, 2009, mediamatters.org/research/200901290026.

47. *Glenn Beck,* Fox News Channel, February 4, 2009; "Beck on Bank 'Nationaliz[ation],' Executive Pay Caps, EFCA, SCHIP," MediaMatters .org, February 4, 2009, mediamatters.org/mmtv/200902040022.

48. *The O'Reilly Factor,* Fox News Channel, February 6, 2009; "Beck on *O'Reilly Factor:* 'We Are Really Truly Stepping Beyond Socialism and Starting to Look at Fascism'; Compares Proposals to Nazi Germany," MediaMatters .org, February 6, 2009, mediamatters.org/mmtv/200902060027.

49. *Fox & Friends,* Fox News Channel, February 10, 2009; "Beck Says of Stimulus Package, 'It Is Slavery,' " MediaMatters.org, February 10, 2009, media matters.org/mmtv/200902100007.

50. *Glenn Beck,* Fox News Channel, February 11, 2009; "Beck: 'You Know What This President Is Doing Right Now? He Is Addicting This Country to Heroin—the Heroin That Is Slavery,' " MediaMatters.org, February 11, 2009, mediamatters.org/mmtv/200902110028.

51. *Your World,* Fox News Channel, February 11, 2009; "Fox News Jumps at GOP's Mouse Tale," MediaMatters.org, February 12, 2009, mediamatters .org/research/200902120023.

52. *Fox & Friends,* Fox News Channel, February 12, 2009; "Fox News Jumps at GOP's Mouse Tale."

53. Greg Sargent, "Pelosi's Office: Conservative Talking Point About $30 Million for Mice Is Fabrication," *The Plum Line* (blog), *Washington Post,* February 12, 2009, theplumline.whorunsgov.com/stimulus-package/pelosi-staff -conservative-talking-point-about-30-million-for-mice-is-fabrication/.

54. *Glenn Beck,* Fox News Channel, February 12, 2009; "Fox News Jumps at GOP's Mouse Tale."

55. *Trillion with a T,* Fox News Channel, February 14–16, 2009; "Fox Special Promoted Numerous Myths and Falsehoods About Obama and the Economic Recovery Bill," MediaMatters.org, February 18, 2009, mediamatters .org/research/200902180019.

56. Remarks by President Obama at Strasbourg Town Hall, White House, April 3, 2009, www.whitehouse.gov/the_press_office/Remarks-by -President-Obama-at-Strasbourg-Town-Hall/.

57. Ibid.

58. *Hannity,* Fox News Channel, April 6, 2009; "Hannity Falsely Claimed Obama 'Seemingly Apologiz[ed] for Our Engagement in the War on Terror,' " MediaMatters.org, April 7, 2009, mediamatters.org/research/200904070002.

59. *Hannity,* Fox News Channel, April 8, 2009; "Fox News Figures Outraged over Obama's 'Christian Nation' Comment," MediaMatters.org, April 9, 2009, mediamatters.org/research/200904090033.

60. "Joint Press Available with President Obama and President Gul of Turkey," Cankaya Palace, Ankara, Turkey, April 6, 2009, www.whitehouse .gov/the_press_office/Joint-Press-Availability-With-President-Obama -And-President-Gul-Of-Turkey.

61. Liz Peek, "Chavez Handshake May Cost U.S. Billions," FoxNews.com, April 22, 2009; "FoxNews.com Financial Columnist Claims 'Chavez Handshake May Cost U.S. Billions,' Because It Signifies Obama Will 'Buy Chavez' Friendship,' " *County Fair* (blog), MediaMatters.org, April 22, 2009, mediamatters.org/blog/200904220007.

62. Nicholas Johnston, "Lieberman Says Obama Off to 'Good Start,' Cites Cairo Speech," *Bloomberg,* June 13, 2009, www.bloomberg.com/apps/news ?pid=ewsarchive&sid=ak5htM4suvD8.

63. Hans Nichols, "Obama Cairo Speech 'Signal Achievement,' Republican Lugar Says," *Bloomberg,* June 6, 2009, www.bloomberg.com/apps/news ?pidewsarchive&sid=anR10RbcGdeQ.

64. Bill Sammon e-mail, obtained by Media Matters for America.

65. *America's Newsroom,* Fox News Channel, June 4, 2009; Simon Maloy, "FOXLEAKS: How Bill Sammon Slanted Fox's Cairo Speech Coverage," *County Fair* (blog), MediaMatters.org, February 8, 2011, mediamatters.org/ blog/201102080014.

66. *Special Report,* Fox News Channel, June 4, 2009; Maloy, "FOXLEAKS: How Bill Sammon Slanted Fox's Cairo Speech Coverage."

67. *The O'Reilly Factor,* Fox News Channel, June 4, 2009; Maloy, "FOXLEAKS: How Bill Sammon Slanted Fox's Cairo Speech Coverage."

68. *Hannity,* Fox News Channel, June 4, 2009; Maloy, "FOXLEAKS: How Bill Sammon Slanted Fox's Cairo Speech Coverage."

69. *Fox & Friends,* Fox News Channel, June 5, 2009; Maloy, "FOXLEAKS: How Bill Sammon Slanted Fox's Cairo Speech Coverage."

70. "Remarks by the President on a New Beginning," Cairo University, White House, June 4, 2009; www.whitehouse.gov/the-press-office/remarks -president-cairo-university-6–04–09.

71. *Fox & Friends,* Fox News Channel, April 29, 2009, www.youtube.com/ watch?v=35eRxxZ-Ar0.

Chapter 5: Time for a Tea Party

1. *Squawk Box,* CNBC, February 19, 2009; "Politico Falsely Claimed that Santelli's 'Rant' Criticized 'Careless Banks,' " MediaMatters.org, February 25, 2009, mediamatters.org/research/200902250011.

2. Ibid.

3. *Glenn Beck,* Fox News Channel, April 6, 2009; "Beck Says You Can 'Celebrate with Fox News' at Any of Four 'FNC Tax Day Tea Parties,' " Media Matters.org, April 6, 2009, mediamatters.org/mmtv/200904060023.

4. Kate Zernike and Megan Thee-Brenan, "Poll Finds Tea Party Backers Wealthier and More Educated," *New York Times,* April 14, 2010, www .nytimes.com/2010/04/15/us/politics/15poll.html.

5. "Fox Promotion of Tea Parties Follows Years of Attacking Progressive Demonstrators," MediaMatters.org, April 17, 2009, mediamatters.org/ research/200904170036.

6. Interview with Media Matters conducted by Joe Strupp. May 17, 2011.

7. *On the Record,* Fox News Channel, February 27, 2009; "Report: 'Fair and Balanced' Fox News Aggressively Promotes 'Tea Party' Protests," Media Matters.org, April 8, 2009, mediamatters.org/reports/200904080025.

8. *Special Report,* Fox News Channel, March 25, 2009; "Report: 'Fair and Balanced' Fox News Aggressively Promotes 'Tea Party' Protests."

9. *America's Newsroom,* Fox News Channel, April 6, 2009; "Report: 'Fair and Balanced' Fox News Aggressively Promotes 'Tea Party' Protests."

10. *Glenn Beck,* Fox News Channel, April 6, 2009; "Report: 'Fair and Balanced' Fox News Aggressively Promotes 'Tea Party' Protests."

11. Ibid.

12. *Hannity,* Fox News Channel, April 2, 2009; "Report: 'Fair and Balanced' Fox News Aggressively Promotes 'Tea Party' Protests."

13. "Report: 'Fair and Balanced' Fox News Aggressively Promotes 'Tea Party' Protests."

14. Ibid.

15. Jeanne Jakle, "Glenn Beck to Broadcast TV Show in Front of Alamo," *Jakle's Jacuzzi* (blog), *San Antonio Express-News,* April 2, 2009, blog.mysan antonio.com/jakle06/2009/04/glenn-beck-to-broadcast-show-in-front -of-alamo/.

16. "Report: 'Fair and Balanced' Fox News Aggressively Promotes 'Tea Party' Protests."

17. Ibid.

18. *America's Newsroom,* Fox News Channel, March 24, 2009; "Report: 'Fair and Balanced' Fox News Aggressively Promotes 'Tea Party' Protests."

19. "On the House: Fox Aired 107 Ads for Its Coverage of Tea Party Protests over 10 Days," MediaMatters.org, April 17, 2009, mediamatters.org/ research/200904170011.

20. Ibid.

21. Ibid.

22. *Fox & Friends,* Fox News Channel, April 15, 2009; "Carlson's Suggestion on How to Show Support for Tea Parties: 'You Can Hang [a Teabag] from Your Mirror, Too, Like Fuzzy Dice,' " MediaMatters.org, April 15, 2009, mediamatters.org/mmtv/200904150008.

23. *America's Newsroom,* Fox News Channel, April 15, 2009; "Fox News' Tea Party Coverage Makes Mockery of Claim That Network Provides 'Straight . . . News' in Daytime," MediaMatters.org, April 16, 2009, mediamatters.org/research/200904160022.

24. *Happening Now,* Fox News Channel, April 15, 2009; "Fox News' Tea Party Coverage Makes Mockery."

25. *New York Times*/CBS National Survey of Tea Party Supporters, April 5–10, 2010, s3.amazonaws.com/nytdocs/docs/312/312.pdf#page=35.

26. *The Situation Room,* CNN, April 13, 2009; "Kurtz: 'The Question Is Whether Rupert Murdoch's Network Wants to Be So Closely Identified with What Has Become an Anti-Obama Protest Movement," MediaMatters.org, April 13, 2009, mediamatters.org/mmtv/200904130027.

27. James Rainey, "Fox News, MSNBC Prejudge 'Tea Parties,' " *Los Angeles Times,* April 15, 2009, articles.latimes.com/2009/apr/15/entertainment/et-onthemedia15.

28. Ari Rabin-Havt, "Rupert Murdoch Lied to Me (Personally)," *Huffington Post,* August 17, 2010, www.huffingtonpost.com/ari-rabin-havt/rupert-murdoch-lied-to-me_b_685180.html.

29. Flyer for Cincinnati Tea Party Tax Day Tea Party 2010, www.cincinnatiteaparty.org/Media/CTP_TAX_DAY_RALLY_FLIER.pdf.

30. Jane Prendergast, "Sean Hannity, Tax Day Rally Expected to Draw Thousands," *Cincinnati Enquirer,* April 13, 2010, news.cincinnati.com/article/20100413/NEWS0108/4140317/Sean-Hannity-Tax-Day-rally-expected-to-draw-thousands.

31. Matea Gold, "Fox News Yanks Sean Hannity from Cincinnati Tea Party Rally He Was Set to Star in," *Show Tracker* (blog), *Los Angeles Times,* April 15, 2010, latimesblogs.latimes.com/showtracker/2010/04/fox-news-cancels-hannity-taping-at-cincinnati-tea-party-rally-.html.

32. Interview with Media Matters for America conducted by Joe Strupp, May 16, 2011.

33. *Fox & Friends,* Fox News Channel, July 30, 2009; "Out of Touch: Conservative Media Argue Insured Don't Need Health Care Reform," MediaMatters.org, August 4, 2009, mediamatters.org/research/200908040021.

34. *Hannity,* Fox News Channel, July 19, 2009; "Hannity Fear-Mongering on Health Care: Gov't Rationing Body Will Tell Women with Breast Cancer, 'You're Dead,' " MediaMatters.org, June 19, 2009, mediamatters.org/mmtv/200906190039.

35. *Hannity,* Fox News Channel, July 29, 2009; "Rove's Latest Distortion:

Dems Plan $1T 'Price Tag' for Health Reform," MediaMatters.org, July 30, 2009, mediamatters.org/research/200907300005.

36. *Special Report,* Fox News Channel, June 29, 2009; "Fox's Baier Falsely Suggests Obama Has Cited Canada as Possible Health Reform Model," Media Matters.org, June 30, 2009, mediamatters.org/research/200906300005.

37. *Hannity,* Fox News Channel, June 16, 2009; "Conservative Media Run with False *IBD* Claim that Health Bill Outlaws Private Coverage," Media Matters.org, July 17, 2009, mediamatters.org/research/200907170005.

38. Interview with Media Matters for America conducted by Joe Strupp, May 17, 2011.

39. Tom Wolfe, "Revolutionaries," *New York Post,* June 30, 2003, www .manhattan-institute.org/html/_nypost-revolutionaries.htm.

40. Legacy Tobacco Documents Library, University of California, San Francisco, legacy.library.ucsf.edu/tid/tfu82e00/pdf?search=%22betsy%20 mccaughey%22.

41. Andy Plattner, "Big Tobacco's Toughest Road," *US News & World Report,* April 17, 1989, available at Legacy Tobacco Documents Library, University of California, San Francisco, legacy.library.ucsf.edu/tid/buq37b00/pdf.

42. Legacy Tobacco Documents Library, University of California, San Francisco, legacy.library.ucsf.edu/tid/sqr86d00/pdf?search=%22cauti%20ailes %20communications%22.

43. Legacy Tobacco Documents Library, University of California, San Francisco, legacy.library.ucsf.edu/tid/uhb03e00/pdf.

44. Legacy Tobacco Documents Library, University of California, San Francisco, legacy.library.ucsf.edu/tid/mgs57c00/pdf.

45. Legacy Tobacco Documents Library, University of California, San Francisco, legacy.library.ucsf.edu/tid/kqq74e00/pdf?search=%22ailes%22.

46. Ibid.

47. Legacy Tobacco Documents Library, University of California, San Francisco, legacy.library.ucsf.edu/tid/ptk53e00/pdf.

48. Legacy Tobacco Documents Library, University of California, San Francisco, legacy.library.ucsf.edu/tid/upq91a00/pdf.

49. *The Fred Thompson Show,* July 16, 2009; "Media Echo Serial Misinformer McCaughey's False End-of-Life Counseling Claim," MediaMatters.org, July 31, 2009, mediamatters.org/research/200907310051.

50. "McCaughey Claims End-of-Life Counseling Will Be Required for Medicare Patients," Politifact.com, July 16, 2009, politifact.com/truth-o-meter/ statements/2009/jul/23/betsy-mccaughey/mccaughey-claims-end-life -counseling-will-be-requi/.

51. "Statement on the Current Health Care Debate," Sarah Palin's Facebook page, August 7, 2009, www.facebook.com/note.php?note_id=113851103434.

52. *Fox & Friends,* Fox News Channel, August 10, 2009; "Echoing Palin, Kilmeade Said Health Care Bill Mandates Elderly Go 'in Front of

Death Panel,' " MediaMatters.org, August 10, 2009, mediamatters.org/mmtv/200908100002.

53. *Special Report,* Fox News Channel, August 13, 2009; "*Special Report* Portrays 'Death Panels' Issue as He Said/She Said Issue," MediaMatters.org, August 14, 2009, mediamatters.org/research/200908140026.

54. *Fox & Friends,* Fox News Channel, August 19, 2009; "After Repeated Debunkings of 'Death Panels,' Conservative Media Backtrack to 'De Facto Death Panels,' " MediaMatters.org, August 19, 2009, mediamatters.org/research/200908190053.

55. CNN/Opinion Research Poll, September 14, 2009, i2.cdn.turner.com/cnn/2009/images/09/14/rel14b2.pdf.

56. *Glenn Beck,* Fox News Channel, January 3, 2011; "Napolitano Falsely Claims There Are Now Death Panels That Will 'Tell Grandma and Grandpa . . . How and When to Die,' " *MediaMatters.org,* January 3, 2011, mediamatters.org/mmtv/201101030034.

57. *The Glenn Beck Program,* Premiere Radio Networks, November 19, 2009, "Beck Insists Audience "Must Not Allow" Health Care Bill to Pass, Warns It Would Mean "the End of America as You Know It," mediamatters.org/mmtv/200911190012.

58. *Hannity,* Fox News Channel, March 21, 2010; "Hannity: Health Care Reform Is 'the Most Irresponsible Piece of Domestic Legislation in Our Lifetime,' " MediaMatters.org, March 21, 2010, mediamatters.org/mmtv/201003210024.

59. *Fox Nation,* August 14, 2009: " 'Fox Nation Victory!' Declared: 'Senate Removes "End of Life" Provision,' " *MediaMatters.org,* August 14, 2009, mediamatters.org/mmtv/200908140001.

60. FoxNation.com, August 17, 2009; " 'Fox Nation Victory!' Declared: 'Obama Backs Down from Gov't-Run Health Care!' " MediaMatters.org, August 17, 2009, mediamatters.org/blog/200908170001.

61. FoxNation.com, July 24, 2009; "Yet Another Fox Nation 'Victory!': 'Congress Delays Health Care Rationing Bill,' " MediaMatters.org, July 24, 2009, mediamatters.org/mmtv/200907240003.

62. *The Sean Hannity Show,* Premiere Radio Networks, July 29, 2009; "CBS, Fox Reports on Town Hall Disruptions Ignore Conservative Strategy," Media Matters.org, August 5, 2009, mediamatters.org/research/200908050017.

63. *Fox & Friends,* Fox News Channel, August 3, 2009; "Fair & Balanced: *Fox & Friends* Guest-Host Fearmongers over Euthanasia, Hosts Urge Listeners to Contact Congress," MediaMatters.org, August 3, 2009, mediamatters.org/mmtv/200908030014.

64. Rachel Slajda, "Teabaggers Try to Shout Down Health Care Reform at Town Halls," *TPMDC* (blog), *Talking Points Memo,* August 3, 2009, tpmdc.talkingpointsmemo.com/2009/08/teabaggers-try-to-shout-down-health-care-reform-at-town-halls.php.

65. *Fox & Friends,* Fox News Channel, August 3, 2009; "Fair & Balanced: *Fox & Friends* Guest-Host Fearmongers."

66. *Fox & Friends,* Fox News Channel, August 4, 2009; "Fox at It Again: Now Promoting Anti–Health Reform Disruptions of Town Halls," Media Matters.org, August 4, 2009, mediamatters.org/research/200908040054.

67. *Hannity,* Fox News Channel, August 3, 2009; ibid.

68. Nancy Pelosi and Steny Hoyer, "Drowning Out Opposing Views Is Simply Un-American," *USA Today,* August 10, 2009.

69. *Fox & Friends,* Fox News Channel, August 10, 2009; "Carlson, Doocy Falsely Claim Pelosi Called Health Reform Opponents 'Un-American,' " Media Matters.org, August 10, 2009, mediamatters.org/research/200908100007.

70. Ibid.

71. *Hannity,* Fox News Channel, August 11, 2009; "Hannity Falsely Claims 'We've Had Hard-Working Americans Called Nazis and Brownshirts and un-American by Pelosi,' " MediaMatters.org, August 11, 2009, media matters.org/mmtv/200908110054?lid=1058105&rid=33202694.

72. "After Pelosi Noted that Protesters Had Swastika Signs, Media Claim She Called Them Nazis," MediaMatters.org, August 11, 2009, mediamatters .org/research/200908110023.

73. *Fox & Friends,* Fox News Channel, August 24, 2009; "Fox News Freak-Out: Guests Make Extreme Claims and Accusations About Health Care," Media Matters.org, August 24, 2009, mediamatters.org/research/200908240129.

74. *Fox & Friends,* Fox News Channel, August 19, 2009; "Doocy Finds Fault with 'Rude' Frank, Not Protester Who Compared Obama to Hitler," Media Matters.org, August 19, 2009, mediamatters.org/research/200908190020.

75. "Rep. Frank Condemns Those Comparing Obama to Hitler," NECN.com (New England Cable News), April 18, 2009, www.necn.com/Boston/ NECN-Extra/2009/08/18/Rep-Frank-condemns-those/1250643022 .html.

76. *Fox & Friends,* Fox News Channel, August 31, 2009; "Will *Fox & Friends* Set Story Straight on NH Town Hall?" MediaMatters.org, September 3, 2009, mediamatters.org/research/200909030055?lid=1062390&rid=34213490.

77. John DiStaso, "John DiStaso's Granite Status: Another National GOP Boost for Ayotte," *New Hampshire Union Leader,* September 8, 2009, via "Will Fox & Friends Set Story Straight on NH Town Hall?" MediaMatters .org, September 3, 2009, http://mediamatters.org/research/200909030055.

78. Howard Kurtz, "Journalists, Left Out of the Debate," *Washington Post,* August 24, 2009; www.washingtonpost.com/wp-dyn/content/article/ 2009/08/23/AR2009082302173.html.

79. "Report: Fox News' Town Hall Coverage Amplifies Opponents of Health Care Reform, Ignores Supporters," MediaMatters.org, September 8, 2009, mediamatters.org/research/200909080004.

80. *On the Record,* Fox News Channel, August 25, 2009.

81. *America's Newsroom,* Fox News Channel, August 28, 2009.

82. Ibid.

83. "Report: Fox News' Town Hall Coverage Amplifies Opponents."

84. *CNN Newsroom,* CNN, August 25, 2009, transcripts.cnn.com/transcripts/0908/25/cnr.07.html.

85. Bachmann Healthcare Town Hall, August 27, 2009, Lake Elmo, MN, www.youtube.com/watch?v=9ybA8aWPyEA.

86. C-SPAN, August 25, 2009; Jamison Foser, "Hey, MSNBC/CNN: Let's See You Play *This* Clip All Week," *County Fair* (blog), MediaMatters.org, August 25, 2009, mediamatters.org/blog/200908250059.

87. "Report: Fox News' Town Hall Coverage Amplifies Opponents."

88. Ibid.

89. Rosalind S. Helderman, "U.S. Rep. James P. Moran, Howard Dean Appear at Health-Care Town Hall in Reston," *Washington Post,* August 26, 2009, www.washingtonpost.com/wp-dyn/content/article/2009/08/25/AR2009082503413.html.

90. "Report: Fox News' Town Hall Coverage Amplifies Opponents."

91. Ibid.

92. William Kristol, "Defeating President Clinton's Health Care Proposal," December 2, 1993, viewed at *Brad DeLong's Egregious Moderation* (blog), delong.typepad.com/egregious_moderation/2009/03/william-kristol-defeating-president-clintons-health-care-proposal.html.

93. *The Rush Limbaugh Show,* EIB Network, February 8, 2010, www.rushlimbaugh.com/home/daily/site_020810/content/01125108.guest.html.

94. *Fox & Friends,* Fox News Channel, February 11, 2010; "Fox's Johnson Jr. Calls Health Care Summit a 'Trap,' Says Bill Must 'Start from Scratch' to Be Bipartisan," MediaMatters.org, February 11, 2010, mediamatters.org/mmtv/201002110009.

95. *Brian and the Judge,* Fox News Radio, February 10, 2010; "Napolitano Agrees with Limbaugh: Health Care Summit 'a Trap [Obama's] Setting for the Republicans' on Road to Socialism," *MediaMatters.org,* February 10, 2010, mediamatters.org/mmtv/201002100026.

96. *The O'Reilly Factor,* Fox News Channel, February 24, 2010; "An *O'Reilly Factor* Hat Trick: Rove, Morris, and Schoen Repeat Falsehoods on the Eve of Health Care Summit," MediaMatters.org, February 25, 2010, www.mediamattersinstitute.org/research/201002250003.

97. Ibid.

98. *The O'Reilly Factor,* Fox News Channel, February 25, 2010; "Right-Wing Media 'Bor[ed]' by Health Care Summit," MediaMatters.org, February 25, 2010, mediamatters.org/research/201002250074.

99. Glenn Beck e-mail newsletter, February 25, 2010; "Right-Wing Media 'Bor[ed]' by Health Care Summit."

100. *Special Report,* Fox News Channel, February 25, 2010; "Conservatives Say

Obama 'Lowered Himself' with Participation in Health Summit 'Beneath' His Office," MediaMatters.org, February 25, 2010, mediamatters.org/research/201002250073.

101. *The O'Reilly Factor,* Fox News Channel, February 25, 2010; "Conservatives Say Obama 'Lowered Himself' with Participation in Health Summit 'Beneath' His Office."

102. *Special Report,* Fox News Channel, February 25, 2010; "Garrett Presents Obama's Rebuttal of GOP Health Care Falsehoods as He-Said/He-Said," MediaMatters.org, February 25, 2010, mediamatters.org/research/201002250069.

103. Ibid.

104. *Fox & Friends,* Fox News Channel, March 11, 2010; "Doocy Baselessly Claims Slaughter Is Angling to Pass Health Care Reform Without a Vote," MediaMatters.org, March 11, 2010, mediamatters.org/research/201003110037.

105. *Special Report,* Fox News Channel, February 24, 2010; "Baier Claims Reconciliation 'Was Once Called the Nuclear Option' to Falsely Suggest Dem Hypocrisy," MediaMatters.org, February 24, 2010, mediamatters.org/research/201002240062.

106. *Hannity,* Fox News Channel, February 25, 2010; "Myths and Falsehoods on Budget Reconciliation," MediaMatters.org, March 15, 2010, mediamatters.org/research/201003150034#5.

107. *Glenn Beck,* Fox News Channel, March 16, 2010; "Beck on Health Bill: 'If This Passes, They Will Control Every Aspect of Your Life,' Including Whether You Can Have Children," MediaMatters.org, March 16, 2010, mediamatters.org/mmtv/201003160046.

108. *Glenn Beck,* Fox News Channel, March 19, 2010; "Beck: If Health Care Passes, 'Don't We Lose Really the Democratic Party to the Socialists?' " MediaMatters.org, March 19, 2010, mediamatters.org/mmtv/201003190075.

109. *America's Newsroom,* Fox News Channel, March 19, 2010; "Hemmer Perpetuates Debunked Health Care Myth: 'Could People Be Going to Jail for Not Owning Health Insurance?' " MediaMatters.org, March 19, 2010, mediamatters.org/mmtv/201003190031.

110. *Fox & Friends,* Fox News Channel, March 18, 2010; "*Fox & Friends*' Chyron on Health Care Reform: 'Don't Do It!' " MediaMatters.org, March 18, 2010, mediamatters.org/blog/201003180005.

111. Laura Ingraham, Twitter, March 19, 2010; "Kitchen Sink: Fox's Last-Ditch Effort to Rally Opposition to Health Care Reform," *MediaMatters.org,* March 19, 2010, mediamatters.org/research/201003190058.

112. Bill O'Reilly, "Obamacare: Truth vs. Propaganda," FoxNews.com, March 5, 2010, www.foxnews.com/story/0,2933,588139,00.html.

113. "Keep Calling Congress": " 'Kill the Bill': Fox's Year-Long Open Activism

Against Health Care Reform," MediaMatters.org, March 22, 2010, media matters.org/research/201003220077.

114. *Glenn Beck,* Fox News Channel, March 17, 2010; " 'Kill the Bill': Fox's Year-Long Open Activism Against Health Care Reform," MediaMatters .org, March 22, 2010, mediamatters.org/research/201003220077.

115. *Glenn Beck,* Fox News Channel, March 18, 2010; " 'Kill the Bill': Fox's Year-Long Open Activism Against Health Care Reform."

116. Interview with Media Matters for America conducted by Joe Strupp, May 16, 2011.

Chapter 6: Violent Rhetoric

1. *Fox & Friends,* Fox News Channel, July 28, 2009; "Beck: Obama Has 'Exposed Himself as a Guy' with 'a Deep-Seated Hatred for White People,' " MediaMatters.org, July 28, 2009, mediamatters.org/mmtv/200907280008.

2. Ibid.

3. *Glenn Beck,* CNN Headline News, November 14, 2006; "CNN's Beck to First-Ever Muslim Congressman: '[W]hat I Feel Like Saying Is, "Sir, Prove to Me that You Are Not Working with Our Enemies," ' " MediaMatters .org, November 15, 2006, mediamatters.org/mmtv/200611150004.

4. Tom Junod, "Roger Ailes on Roger Ailes: The Interview Transcripts, Part 2," *The Politics Blog, Esquire,* January 27, 2011, www.esquire.com/blogs/politics/roger-ailes-quotes-5072437.

5. "Nixon's Roger Ailes," *Washington Post,* February 13, 1972, www.scribd .com/doc/53543922/Roger-Ailes-I-Dont-Try-to-Fool-Voters.

6. David Axelrod at First Draft of History Conference, video at link.bright cove.com/services/player/bcpid42953000001?bctid=44135339001 (thirty-four-minute mark).

7. *Glenn Beck,* Fox News Channel, August 27, 2009; "Beck Crops Obama to Fearmonger About 'Crazy Things' Like 'Civilian National Security Force,' " MediaMatters.org, August 27, 2009, mediamatters.org/mmtv/200908270033.

8. *Glenn Beck,* Fox News Channel, August 27, 2009; "Beck Claims Obama's 'Civilian National Security Force' Is 'What Hitler Did with the SS,' 'What Saddam Hussein Did,' " MediaMatters.org, August 27, 2009, mediamatters .org/mmtv/200908270036.

9. Simon Greer, "Government Is Essential to Quest for Social Justice," *On Faith* (blog) *Washington Post,* April 14, 2010, newsweek.washingtonpost .com/onfaith/guestvoices/2010/04/mr_beck_-_you_are.html.

10. *The Glenn Beck Program,* Premiere Radio Networks, May 28, 2010; "Beck Attacks Jewish Funds for Justice's Simon Greer; Says Putting 'the Common Good' First 'Leads to Death Camps,' " MediaMatters.org, May 28, 2010, mediamatters.org/mmtv/201005280022.

11. Letter from Jewish leaders to Rupert Murdoch, obtained by Media Matters, July 1, 2010.

12. Letter from Roger Ailes to Jewish leaders, obtained by Media Matters, July 9, 2010.

13. Howard Kurtz, "Fox News Chief Blasts NPR 'Nazis,'" *Daily Beast,* November 17, 2010, www.thedailybeast.com/blogs-and-stories/2010–11–17/fox-news-chief-roger-ailes-blasts-national-public-radio-brass-as-nazis/.

14. Michael Calderone, "Fox News Chief Apologizes to ADL for Nazi Remark," *The Cutline* (blog), Yahoo News, November 18, 2010; news.yahoo.com/s/yblog_thecutline/20101118/bs_yblog_thecutline/fox-news-chief-apologizes-to-adl-for-nazi-remark.

15. Howard Kurtz, "Roger Ailes Lets Rip," *Daily Beast,* November 16, 2010; www.thedailybeast.com/blogs-and-stories/2010–11–16/fox-news-chairman-roger-ailes-slams-white-house-in-exclusive-interview/.

16. "Stop the Race Baiting," ColorofChange.org, June 30, 2009, orig.colorofchange.org/beck/message.html.

17. Eliza Strickland, "The New Face of Environmentalism: Van Jones Renounced His Rowdy Black Nationalism on the Way Toward Becoming an Influential Leader of the New Progressive Politics," *East Bay Express,* November 2, 2005.

18. *Glenn Beck,* Fox News Channel, July 23, 2009.

19. David Weigel, " Far-Right Site Gains Influence in Obama Era," *Washington Independent,* September 4, 2009, washingtonindependent.com/57776/far-right-site-gains-influence-in-obama-era.

20. Ibid.

21. *The O'Reilly Factor,* Fox News Channel, August 26, 2009; "O'Reilly Says Van Jones 'Reminds Me of Rev. Wright . . . He's an Anti-American Guy, We Think,' " MediaMatters.org, August 26, 2009, mediamatters.org/mmtv/200908260051.

22. *Glenn Beck,* Fox News Channel, September 1, 2010.

23. Van Jones, "Shirley Sherrod and Me," *New York Times,* July 24, 2010; www.nytimes.com/2010/07/25/opinion/25jones.html.

24. Garance Franke-Ruta and Anne E. Kornblut, "White House Says Little About Embattled Jones," *Washington Post,* September 5, 2009, www.washingtonpost.com/wp-dyn/content/article/2009/09/04/AR2009090403563.html.

25. Ibid.

26. Scott Wilson and Garance Franke-Ruta, "White House Adviser Van Jones Resigns amid Controversy over Past Activism," *Washington Post,* September 6, 2009, voices.washingtonpost.com/44/2009/09/06/van_jones_resigns.html.

27. Ibid.

28. Ben Smith and Nia-Malika Henderson, "Glenn Beck Up, Left Down and Van Jones Defiant," *Politico,* September 8, 2009, www.politico.com/news/stories/0909/26813_Page2.html.

29. *Reliable Sources,* CNN, September 20, 2009.

30. Will Bunch, " 'Pop' Poplawski, the High-Def Hucksters, and the Downward Cycle of Violence," *County Fair* (blog), MediaMatters.org, August 9, 2010, mediamatters.org/blog/201008090022.

31. Sarah Pavlus, "Relative: Man Convicted of Threatening Sen. Murray Was Inspired by Beck," *County Fair* (blog), MediaMatters.org, October 28, 2010, mediamatters.org/blog/201010280036.

32. John Hamilton, " 'Progressive Hunter,' " MediaMatters.org, October 11, 2010, mediamatters.org/research/201010110002.

33. Will Bunch, "Beck, Palin to Restore Honor to 9/11 by Cashing In with $225 'Meet and Greet,' " *County Fair* (blog), MediaMatters.org, September 8, 2010, mediamatters.org/blog/201009080028.

34. *Glenn Beck,* Fox News Channel, August 12, 2009; "Beck Announces He Will Anchor Fox News' Live Coverage of 'the Biggest 9–12 Tea Party Yet, on Capitol Hill,' " MediaMatters.org, August 13, 2009, mediamatters.org/mmtv/200908130005.

35. *Glenn Beck,* Fox News Channel, August 27, 2009; " 'Voice of the Opposition': Fox News Openly Advocates Against Democratic Congress, White House," MediaMatters.org, September 11, 2009, mediamatters.org/reports/200909110016.

36. *Glenn Beck,* Fox News Channel, August 28, 2009; "Beck's Mutually Beneficial Partnership with FreedomWorks," MediaMatters.org, June 14, 2010, mediamatters.org/research/201006140030.

37. Howard Kurtz, "Fox News Ad Draws Protests," *Washington Post,* September 18, 2009, www.washingtonpost.com/wp-dyn/content/article/2009/09/18/AR2009091801102.html.

38. Glenn Beck, Twitter, September 3, 2009, twitter.com/#!/glennbeck/status/3749169499.

39. Eric Bolling, Twitter, September 6, 2009, twitter.com/#!/ericbolling/status/3799500889.

40. Amanda Terkel, "Hannity: Starting Now, My 'Job' Is to 'Get Rid of Every Other One' of Obama's Czars," ThinkProgress.org, September 8, 2009, thinkprogress.org/2009/09/08/hannity-czars-job/.

41. *America's Newsroom,* Fox News Channel, September 8, 2009; "Oops . . . In Report on 'Science Czar' and 'Regulatory Czar,' Fox's Kelly Acknowledges They're 'Not Really' Czars," MediaMatters.org, September 8, 2009, mediamatters.org/mmtv/200909080037.

42. *Hannity,* Fox News Channel, September 8, 2009; "Hannity Falsely Claims Science Adviser Holdren 'Advocated Compulsory Abortion,' " MediaMatters.org, September 9, 2009, mediamatters.org/research/200909090028.

43. "Glenn Beck Claims Science Czar John Holdren Proposed Forced Abortions and Putting Sterilants in the Drinking Water to Control Population," Politifact.com, July 22, 2009; www.politifact.com/truth-o-meter/ statements/2009/jul/29/glenn-beck/glenn-beck-claims-science-czar -john-holdren-propos/.

44. *Glenn Beck,* Fox News Channel, September 8, 2009; "Fox News on a Witch Hunt for Obama Czars," MediaMatters.org, September 9, 2009, media matters.org/print/research/200909090051.

45. *Glenn Beck,* Fox News Channel, August 25, 2009; "Fox News on a Witch Hunt for Obama Czars."

Chapter 7: Six Steps

1. www.mprerc.com/programs.htm.

2. *America's Newsroom,* Fox News Channel, October 14, 2008; "Fox News' Kelly Mocked ACORN for Accurate Statement About Florida Registration Law," MediaMatters.org, October 14, 2008, mediamatters.org/ research/200810140010.

3. "Fox News' Kelly Mocked ACORN for Accurate Statement."

4. *Saving Our Economy,* Fox News Channel, October 5, 2008; "Fox News' Baier Advanced Conservative Attacks on CRA, Repeated Falsehood About Rep. Frank," MediaMatters.org, October 7, 2008, mediamatters .org/research/200810070033.

5. Ibid.

6. Letter from Chairman Ben Bernanke to Senator Robert Menendez, November 25, 2008, menendez.senate.gov/pdf/112508Responsefrom BernankeonCRA.pdf.

7. Greg Sandoval, "Breitbart.com Has Drudge to Thank for Its Success," *CNET News,* November 30, 2005, news.cnet.com/Breitbart.com-has -Drudge-to-thank-for-its-success—page-2/2100–1025_3–5976096–2.html.

8. Ibid.

9. Ibid.

10. *Glenn Beck,* Fox News Channel, September 9, 2009; "Following Beck's Instructions, Fox News Attempts to Change Story from Health Care to ACORN," MediaMatters.org, September 10, 2009, mediamatters.org/ research/200909100058.

11. James O'Keefe, "Chaos for Glory: My Time with ACORN," Big Government.com, September 10, 2009, biggovernment.com/jokeefe/ 2009/09/10/chaos-for-glory/.

12. *Glenn Beck,* Fox News Channel, September 15, 2009; "Report: ACORN Obsession: Beck, Hannity Obsess over ACORN While Virtually Ignoring Major Corruption Scandals," MediaMatters.org, September 23, 2009, mediamatters.org/reports/200909230032.

13. "Report: ACORN Obsession: Beck, Hannity Obsess over ACORN."

14. Eric Boehlert, "Fox News Insider: 'Stuff Is Just Made Up,' " Media Matters.org, February 10, 2011. Interview with Media Matters, mediamatters .org/blog/201102100007.

15. Tom Junod, "Why Does Roger Ailes Hate America?" *Esquire,* January 18, 2011, www.esquire.com/features/roger-ailes-0211.

16. *Fox & Friends.* Fox News Channel, November 29, 2010; "Exclusive: Fox Runs with *Another* Bogus War on Christmas Story?" MediaMatters.org, November 29, 2010, mediamatters.org/research/201011290017.

17. "Exclusive: Fox Runs with *Another* Bogus War on Christmas Story?"

18. *Glenn Beck,* Fox News Channel, September 15, 2009; "Fox News Runs with San Bernardino ACORN Video Without Needed Fact Check," MediaMatters .org, September 16, 2009, mediamatters.org/research/200909160039.

19. Ibid.

20. *The O'Reilly Factor,* Fox News Channel, September 15, 2009; "Fox News Runs with San Bernardino ACORN Video Without Needed Fact Check."

21. *Hannity,* Fox News Channel, September 15, 2009; "Fox News Runs with San Bernardino ACORN Video Without Needed Fact Check."

22. *On the Record,* Fox News Channel, September 15, 2009; "Fox News Runs with San Bernardino ACORN Video Without Needed Fact Check."

23. San Bernardino Police Department News Release, September 15, 2009, www.politico.com/pdf/PPM130_acorn_investigation.pdf.

24. "Ignoring Police Report, Carlson Advanced False Claim that ACORN Employee Killed Husband," MediaMatters.org, September 16, 2009, mediamatters.org/research/200909160003.

25. *Fox & Friends,* Fox News Channel, September 16, 2009; "Ignoring Police Report, Carlson Advanced False Claim," mediamatters.org/research/ 200909160003.

26. "Ignoring Police Report, Carlson Advanced False Claim That ACORN Employee Killed Husband," MediaMatters.org, September 16, 2009.

27. "Police Report Filed by ACORN Exposes False Claims by Individuals Behind Videos," MediaMatters.org, September 17, 2009; "Police: ACORN Worker Sought Advice on Pair," Associated Press, September 22, 2009.

28. "In LA Video, O'Keefe and Giles expose their own dishonesty," Media Matters.org, November 20, 2009.

29. *Good Morning America*, ABC News, June 1, 2010; "Breitbart Falsely Suggests ACORN Employees "Help[ed] Set Up a Prostitution Ring in Every Single Office," MediaMatters.org, June 1, 2010, mediamatters.org/ research/201006010020.

30. Scott Harshbarger and Amy Crafts, "An Independent Governance Assessment of ACORN," December 7, 2009, www.proskauer.com/files/uploads/ report2.pdf.

31. "Brown Releases Report Detailing a Litany of Problems with ACORN, but

No Criminality," Press Release, Office of the Attorney General, California, April 1, 2010, oag.ca.gov/news/press_release?id=1888.

32. Scott Shifrel, "B'klyn ACORN Cleared over Giving Illegal Advice on How to Hide Money from Prostitution," *Daily News* (New York), March 1, 2010, www.nydailynews.com/news/ny_crime/2010/03/01/2010 –03–01_bklyn_acorn_cleared_over_giving_illegal_advice_on_how_to _hide_money_from_prostit.html.

33. *Glenn Beck,* Fox News Channel, September 11, 2009; "The Fox Cycle: From Bogus Right-Wing Attack to Mainstream News," MediaMatters.org, July 12, 2010, mediamatters.org/research/201007120005.

34. *Reliable Sources,* CNN, September 20, 2009; "The Fox Cycle: From Bogus Right-Wing Attack to Mainstream News."

35. *Hannity,* Fox News Channel, June 26, 2009; "Hannity Continues to Push Debunked Cap and Trade Cost Figure," MediaMatters.org, June 29, 2009, mediamatters.org/research/200906290001.

36. "Cap-and-Trade Cost Inflation," FactCheck.org, May 28, 2009; www .factcheck.org/politics/cap-and-trade_cost_inflation.html.

37. *Hannity,* Fox News Channel, November 24, 2009; "Hannity Says Stolen Emails Are Evidence Global Warming Is a 'Hoax,' " MediaMatters.org, November 24, 2009, mediamatters.org/mmtv/200911240055.

38. Kim Zetter, "Hacked E-mails Fuel Climate Change Debate," *Threat Level* (blog), *Wired,* November 20, 2009, www.wired.com/threatlevel/2009/11/ climate-hack.

39. E-mail from Bill Sammon, December 8, 2009, obtained by Media Matters for America.

40. *Happening Now,* Fox News Channel, December 8, 2009; Ben Dimiero, "Foxleaks: Fox Boss Ordered Staff to Cast Doubt on Climate Science," *County Fair* (blog), MediaMatters.org, mediamatters.org/blog/ 201012150004.

41. "Climategate," FactCheck.org, December 10, 2009, www.factcheck.org/ 2009/12/climategate/.

42. "Impact of CRU Hacking on the AMS Statement on Climate Change," American Meteorological Society, November 25, 2009, ametsoc.org/ policy/climatechangeclarify.html.

43. "Remarks by Rupert Murdoch, Chairman and Chief Executive Officer, News Corporation," New York, May 9, 2007, www.newscorp.com/ energy/full_speech.html.

44. Amanda Griscom Little, "Rupert Murdoch Joins Climate Crusade," *Grist,* May 24, 2007, www.msnbc.msn.com/id/18746241/.

45. "Pollster Frank Luntz Points to Bipartisan Support for Climate Legislation," SustainableBusiness.com, January 21, 2010, www.sustainablebusiness.com/ index.cfm/go/news.display/id/19608.

46. *Hannity's America,* Fox News Channel, April 29, 2007; "Murdoch to Achieve Carbon Neutrality with Credits, but Fox Employees Call Them a Sham," MediaMatters.org, May 14, 2005, mediamatters.org/research/200705140007.
47. *Hannity & Colmes,* Fox News Channel, July 9, 2007; "Hannity Continued to Bash Carbon Offsets—No Mention of Murdoch's Purported Plans to Use Them," MediaMatters.org, July 10, 2007, mediamatters.org/research/200707100012.
48. *The O'Reilly Factor,* Fox News Channel, May 1, 2009; "Ingraham Uses Doctored Video to Smear Gore," MediaMatters.org, May 1, 2009, mediamatters.org/research/200905010049.
49. Ibid.
50. Al Gore Congressional Testimony, April 24, 2009, www.youtube.com/watch?v=NXGkI-mw7Pw.
51. *The O'Reilly Factor,* Fox News Channel, June 4, 2009; *"O'Reilly Factor* Still Smearing Gore, Misrepresenting His Testimony on Profiting from Advocacy," MediaMatters.org, June 4, 2009, mediamatters.org/research/200906040051.
52. *Hannity,* Fox News Channel, September 18, 2009.
53. *Hannity,* Fox News Channel, September 25, 2009.
54. *Fox & Friends,* Fox News Channel, September 24, 2009.
55. Maxim Lott, "Critics Assail Obama's 'Safe Schools' Czar, Say He's Wrong Man for the Job," FoxNews.com, September 23, 2009, www.foxnews.com/politics/2009/09/23/critics-assail-obamas-safe-schools-czar-say-hes-wrong-man-job/.
56. Hannity, Fox News Channel, September 30, 2009; "Despite Evidence to Contrary, Fox News Machine Claims Jennings 'Cover[ed] Up Statutory Rape,' " MediaMatters.org, September 30, 2009, mediamatters.org/research/200909300050.
57. Karl Frisch, "Exclusive: Statement from Former Student at Center of Fox-Fueled Jennings Controversy," *County Fair* (blog), MediaMatters.org, October 2, 2009, mediamatters.org/blog/200910020029.
58. Chris Good, "How Kevin Jennings Survived," *TheAtlantic.com,* October 21, 2009, www.theatlantic.com/politics/archive/2009/10/how-kevin-jennings-survived/28754/.

Chapter 8: Willie Horton . . . Times a Thousand

1. Andrew Breitbart, "Video Proof: The NAACP Awards Racism—2010," BigGovernment.com, July 19, 2010, biggovernment.com/abreitbart/2010/07/19/video-proof-the-naacp-awards-racism2010/.
2. "Timeline of Breitbart's Sherrod Smear," MediaMatters.org, July 22, 2010, mediamatters.org/research/201007220004.
3. "Timeline of Breitbart's Sherrod Smear," MediaMatters.org, July 22, 2010, mediamatters.org/research/201007220004.
4. *The O'Reilly Factor,* Fox News Channel, July 19, 2010; Matt Gertz,

"Fox Smears Sherrod as Racist, Sherrod Cancels Fox Interview," *County Fair* (blog), MediaMatters.org, July 20, 2010, mediamatters.org/blog/201007200060.

5. *Hannity,* Fox News Channel, July 19, 2010.

6. *Fox & Friends,* Fox News Channel, July 20, 2010.

7. *American Morning,* CNN, July 20, 2010, transcripts.cnn.com/transcripts/1007/20/ltm.01.html.

8. *America's Newsroom,* Fox News Channel, July 20, 2010; MediaMatters.org, mediamatters.org/embed/clips/2010/07/21/7760/fnc-20100720-york_sherrod.

9. *Rick's List,* CNN, July 20, 2010; " 'White Farmer' Spooner: Sherrod Smearers 'Don't Know What They're Talking About,' Sherrod Did 'Her Level Best' to Help," MediaMatters.org, July 20, 2010, mediamatters.org/mmtv/201007200058.

10. *Glenn Beck,* Fox News Channel, July 20, 2010; Matt Gertz, "Beck Blasts Administration for Believing Fox News, Breitbart," *County Fair* (blog), MediaMatters.org, July 20, 2010, mediamatters.org/blog/201007200065.

11. *Special Report,* Fox News Channel, July 20, 2010; "Baier Absurdly Claims Fox News 'Didn't Even Do' the Sherrod Story," MediaMatters.org, July 20, 2010, mediamatters.org/mmtv/201007200072.

12. Joe Strupp, "Sherrod: I'm a Victim of Breitbart, Fox 'Racism,' " *County Fair* (blog), MediaMatters.org, July 21, 2010, mediamatters.org/blog/201007210037.

13. *Fox & Friends,* Fox News Channel, July 22, 2010; "Doocy's Deception: 'Fox News Channel' Did Not Touch Sherrod Story 'Until She Had Actually Quit,' " MediaMatters.org, July 22, 2010, mediamatters.org/research/201007220003.

14. *The O'Reilly Factor,* Fox News Channel, July 22, 2010; MediaMatters.org, July 29, 2010, mediamatters.org/embed/clips/2010/07/29/8048/o-reilly-20100722-rosensherrod.

15. *Studio B,* Fox News Channel, July 22, 2010; Joe Strupp, "Fox News' Shep Smith: I Never Trusted Breitbart Video," *County Fair* (blog), MediaMatters.org, July 22, 2010, mediamatters.org/blog/201007220016.

16. Keach Hagey, "Fox News Admits 'a Breakdown' on Shirley Sherrod Story," *Politico,* July 28, 2010, www.politico.com/news/stories/0710/40374.html.

17. *The O'Reilly Factor,* Fox News Channel, March 13, 2008; "Morris: McCain 'Doesn't Have to' Engage in Willie Horton–Like Campaign Because O'Reilly Is Already Doing So," MediaMatters.org, March 14, 2008, mediamatters.org/research/200803140006.

18. Ibid.

19. *The O'Reilly Factor,* Fox News Channel, May 7, 2008; "Dick Morris: Election Hinges on Whether 'We Believe' Obama Is 'Sort of a Sleeper Agent Who Really Doesn't Believe in Our System,' " MediaMatters.org, May 8, 2008, mediamatters.org/research/200805080003.

20. J. Christian Adams, "Adams: Inside the Black Panther Case," *Washington Times,* June 25, 2010, www.washingtontimes.com/news/2010/jun/25/inside-the-black-panther-case-anger-ignorance-and/.

21. Ibid.

22. Testimony of Assistant Attorney General Thomas Perez, Hearing on the Department of Justice's Actions Related to the New Black Panther Party Litigation and Its Enforcement of Section 11(b) of the Voting Rights Act, U.S. Commission on Civil Rights, May 14, 2010, page 18, www.usccr.gov/NBPH/05–14–2010_NBPPhearing.pdf#page=18.

23. Ibid.

24. *Austin American-Statesman,* November 8, 2006; Jeremy Holden, "Christian Adams' Case Continues to Implode: Bush-Era DOJ Declined to Charge Minutemen for Voter Intimidation," *County Fair* (blog), MediaMatters.org, July 01, 2010, mediamatters.org/blog/201007010023.

25. Testimony of Assistant Attorney General Thomas Perez.

26. Ryan J. Reilly, "The Black Panther Case: A Legacy of Politicized Hiring," *Main Justice,* December 23, 2009, www.mainjustice.com/2009/12/23/the-black-panther-case-a-legacy-of-politicized-hiring/.

27. Ryan J. Reilly, "Adams Hired for Conservative Credentials, Former DOJ Official Says," *Main Justice,* July 6, 2010, www.mainjustice.com/2010/07/06/adams-hired-for-conservative-credentials-former-doj-official-says/.

28. *America's Newsroom,* Fox News Channel, June 30, 2010; "Fox Hypes GOP Activist's 'Explosive New Allegations' Against Obama DOJ," MediaMatters.org, June 30, 2010, mediamatters.org/research/201006300064.

29. Erick Erickson, "King Samir Shabazz Should Be 2010's Willie Horton," *RedState* (blog), July 13, 2010, www.redstate.com/erick/2010/07/13/king-samir-shabazz-should-be-2010s-willie-horton/.

30. *The Glenn Beck Program,* Premiere Radio Networks, July 9, 2010; "Beck Says New Black Panthers Are Part of Obama's 'Party of Thugs,' " MediaMatters.org, July 9, 2010, mediamatters.org/mmtv/201007090026.

31. *The Glenn Beck Program,* Premiere Radio Networks, July 12, 2008; "Beck: They Want a Race War . . . and Our Government Is Going to Stand By and Let Them Do It," MediaMatters.org, July 12, 2010, mediamatters.org/mmtv/201007120021.

32. Ben Smith, "A Conservative Dismisses Right-Wing Black Panther 'Fantasies,' " *Politico,* July 19, 2010, www.politico.com/news/stories/0710/39861.html.

Chapter 9: A Vote for Liberty

1. *Hannity,* Fox News Channel, January 8, 2010; "Fox News Provides MA Senate Candidate Brown a Forum to Raise Funds and Misinform," Media Matters.org, January 12, 2010, mediamatters.org/research/201001120029.

2. *On the Record,* Fox News Channel, January 11, 2010; "Fox News Provides MA Senate Candidate Brown a Forum."

3. *Fox & Friends,* Fox News Channel, January 14, 2010; "Fox News' Campaign for Brown," MediaMatters.org, January 19, 2010, mediamatters.org/ research/201001190049.

4. "Huckabee Sends Viewers to His PAC Under Guise of Signing a Petition," MediaMatters.org, October 5, 2009, mediamatters.org/ research/200910050002.

5. *Huckabee,* Fox News Channel, October 4, 2009; "Huckabee Sends Viewers to His PAC."

6. E-mail from Mike Huckabee; "Huck PAC—Which Huckabee Promoted on Fox News—Now Soliciting Donations for Campaigns Against Democrats," MediaMatters.org, November 10, 2009, mediamatters.org/ research/200911100002.

7. *Hannity,* Fox News Channel, January 11, 2010; "More Fox Advocacy: Morris Tells Hannity Audience to 'Please, Please Help' Brown Win MA Senate Seat," MediaMatters.org, January 11, 2010, mediamatters.org/ mmtv/201001110059.

8. Dick Morris and Eileen McGann, "Urgent: Help Us Win in Massachusetts," *DickMorris.com* (blog), dickmorris.com/blog/urgent-help-us-win-in -massachusetts.

9. "Keith Olbermann Suspended over Political Donations," MSNBC.com, November 5, 2010, www.msnbc.msn.com/id/40028929/ns/politics -decision_2010/t/keith-olbermann-suspended-over-political-donations/.

10. "Fox News' Campaign for Brown."

11. *State of the Union,* CNN, October 4, 2009, transcripts.cnn.com/transcripts/ 0910/04/sotu.05.html.

12. *State of the Union,* CNN, May 10, 2009, transcripts.cnn.com/transcripts/ 0905/10/sotu.01.html.

13. *Fox & Friends,* Fox News Channel, January 11, 2010; "Fox News' Campaign for Brown."

14. *Hannity,* Fox News Channel, January 18, 2010; "Quick Fact: Hannity Revives Distortions of Coakley's Remarks About 'Terrorists' and Catholics in ERs," MediaMatters.org, January 19, 2010, mediamatters.org/ research/201001190001.

15. *Glenn Beck,* Fox News Channel, January 18, 2010; " 'Religious Bigotry': Beck Smears Coakley over Her Remarks on Emergency Room Procedures and Treatments," MediaMatters.org, January 18, 2010, mediamatters.org/ mmtv/201001180017.

16. Jim Hoft, "Game-Changer—Martha Coakley: Devout Catholics 'Probably Shouldn't Work in the Emergency Room' " *Gateway Pundit* (blog), January 14, 2010, gatewaypundit.rightnetwork.com/2010/01/game

-changer-martha-coakley-devout-catholics-probably-shouldnt-work-in
-the-emergency-room-video/; "Coakley: Catholics Shouldn't Work in the
ER," FoxNation.com, January 15, 2010, nation.foxnews.com/Martha
-coakley/2010/01/15/coakley-catholics-shouldnt-work-er.

17. *Ken Pittman Show,* WBSM-AM, January 14, 2010; "Fox News' Campaign for
    Brown."

18. *Fox & Friends,* Fox News Channel, January 19, 2010; MediaMatters.org,
    January 19, 2010, mediamatters.org/mmtv/201001190006.

19. "Brown Win Could Cause Huge Stock Rally," FoxNation.com, January
    18, 2010, nation.foxnews.com/business/2010/01/18/brown-win-could
    -cause-huge-stock-rally.

20. FoxNation.com, January 18, 2010; "Non-'Biased' Fox Nation Promotes
    Video Claiming a 'Vote for Scott Brown Is a Vote for Liberty,' " *County
    Fair* (blog), MediaMatters.org, January 18, 2010, mediamatters.org/blog/
    201001180015.

21. Lee Fang, "Carl Cameron Gets Chummy with Brown Supporters, Ducks
    Question of Fox News' Ethics," *ThinkProgress.org,* January 19, 2010, think
    progress.org/politics/2010/01/19/77913/fox-ethics-brown/.

22. Philip Rucker and Eli Saslow, "Gov. Palin Says She Will Quit, Citing
    Probes, Family Needs," *Washington Post,* July 4, 2009, www.washingtonpost
    .com/wp-dyn/content/article/2009/07/03/AR2009070301738.html.

23. Ibid.

24. Katie Couric, CBS News interview with Sarah Palin, September 30, 2008.

25. Rich Lowry, "Palin on CBS," *The Corner* (blog), *National Review Online,* Sep-
    tember 27, 2008, www.nationalreview.com/corner/170741/palin-cbs/
    rich-lowry.

26. David Carr, "AP Fact-Checks Sarah Palin Book," *Media Decoder* (blog),
    New York Times, November 16, 2009, mediadecoder.blogs.nytimes
    .com/2009/11/16/the-ap-fact-checks-palins-book/.

27. *The Glenn Beck Program,* Premiere Radio Networks, January 14, 2010, www
    .glennbeck.com/content/articles/article/198/35049/.

28. Brian Stelter, "A Host Defends Her Brand," *New York Times,* May 24, 2009,
    www.nytimes.com/2009/05/25/business/media/25greta.html.

29. Ibid.

30. Interview with Media Matters for America conducted by Joe Strupp.
    May 16, 2010.

31. Ibid.

32. *The O'Reilly Factor,* Fox News Channel, November 19, 2009.

33. Chris Ariens, "Ratings for Sarah Palin Debut on Fox News," *TVNewser*
    (blog), MediaBistro.com, April 2, 2010, www.mediabistro.com/tvnewser/
    ratings-for-sarah-palin-debut-on-fox-news_b24948.

Chapter 10: One Million Dollars

1. Lauren Weppler, "A FOX News Analyst Comes to Town," WTAP-TV, September 1, 2010, www.wtap.com/news/headlines/102032563.html?ref=563.
2. "Report: More Than 30 Fox Newsers Support GOP in 600-Plus Instances During Midterms," MediaMatters.org, October 27, 2010, mediamatters .org/research/201010270005.
3. Ibid.
4. Ibid.
5. Dara Kam, "Attorney General Candidate Bondi Makes Final Push for GOP Support," *Palm Beach Post,* August 20, 2010, www.palmbeachpost .com/news/state/attorney-general-candidate-bondi-makes-final-push -for-870595.html.
6. Legacy Tobacco Documents Library, University of California, San Francisco, legacy.library.ucsf.edu/tid/wra83b00/pdf?search=%22ailes%22.
7. Legacy Tobacco Documents Library, University of California, San Francisco, legacy.library.ucsf.edu/tid/htu63b00/pdf?search=%22ailes%22.
8. *The Glenn Beck Program,* Premiere Radio Networks, October 14, 2009; Media Matters.org, October 14, 2009, mediamatters.org/mmtv/200910140013.
9. Joe Strupp, "News Corp. Million Dollar Donation Sparks Ethics Concerns," *County Fair* (blog), MediaMatters.org, August 18, 2010, mediamatters .org/blog/201008180066.
10. Ben Smith, "Fox Parent Gives $1 Million to RGA," *Politico,* August 16, 2010, www.politico.com/blogs/bensmith/0810/Fox_parent_gives_1_mil lion_to_RGA.html.
11. Keach Hagey, "Kasich Inspired News Corp.'s RGA Gift," *Politico,* October 6, 2010, www.politico.com/blogs/onmedia/1010/Kasich_inspired _News_Corps_RGA_gift.html.
12. "The Chamber's Latest Ad Aims to Mislead AZ Voters," PoliticalCorrection .org, October 22, 2010, politicalcorrection.org/adcheck/201010220012.
13. "The Chamber of Commerce's Health Care Lies Keep Getting 'Worse,' " PoliticalCorrection.org, October 8, 2010, politicalcorrection.org/adcheck/ 201010080009.
14. "The Chamber of Commerce's Deeply Dishonest Attack on Grayson," PoliticalCorrection.org, October 8, 2010, politicalcorrection.org/ adcheck/201010080016.
15. Alan Pike, "Astroturfing the Airwaves: 20 Largest Right-Wing Groups Bought 144,000 TV Ads, 77% Anonymously Funded," blog at PoliticalCorrection.org, November 9, 2010, politicalcorrection.org/blog/ 201011090001.
16. Keach Hagey, "Kasich Inspired News Corp.'s RGA Gift," *Politico,* October 6, 2010, www.politico.com/blogs/onmedia/1010/Kasich_inspired _News_Corps_RGA_gift.html.
17. Sarah Pavlus, "AUDIO: Murdoch Says News Corp. Donations Were

in Interest of 'Shareholders and the Country,' " *County Fair* (blog), Media Matters.org, October 15, 2010, mediamatters.org/blog/201010150017.

18. *The Glenn Beck Program,* Premiere Radio Networks, October 14, 2010; "Beck: The Chamber of Commerce Is 'Our Parents, Our Grandparents—They Are Us,' " MediaMatters.org, October 14, 2010, mediamatters.org/mmtv/201010140033.

19. Paul Bedard, "Glenn Beck Sparks Record Donations to Chamber of Commerce," *US News and World Report,* October 21, 2010, www.usnews.com/news/blogs/washington-whispers/2010/10/21/glenn-beck-sparks-record-donations-to-chamber-of-commerce.

20. Glenn Beck Tracking Footage, November 21, 2009, www.youtube.com/watch?v=5VSwvt778rY.

21. Ibid.

22. *The Glenn Beck Program,* Premiere Radio Networks, June 18, 2010; "Beck Says It's 'Divine Providence' 8–28 Rally Is on Same Day as MLK Speech, Adds: 'It's Time We Picked That Dream Back Up,' " MediaMatters.org, June 18, 2010, mediamatters.org/mmtv/201006180017.

23. *The Glenn Beck Program,* Premiere Radio Networks, June 15, 2010; "Beck: At 8–28 Rally, We Will 'Pick Up Martin Luther King's Dream That Has Been Distorted,' " MediaMatters.org, June 15, 2010, mediamatters.org/mmtv/201006150013.

24. *The O'Reilly Factor,* Fox News Channel, August 19, 2010; "O'Reilly Hosts Beck to Promote 8–28 Rally: 'I Don't Think Black People Own the Legacy of Dr. Martin Luther King,' " MediaMatters.org, August 19, 2010, mediamatters.org/mmtv/201008190066.

25. *Glenn Beck,* Fox News Channel, May 7, 2010; "Beck Pushes His August 28 Rally in D.C.: 'The Capitol Will Fix Itself if We Just Stand Between Washington and Lincoln,' " MediaMatters.org, May 7, 2010, mediamatters.org/mmtv/201005070040.

26. *Restoring Honor,* C-SPAN, August 28, 2010; "Beck Introduces the New 'Black Robe Regiment,' " MediaMatters.org, August 28, 2010, mediamatters.org/mmtv/201008280018.

27. *Restoring Honor,* C-SPAN, August 28, 2010; "Beck: 25 Years from Now, 'the Next George Washington' in His Audience Will Stand at Lincoln Memorial and Proclaim, 'I Have a New Dream,' " MediaMatters.org, August 28, 2010, mediamatters.org/mmtv/201008280021.

28. *The O'Reilly Factor,* Fox News Channel, September 15, 2010; "Fox News Contributor Sarah Palin Advises GOP Candidate O'Donnell to 'Speak Through Fox News,' " MediaMatters.org, September 15, 2010, mediamatters.org/mmtv/201009150072.

29. *Hannity,* Fox News Channel, September 21, 2010; "O'Donnell Follows Palin's Advice, Speaks Through Sean Hannity," *County Fair* (blog), Media Matters.org, September 21, 2010, mediamatters.org/blog/201009210070.

30. Ibid.

31. Felicia Sonmez, "Christine O'Donnell: I'm Not Doing Any More National TV Interviews," *The Fix* (blog), *Washington Post,* September 21, 2010, voices .washingtonpost.com/thefix/christine-odonnell-im-not-doin.html.

32. Joe Strupp, "Fox News Source: O'Donnell Chose Hannity to Get 'Certain Kind of Treatment,' " *County Fair* (blog), MediaMatters.org, September 22, 2010, mediamatters.org/blog/201009220037.

33. *The O'Reilly Factor,* Fox News Channel, September 15, 2010; "Fox News Contributor Sarah Palin Advises GOP Candidate O'Donnell."

34. Howard Fineman, "Christine O'Donnell Tells GOPers: 'I've Got Sean Hannity in My Back Pocket,' " *Huffington Post,* October 14, 2010, www .huffingtonpost.com/2010/10/14/christine-odonnell-sean-hannity -republicans-fundraising_n_763487.html.

35. *Hannity,* Fox News Channel, September 15, 2010; "Hannity Hosts O'Donnell to Thank Him and Direct His Viewers to Her Website," MediaMatters.org, September 15, 2010, mediamatters.org/mmtv/201009150067.

36. *Hannity,* Fox News Channel, October 7, 2010; "Hannity: Nevada Voters 'Have a Duty' to Throw Reid out of Congress," MediaMatters.org, October 7, 2010, mediamatters.org/mmtv/201010070058.

37. *Hannity,* Fox News Channel, June 14, 2010; "HannityPAC: The GOP's Man Inside Fox," MediaMatters.org, November 2, 2010, mediamatters .org/research/201011020013.

38. Jon Ralston, "I Made $236,000 off Rush Limbaugh, and Hannity Was Profitable, Too," *Las Vegas Sun,* September 21, 2010, www.lasvegassun.com/ blogs/ralstons-flash/2010/sep/21/angle-i-made-236000-rush-limbaugh -and-hannity-was-/.

39. David Brody, "Exclusive: Sharron Angle Talks to the Brody File," *The Brody File* (blog), CBN News, July 14, 2010, blogs.cbn.com/thebrodyfile/ archive/2010/07/14/exclusive-sharron-angle-talks-to-the-brody-file.aspx.

40. *Hannity,* Fox News Channel, October 8, 2010; MediaMatters.org, October 8, 2010, mediamatters.org/blog/201010080003.

41. *Hannity,* Fox News Channel, June 10, 2010; MediaMatters.org, June 10, 2010, mediamatters.org/mmtv/201006100066.

42. Emily Cadei, "NRCC Raises $7 Million at Annual Dinner," *CQ Roll Call's The Eye,* March 23, 2010, blogs.cqrollcall.com/eyeon2010/2010/03/nrcc -raises-7-million-for-tues.html. This blog post has since been taken down.

43. David Saltonstall, "Giuliani's Fox-y Pal Cash Flap," *Daily News* (New York), August 19, 2007, www.nydailynews.com/news/national/2007/08/ 19/2007–08–19_giulianis_foxy_pal_cash_flap.html.

44. *The Sean Hannity Show,* ABC News Radio, September 20, 2005; "Hannity Pledged 'Maximum' Contribution to Clinton Challenger Pirro, Asked Listeners to Donate Too," MediaMatters.org, September 20, 2005, mediamatters .org/mmtv/200509200007.

45. Saltonstall, "Giuliani's Fox-y Pal Cash Flap."

46. Jana Winter, "EXCLUSIVE: Aide to Harry Reid Lied to Feds, Submitted False Documents About Sham Marriage," FoxNews.com, October 25, 2010, www.foxnews.com/politics/2010/10/25/exclusive-aide-to-harry-reid -lied-to-feds-submitted-false-documents-about-sham-marriage/.

47. Ibid.

48. *Special Report,* Fox News Channel, October 27, 2010; "Hatchet Job: Fox Crops Reid Statement to Pretend He Has a Political Scandal," October 28, 2010, mediamatters.org/research/201010280001.

49. Ibid.

50. *Fox & Friends,* Fox News Channel, October 26, 2010; "Fox Kicks Off GOP GOTV Efforts by Almost Exclusively Hosting Republicans," MediaMatters .org, October 27, 2010, mediamatters.org/research/201010270027.

51. *Glenn Beck,* Fox News Channel, October 26, 2010; "Fox Kicks Off GOP GOTV Efforts."

52. *Hannity,* Fox News Channel, October 26, 2010; "Fox Kicks Off GOP GOTV Efforts."

53. Ibid.

54. Ibid.

55. *Fox & Friends,* Fox News Channel, October 26, 2010; "Fox Kicks Off GOP GOTV Efforts," MediaMatters.org, October 27, 2010, mediamatters.org/ research/201010270027.

56. Interview with Media Matters for America conducted by Joe Strupp, May 17, 2011.

57. Michael Tomasky, "Obama and the Bus, Which Was Not a Bus at All," Guardian.co.uk, October 28, 2010, www.guardian.co.uk/commentisfree/ michaeltomasky/2010/oct/28/barack-obama-fox-news-back-seat-of-car.

58. *Hannity,* Fox News Channel, October 26, 2010; "Unreal: Fox News Claims Obama Invoked Racial Segregation with His Car Analogy," MediaMatters .org, October 27, 2010, mediamatters.org/research/201010270029.

59. Ibid.

60. *Fox & Friends,* Fox News Channel, October 27, 2010; "Seriously!? Fox Claims Obama Was Referring to Racial Segregation with His Car Analogy," Media-Matters.org, October 27, 2010, mediamatters.org/mmtv/201010270009.

61. *America Live,* Fox News Channel, October 27, 2010; "Fox's Monica Crowley: Obama's Car Analogy Comments Were 'Appalling' and Had 'Racial Overtones,' " MediaMatters.org, October 27, 2010, mediamatters.org/ mmtv/201010270025.

62. *America's Newsroom,* Fox News Channel, October 27, 2010; "Day 2: Fox Continues Its Relentless GOP GOTV Efforts," MediaMatters.org, October 28, 2010, mediamatters.org/research/201010280024.

63. *America Live,* Fox News Channel, October 27, 2010; "Day 2: Fox Continues Its Relentless GOP GOTV Efforts."

64. *Hannity,* Fox News Channel, October 27, 2010; "Day 2: Fox Continues Its Relentless GOP GOTV Efforts."

65. *America's Newsroom,* Fox News Channel, October 28, 2010; "FOX GOTV Day Three: Fox Continues Its Week of Relentless Campaigning for Republicans," MediaMatters.org, October 29, 2010, mediamatters.org/research/201010290024.

66. *Your World,* Fox News Channel, November 1, 2010; "The Final Push: Fox Provides Forum for GOP Candidates' Last-Minute Appeals," MediaMatters.org, November 2, 2010, mediamatters.org/research/201011020026.

67. *Hannity,* Fox News Channel, November 1, 2010; "The Final Push: Fox Provides Forum for GOP Candidates' Last-Minute Appeals."

68. *America's Newsroom,* Fox News Channel, November 1, 2010; "The Final Push: Fox Provides Forum for GOP Candidates' Last-Minute Appeals."

Chapter 11: The Puppet Master

1. *The Daily Show,* November 3, 2010, www.thedailyshow.com/watch/wed-november-3–2010/chris-wallace.

2. Alex Spillius, "Karl Rove Questions Sarah Palin's Suitability for President," *Daily Telegraph,* October 27, 2010, www.telegraph.co.uk/news/worldnews/us-politics/8090279/Karl-Rove-questions-Sarah-Palins-suitability-for-president.html.

3. *On the Record,* Fox News Channel, October 31, 2010; "Fox Primary: Palin and Van Susteren Lash Out at *Politico* 'Trash Piece' and Rove," MediaMatters.org, October 31, 2010, mediamatters.org/mmtv/201010310029.

4. Jonathan Martin and Keach Hagey, "Fox Primary: Complicated, Contractual," *Politico,* September 27, 2010, www.politico.com/news/stories/0910/42745.html.

5. Ibid.

6. *Varney & Co.,* Fox Business Channel, September 9, 2010, video.fox business.com/v/4333060/bolton-for-president-im-thinking-about-it.

7. "Updated Report: Fox News' $55 Million Presidential Donation," Media Matters.org, January 24, 2011, mediamatters.org/research/201101240010.

8. *Glenn Beck,* Fox News Channel, October 2, 2010; "Beck Revives Anti-Semitic Soros Conspiracy Theory," MediaMatters.org, October 6, 2010, mediamatters.org/research/201010060033.

9. Berita Harian (excerpted by BBC Summary of World Broadcasts), October 10, 1997; "Beck Revives Anti-Semitic Soros Conspiracy Theory," media-matters.org/research/201010060033.

10. *Glenn Beck,* Fox News Channel, November 9, 2010; " 'Puppet Master': Beck Lies About Soros, Day 1," MediaMatters.org, November 10, 2010, media matters.org/research/201011100002.

11. James Besser, "Glenn Beck's 'Monstrous' Soros Accusations Rile Holocaust Survivors, Jewish Groups," *Jewish Week,* November 11, 2010, www

.thejewishweek.com/blogs/political_insider/glenn_becks_monstrous _soros_accusations_rile_holocaust_survivors_jewish.

12. "Fox News' Ailes Tells Team to Tone Down Rhetoric," *Roll Call*, January 10, 2011, www.rollcall.com/news/-202342–1.html.

13. *Glenn Beck*, Fox News Channel, January 11, 2011; "Beck: Lawmakers Are 'Pushing a Ban on Certain Symbols and Words, a Ban on Guns, a Ban on Talk Radio," MediaMatters.org, January 11, 2011, mediamatters.org/ mmtv/201101110038.

14. Sarah Palin Twitter Account: https://twitter.com/#!/sarahpalinusa/ status/29677744457.

15. Gabriel Sherman, "The Elephant in the Green Room," *New York*, May 22, 2011, nymag.com/print/?/news/media/roger-ailes-fox-news-2011–5/.

16. "America's Enduring Strength," Sarah Palin's Facebook page, January 12, 2011, www.facebook.com/notes/sarah-palin/americas-enduring -strength/487510653434.

17. Sherman, "The Elephant in the Green Room."

18. *Glenn Beck*, Fox News Channel, January 31, 2011; Sean Easter and Todd Gregory, "In Egypt Protests, Beck Sees . . . a New Islamic Caliphate and Communist Revolution?" *County Fair* (blog), MediaMatters.org, February 1, 2010, mediamatters.org/blog/201102010001.

19. William Kristol, "Stand for Freedom," *The Weekly Standard*, February 14, 2011, www.weeklystandard.com/articles/stand-freedom_541404.html.

20. Joe Klein, "How Long, Glenn Beck, How Long?" *Swampland* (blog), *Time*, February 5, 2011, swampland.time.com/2011/02/05/how-long-glenn -beck-how-long/.

21. "Glenn Beck to End Daily Fox News Program," FoxNation.com, April 6, 2011, nation.foxnews.com/glenn-beck/2011/04/06/glenn-beck-end-daily -fox-news-program.

22. Ibid.

23. *The O'Reilly Factor*, Fox News Channel, August 3, 2009.

24. Eric Boehlert, "How Fox Teamed Up with Trump for Birtherpalooza," MediaMatters.org, April 27, 2011, mediamatters.org/blog/201104270016.

25. "Report: Fox Promotes Birther Myth in at Least 52 Segments," Media Matters.org, April 27, 2011, mediamatters.org/research/201104270009.

26. *Justice with Judge Jeanine*, Fox News Channel, April 9, 2011, mediamatters .org/mmtv/201104100003.

27. *Hannity*, Fox News Channel, March 25, 2011; "Hannity Says It's 'Not True' that Obama Has Shown His Birth Certificate," MediaMatters.org, March 25, 2011, mediamatters.org/mmtv/201103250044.

28. Kirk Johnson, "Evidence Aside, State Lawmakers Debate 'Birther' Bills," *New York Times*, April 21, 2011, www.nytimes.com/2011/04/22/us/ politics/22birthers.html?_r=2&scp=2&sq=birther&st=cse.

29. Interview with Media Matters for America conducted by Joe Strupp, May 16, 2011.

30. *Fox News Sunday,* Fox News Channel, November 29, 2009; "Huckabee: If I Don't Run for President, It's Because 'This Fox Gig I Got Right Now' Is 'Really, Really Wonderful,' " MediaMatters.org, November 29, 2009, media matters.org/mmtv/200911290002.

31. Matea Gold, "Fox News Pulls Newt Gingrich, Rick Santorum off the Air Because of Their Interest in Running for President," *Los Angeles Times,* March 2, 2011, articles.latimes.com/2011/mar/02/news/la-pn-fox -candidates-suspended-20110303.

32. Gabriel Sherman, "The Elephant in the Green Room," *New York,* May 22, 2011, nymag.com/print/?/news/media/roger-ailes-fox-news-2011-5/.

33. Interview with Media Matters for America conducted by Joe Strupp, May 17 , 2011.

Epilogue

1. Mark Joyella, "Spin Cycle: How the Cable Nets Would Like Us to Report May's Ratings," *Mediaite,* June 2, 2011, www.mediaite.com/tv/spin-cycle -how-the-cable-nets-would-like-us-to-report-mays-ratings/.

2. *The Radio Factor,* Westwood One, December 14, 2004; "O'Reilly to *Media Matters*: '[You] Character Assassins . . . You Guys Really Are Despicable Weasels,' " MediaMatters.org, December 15, 2004, mediamatters.org/ research/200412150005.

3. C. Boyden Gray, "Taxpayers' Subsidization of War on Fox News," *Washington Times,* June 21, 2011, www.washingtontimes.com/news/2011/jun/21/ gray-taxpayers-subsidization-of-war-on-fox-news/.

4. "Fox "News" Judgment: Media Matters Tax Status More Important Than NY Same-Sex Marriage Bill," MediaMatters.org, July 12, 2011, mediamatters .org/research/201107120012.

5. *Fox & Friends,* Fox News Channel, July 5, 2011.

6. Ibid.

7. Ibid.

8. Media Matters 2009 IRS Form 990.

9. Keach Hagey, "Fox News Takes on Media Matters," *Politico,* July 7, 2011, www.politico.com/news/stories/0711/58468.html.

10. "Stories Which Raised Prince William's Suspicions," *Daily Mail,* August 9, 2006, www.dailymail.co.uk/news/article-399818/Stories-raised-Prince -Williams-suspicions.html.

11. Paul LaRosa, "*News of the World* Hacking Scandal Began with Prince William," CBS News, July 18, 2011, www.cbsnews.com/8301–504083_162 –20080329–504083.html.

12. Nick Davis and Amelia Hill, "Missing Milly Dowler's Voicemail Was

Hacked by *News of the World,*" *Guardian,* July 4, 2011, www.guardian
.co.uk/uk/2011/jul/04/milly-dowler-voicemail-hacked-news-of
-world.

13. Ibid.

14. "U.K. Government Turns Against Murdoch's Bid for British Sky Broadcasting," Associated Press, July 12, 2011, bostonherald.com/business/
media/view.bg?articleid=1351351.

15. Sarah Lyall and Graham Bowley, "Murdoch Veterans Portray an Engaged
Boss," *New York Times,* July 25, 2011, www.nytimes.com/2011/07/26/
world/europe/26murdoch.html.

16. Kenneth Lovett, "Chalk It Up to the Hacks: New York Scraps $27 Million
Education Contract with Murdoch Firm," *Daily News* (New York), August 27, 2011, articles.nydailynews.com/2011–08–27/news/30103709_1_
wireless-generation-phone-hacking-scandal-murdoch.

17. Bruce Orwall, "In Interview, Murdoch Defends News Corp.," *Wall Street
Journal,* July 14, 2011, online.wsj.com/article/SB100014240527023045213
04576446261304709284.html.

18. Ed Pilkington, "Rebekah Brooks's Departure Puts Les Hinton in the Spotlight," *Guardian,* July 15, 2011, www.guardian.co.uk/media/2011/jul/15/
rebekah-brooks-resignation-les-hinton-news-corps.

19. Tim Walker, "Phone Hacking: 'Rupert Murdoch Tells Rebekah Brooks
to Travel the World,' " *Telegraph,* August 6, 2011, www.telegraph.co.uk/
news/8684463/Phone-hacking-Rupert-Murdoch-tells-Rebekah-Brooks
-to-travel-the-world.html.

20. Reid Epstein, "Rupert Murdoch: 'Most Humble Day of My Life,' " *Politico,*
July 19, 2011, www.politico.com/news/stories/0711/59344.html.

21. "REPORT: How CNN, MSNBC, and Fox Are Covering News Corp.
Hacking Scandal," MediaMatters.org, July 14, 2011, mediamatters.org/
research/201107140013.

22. Eric Hananoki, " 'I'm Not Going to Touch It': Did Fox Admit They're
Avoiding *News of the World* Scandal?" *County Fair* (blog), MediaMatters.org,
July 11, 2011, mediamatters.org/blog/201107110013.

23. "Bill O'Reilly: News Corp Being Attacked By 'Vicious' Opponents Exploit-
ing Hacking Scandal," *Huffington Post,* July 20, 2011, www.huffingtonpost
.com/2011/07/20/bill-oreilly-news-corp-be_n_904258.html.

24. Meg James, "In Lawsuit, Investors Claim 'a Culture Run Amok' at Rupert
Murdoch's News Corp.," *Los Angeles Times,*, July 11, 2011, latimesblogs
.latimes.com/entertainmentnewsbuzz/2011/07/rupert-murdoch-news
-corp-lawsuit-culture-run-amok.html.

25. Adam Shah, "Beck Turns to ADL-Condemned David Barton to Promote
His Israel Rally," MediaMatters.org, May 20, 2011, mediamatters.org/
blog/201105200043.

26. Brian Stelter, "Glenn Beck Contemplates Starting Own Channel," *New York Times,* March 22, 2011, www.nytimes.com/2011/03/23/business/media/23beck.html.

27. Brian Stelter, "Moving Online, Beck Will Charge Viewers a Fee," *New York Times,* June 6, 2011, www.nytimes.com/2011/06/07/business/media/07beck.html.

28. "Glenn Beck and Mercury Radio Arts Announce GBTV—Home of Glenn's NEW Two Hour Show!" GlennBeck.com, June 6, 2011, www .glennbeck.com/2011/06/06/glenn-beck-and-mercury-radio-arts -announce-gbtv-home-of-glenns-new-two-hour-show/.

29. *The Glenn Beck Program,* Premiere Radio Networks, May 16, 2011; Todd Gregory, " 'Restoring Courage' in Jerusalem: Glenn Beck's Latest Self-Aggrandizing Spectacle," *County Fair* (blog), MediaMatters.org, May 16, 2011, mediamatters.org/blog/201105160031.

30. *Glenn Beck,* Fox News Channel, May 16, 2011; Todd Gregory, " 'Restoring Courage' in Jerusalem: Glenn Beck's Latest Self-Aggrandizing Spectacle," *County Fair* (blog), MediaMatters.org, May 16, 2011, mediamatters.org/blog/201105160031.

31. *The Glenn Beck Program,*. Premiere Radio Networks, August 12, 2011; "Beck: 'A Religious Figure That I Respect' Told Me that Restoring Courage 'May Be a Fulfillment of Zechariah Prophecy,' " MediaMatters.org, August 12, 2011, mediamatters.org/mmtv/201108120016.

32. *The Glenn Beck Program,* Premiere Radio Networks, August 10, 2011; "Beck: Restoring Courage 'Will Alter Your Life . . . I Wouldn't Be Surprised if This Did Alter the World,' " MediaMatters.org, August 10, 2011, mediamatters .org/mmtv/201108100013.

33. *Ma Boer,* Israel Defense Force Radio, August 16, 2011.

34. Noam Sheizaf, "Glenn Beck Brings Firebreathing Rhetoric Back to Israel," *Jewish Daily Forward,* August 22, 2011, forward.com/articles/141673/#ixzz1WYpiRnON.

35. Yehoshua Breiner, "Rabbis Against Glenn Beck's Rally in Support of Israel," *Walla News,* August 23, 2011.

36. Madeleine Morgenstern, "Beck Blasts Boehner After Rep. Walsh Says House Members Banned from Israel Event," *The Blaze* (blog), August 18, 2011, www.theblaze.com/stories/beck-lashes-out-at-boehner-after-rep-walsh -says-house-members-banned-from-israel-event/.

37. Ibid.

38. David Weigel, "What Ever Happened to Glenn Beck?" *Slate,* August 19, 2011, www.slate.com/blogs/weigel/2011/08/19/what_ever_happened_to_glenn_beck_.html.

39. "Fox News and *Washington Examiner* to Present Iowa Republican Party Presidential Debate on August 11," FoxNews.com, June 2011, press

.foxnews.com/2011/06/fox-news-and-washington-examiner-to-present
-iowa-republican-party-presidential-debate-on-august-11/.

40. David Zurawik, "Bret Baier, Chris Wallace Make Fox News a Winner
at Iowa Debate," *Baltimore Sun,* August 12, 2011, articles.baltimoresun
.com/2011–08–12/entertainment/bal-bret-baier-chris-wallace-fox-news
-winner-at-iowa-debate-20110812_1_fox-news-gop-candidates-bret-baier.

41. James Poniewozik, "The Morning After: Fox Shows Teeth in Debate," *Tuned
In* (blog), *Time,* August 12, 2011, tunedin.blogs.time.com/2011/08/12/
the-morning-after-fox-shows-teeth-in-debate/#ixzz1WYtI9Fmu.

42. Frances Martel, "GOP Debate Subplot: Newt Gingrich Continues 'Gotcha' Fox News Attack on Bret Baier," *Mediaite,* August 11, 2011, www
.mediaite.com/tv/gop-debate-subplot-newt-gingrich-continues-gotcha
-fox-news-attack-on-bret-baier/.

43. Keach Hagey, "Fox Shifts Its Role in GOP Primary," *On Media* (blog),
Politico, August 12, 2011, www.politico.com/blogs/onmedia/0811/Fox
_shifts_its_role_in_GOP_primary.html.

44. "Report: After Default Crisis Deal Struck, Fox Turned to GOP for Analysis," MediaMatters.org, August 2, 2011, mediamatters.org/research/
201108020021.

45. Rob Savillo, "The Fox Primary by the Numbers, August 8–14," *County
Fair* (blog), MediaMatters.org, August 17, 2011, mediamatters.org/blog/
201108170008.

46. Ibid.

47. Dan Hirschhorn, "Rick Santorum Made $239K from Fox News," *Politico,*
September 29, 2011, www.politico.com/news/stories/0911/64740.html.

48. "Rove to Palin: Get a Slightly Thicker Skin," FoxNews.com, August 24,
2011, www.foxnews.com/on-air/on-the-record/2011/08/25/rove-palin
-get-slightly-thicker-skin#ixzz1WSdYHsDp.

49. Gabriel Sherman, "The Elephant in the Green Room," *New York,* May 22,
2011, nymag.com/print/?/news/media/roger-ailes-fox-news-2011–5/.

50. "Roger Ailes Looks Back on 15 Years of Fox News," Associated Press,
October 5, 2011, www.foxnews.com/us/2011/10/05/roger-ailes-looks
-back-on-15-years-fox-news/.

51. Gabriel Sherman, "Sarah Palin Got Scolded by Roger Ailes for Not
Announcing Her Non-Candidacy on Fox News," NYMag.com Daily
Intel, November 21, 2011, nymag.com/daily/intel/2011/11/sarah-palin
-scolded-furious-roger-ailes-foxnews.html.

52. Michael D. Shear, "Huckabee to Announce Decision on Presidential Run
Saturday," *The Caucus* (blog), *New York Times,* May 13, 2011, thecaucus.blogs
.nytimes.com/2011/05/13/huckabee-teases-decision-on-presidential-run/.

53. Howard Kurtz, "Fox's Reality Show," *Daily Beast,* September 25, 2011,
www.thedailybeast.com/newsweek/2011/09/25/roger-ailes-repositions
-fox-news.html.

54. Ibid.

55. "The Fox Primary by the Numbers, October 10–16," MediaMatters.org, October 18, 2011, mediamatters.org/blog/201110180020.

56. Rob Savillo, "The Fox Primary by the Numbers, November 14–20," Media Matters.org, October 18, 2011, mediamatters.org/blog/201111220014.

57. Joe McGinniss, "Roger Thinks Palin Is an Idiot. He Thinks She's Stupid," JoeMcGinniss.net, May 22, 2011, www.joemcginniss.net/roger-thinks -palin-is-an-idiot-he-thinks-shes-stupid/Joe%20McGinniss.

58. Michael Scherer, "Calling 'Em Out: The White House Takes On the Press," *Time,* October 8, 2009, www.time.com/time/politics/article/ 0,8599,1929058,00.html.

59. Ben Smith, "On Fox, Where's the Outrage?" *Ben Smith* (blog), *Politico,* September 29, 2010, www.politico.com/blogs/bensmith/0910/On_Fox _wheres_the_outrage.html.

60. Kurtz, "Fox's Reality Show."

61. Ibid.

62. " 'Fox News Lies' While Covering Pro-Labor Protests In Wisconsin," Media Matters.org, March 2, 2011, mediamatters.org/research/201103020013.

Acknowledgments

The Fox Effect is in many ways a review of the last several years of Media Matters work and is truly the work of an ensemble cast. There is not a single staff member whose work did not contribute to this book. As such we listed the organization itself as an author.

We are especially grateful to Jeremy Schulman and Melinda Warner who lead our research staff. Their guidance, advice, and leadership show at MediaMatters.org every day.

Matt Finkelstein was invaluable in editing and organizing our thoughts in the first draft of the manuscript. Todd Gregory's advice helped improve and shape later drafts. Additionally we wish to thank Ben Dimiero, Jocelyn Fong, Matt Gertz, Jeremy Holden, Terry Krepel, Sarah Pavlus, Adam Shah, and Oliver Willis for their work fact-checking and editing. Simon Maloy deserves an extra note of thanks for developing "the Fox cycle" and other pieces of analysis featured prominently in *The Fox Effect*. Eric Hananoki's incredible analysis was also critically important.

Alex Zaitchik, Joe Strupp, and Eric Boehlert each provided priceless reporting—their work as investigative journalists is second to none.

Doug Stauffer, Jessica Levin, Danny Herrera, and Angelo Carusone do an amazing job promoting the work of Media Matters. Brad Herring and his incredible team of Jon Salvia and Evan Whitbeck produced the video content in our enhanced eBook.

Our executive team of Matt Butler, Katie Paris, and Este Griffith all work to keep Media Matters humming every day. Additionally Rachel Gaylord, Emma Sprague, and Christine Hammer kept us on schedule. We are indebted to Eric Burns, Marcia Kuntz, Kelly Ronan, and Tate Williams, without whose efforts *The Fox Effect* would not be possible.

Our agent Will Lippincott guided this book from scattered thoughts in our heads onto the page. He is not only the best representation, but also the greatest friend any author could have.

Our editor at Anchor Books, Jeff Alexander, provided exceptional advice and critiques. The publicity team at Vintage/Anchor Russell Perreault and Kate Runde and their production team lead by Nicole Pedersen also did incredible work.

Media Matters would not exist without the dedicated fund-raising efforts of Mary Pat Bonner and her team.

We would like to offer a note of extreme gratitude to Ari's wife, Julie, and David's partner, James, whose love and support sustain us every day.

Also a special note of thanks to Ventnor Sport Cafe in Adams Morgan—Scott and his crew (Julie, Molly, Brian, and Abel) allowed Ari to spend many late nights sitting at their bar writing, while they provided an infinite supply of Diet Coke.

We would be remiss if we did not acknowledge the employees of Fox News who put their livelihood at risk simply by speaking with Media Matters staff members.

In November 2010, Ari, at David's direction, spent $86,000 at a charity auction to purchase a "friendly lunch" with Rupert Murdoch. Sadly that meeting never came to pass. The News Corp. CEO chose to contribute an amount equal to our bid to the charity in question in order to avoid having lunch with us.

Rupert, consider this an open invitation. Anytime you wish to discuss the state of the media and how we can work together to improve it, our door is always open.